A Tale of
Two Utopias

A Tale of Two Utopias

THE POLITICAL JOURNEY OF
THE GENERATION OF 1968

Paul Berman

W. W. NORTON & COMPANY
NEW YORK   LONDON

Portions of this book have appeared in different form in
The New Republic and *The Village Voice*.

For information about permission to reproduce selections from this
book, write to Permissions, W. W. Norton & Company, Inc., 500 Fifth
Avenue, New York, NY 10110.

The text of this book is composed in Garamond
with the display set in Garamond
Composition by Crane Typesetting Service, Inc.
Manufacturing by Quebecor Printing Fairfield.
Book design by Chris Welch

Library of Congress Cataloging-in-Publication Data
Berman, Paul.
A tale of two utopias : the political journey of the generation of
1968 / by Paul Berman.
p.   cm.
Includes index.
ISBN 0-393-03927-7
1. Social history—1960–1970.   2. Social history—1970–
3. Liberalism.   4. Radicalism.   5. Gay liberation movement.
6. Czechoslovakia—Politics and government—1968–1989.
7. History—Philosophy.   I. Title.
HN17.5.B415   1996
306'.09—dc20   95-25321

ISBN 0-393-31675-0 pbk.

W. W. Norton & Company, Inc.
500 Fifth Avenue, New York, N.Y. 10110
www.wwnorton.com

W. W. Norton & Company Ltd.
Castle House, 75/76 Wells Street, London W1T 3QT

4 5 6 7 8 9 0

Contents

The Dream of a
New Society

In the years around 1968, a utopian exhilaration swept across the student universe and across several adult universes as well, and almost everyone in my own circle of friends and classmates was caught up in it. The exhilaration was partly a fury against some well-known social injustices, and against some injustices that had always remained hidden. Partly it was a belief, hard to remember today (except in a cartoon version), that a superior new society was already coming into existence. And it was the belief that we ourselves—the teenage revolutionaries, freaks, hippies, and students, together with our friends and leaders who were five or ten years older and our allies around the world—stood at the heart of a new society.

The exhilaration was brought on by circumstances close to hand—by the activities of two or three tiny left-wing organizations, by several strong personalities whom we loved to deplore, by chance happenings that could just as easily have turned out differently. But it was brought on, most of all, by a confluence of very large events. Four enormous revolutions were roiling the world at that one moment, each of those revolutions different in nature and purpose from the others, each of them far too huge and unprecedented for anyone, no matter how old and experienced, to comprehend at the time. And from each of those revolutions, and from the combination of all four, radiated an intense excitement, which came beaming down on us and on people like ourselves in scattered university towns all over the world.

Our own student uprisings, the building occupations, marches, strikes, battles with the police, the insurrections that were sexual, feminist, and gay, the bursts of ecological passion, the noisy entrance of the first mass group of African-American students into the previously segregated American universities, the slightly crazy effort to raise insubordination into a culture, to eat, dress, smoke, dance differently—all of that counted as merely one of those simultaneous revolutions. It was a political insurrection, but also an insurrection in middle-class customs (a phrase we would have loathed). Revolution Number Two was closely related—a cousin, let us say, of the insurrection in customs. It was an uprising in the zone of the spirit (that phrase we would have liked). In San Francisco and in hippie districts around the country, a handful of adventurous souls were gathering up bits and pieces of Buddhism, Beat poetry, transcendentalism, Mexican folklore, psychedelic mind expansions, and God knows what else, and were funneling those many random oddities into a vague new sensibility, with results that were much less than a religion—something half-hearted, provisional. Yet the half-hearted thing managed to be trembly with expectation, therefore contagious.

The nameless new sensibility spread into the world of rock and roll, which no one would have predicted. And the music, too, proved to be contagious, not just in the United States. No small affair! But the biggest event in the zone of the spirit was going on deep within the Catholic Church. The middle 1960s had been an age of Vatican theological reform, and the reforms went lapping one upon the other until, by that same 1968, the bishops of Latin America were convening at Medellín, Colombia, to give their ecclesiastic blessing to several of the insights of liberation theology. Which was hard to believe. But not every impossibility fails to occur. And so, among the sober Catholics as among the anti-sober freaks and rockers, all kinds of rebellions were strangely afoot, and in several places around the world the conservative instincts of long ago appeared to be sinking into the past, and some crucial flaw in the human personality seemed to be correcting itself before our eyes, and the revolution in the zone of the spirit was nothing you could dismiss.

Revolutions Three and Four were strictly this-worldly. The most violent of all, the worldwide revolution against Western imperialism, was by 1968 reaching a gory climax. Communist dictatorships (another phrase that might not have set too well, except among us left-wing libertarians) had taken over Cuba and half of Vietnam and were spreading outward to no one knew where. The National Liberation Front of South Vietnam launched its Tet Offensive in the early weeks of 1968, in spite of every claim by the American generals that nothing of the sort could possibly occur. And the impression arose that Marxist-Leninist liberation movements were capable of triumphing in every faraway peasant land, and the superpower of the West could do nothing about it, and the high-tech madness of Western civilization had met its nemesis. That was Revolution Number Three.

In Communist Czechoslovakia during several months of 1968 (and, earlier in the sixties, in the inner debates and schisms of Communist Parties and left-wing youth movements all over Western Europe, the United States, Mexico, and elsewhere), the fourth revolution, this one *against* the dictatorships of the left, was meanwhile entering a first, tentative phase. The possibility that left-wing movements might actively turn against Soviet Communism and that Soviet-style tyrannies might be resisted and overthrown was suddenly, in Prague, a reality—for a little while. Communism's defeat became, for the first time, imaginable—even if no one could picture what would happen next. Obviously, Revolutions Three and Four were badly at odds. One of those revolutions was spreading the totalitarianism of Europe to the former colonies; the other was undermining the totalitarianism of Europe. One was peaking; the other, just getting under way.

But the late sixties and early seventies were years

of war and panic, and in the noise and confusion the aspirations from each of those very large political revolutions were somehow projected onto the other, and opposites began to look the same. The effort to throw off the dead weight of totalitarianism (Revolution Number Four) was considered to be in some fashion a goal of Communism's spread into the tropics and the Southern Hemisphere (Revolution Number Three). Imaginary panoramas deployed across the world. The vision that was espoused by the democratic reformers in Czechoslovakia and their supporters and by people with still more libertarian views all over the radical left in the Western countries—the dream of a genuine socialism, uncorrupted, untyrannical, de-Stalinized, ultra-democratic—was pictured even by people who should have known better as flesh-and-blood reality, anyway a lively possibility for the future, in Cuba, in China, and in embattled Vietnam. The dismal old choice between a democratic civilization in the West that appeared to have lost its soul to capitalism and a Soviet civilization in the East that had surely lost its soul to bureaucracy (such was our understanding of the cold war) seemed finally to be a thing of the past. And the new alternative for mankind was thought to be upon us.

It was going to be a society of direct democracy, in a fashion that might be rustic (Third World style), sophisticated (Czechoslovak style), anarchist (workers' council style), or countercultural (hippie style), but admirable in any case. It was going to be a socialism of the poor countries and of their friends around the world, neither Stalinist nor liberal. A worldwide shift in power from the elites to the masses. A society of individual liberty (as per the revolution in middle-class customs). A society of spiritual grandeur (as per the revolution in the zone of the spirit). Something soulful. A moral advance. And in the glow of that very grand and utopian idea, a thousand disparate events from around the world—the student uprisings, the hippie experiments, the religious transformations, the rise of Communism in some places and the first sign of its fall in other places, the Black Power movement, and onward through feminism and every insurrectionary impulse of the age—seemed to merge into a single tide. And the tide swept forward, unstoppable, all-powerful. It was the new society coming into being. That was the source of our exhilaration. Or if the new society seemed, even at the time, more figurative than literal (though some people took everything literally enough), and if the world revolution seemed less than certain, the exhilaration was authentic even so. For something useful was bound to come of those many uprisings. Maybe not a revolution in the major sense; but a revolution in the minor sense. Maybe not an entirely new society; but not the rickety old social system that already existed, either.

Such was the spirit of 1968. It led to a very peculiar aftermath, visible and invisible, during the next decades. In the United States and a number of other countries the cultural half of the old rebellions went on to enjoy a fair amount of success, in a toned-down version. The minor revolution took place. Fashions and customs that were once considered shocking shocked no longer. There were political advances. The barriers that had blocked the paths of women and all sorts of minority groups became a little lower. And because of the prestige that accrued to those achievements, something odd took place in the universities and a few of the bohemian neighborhoods. Rebellions in the '68 style became a kind of ritual, year after year.

Always there were new groups of left-wingers or avant-gardists plotting ever more novel uprisings on behalf of identity politics and a dozen other causes. And always there were the hot red faces of indignant reactionaries, putting up a bitter resistance; always a little circle of left-wing fanatics astounding the world by proclaiming a conversion to right-wing fanaticism; always a conservative politician shaking a wily fist at the odious sixties and gliding to victory at the polls. It was the Battle of Gettysburg in nonstop reenactment. That was 1968's visible aftermath. It endured into the 1990s. And because the culture wars and the endless insurrections attracted a lot of attention, the many combatants on the right and the left could flatter themselves into supposing that issues as grave as those of an earlier moment were still in dispute, and the shape of society was going to depend on the outcome, and 1968 was forever.

The culture wars did have their importance, sometimes. Yet 1968 was not forever. For beneath those wars, something bigger and deeper, 1968's invisible aftermath, was all the while going on. The invisible

aftermath was an undertow of analysis and self-criticism among the rebels themselves. The undertow
pulled steadily at the old left-wing political ideas, and
one by one drew them out to sea, where they quietly
drowned. And where the old ideas had been, newer
thoughts silently bobbed to the surface. The new ideas
came in different versions in different countries, which
made it hard to recognize that, all over the world, an
entire generation was going through the same political
transformation. There was a French version (which
got its shaky start in the movement known as New
Philosophy); an Eastern Bloc version (in which the
student socialists from 1968 evolved, in the course of
their prison terms, into liberal human rights dissidents); a United States version (intellectually muddled,
as is our wont, with everyone claiming not to have
changed any opinions at all); and a Latin American
version (slower and more begrudging than elsewhere,
if only because in Latin America the leftism of the
student movement resulted in guerrilla wars, which
are not like culture wars, and the martyrdom was
staggering, and martyrs impede thought). Yet everywhere the drift was more or less the same.

In place of the old aspirations for direct democracy
and revolutionary socialism you could begin to see a
much livelier appreciation of liberal democracy, social-
democratic style (for some of us) or free-market style
(for some lamentable others), but committed to West-
ern-style political institutions in either case. Sometimes
the old animosity for the United States dropped away.
Sometimes there was even a bit of enthusiasm for

America's culture and political traditions, which was quite a novel development. Naturally, the rise of the new ideas in what had been the precincts of the radical left around the world did not cause everybody to jump for joy. In the remote Peruvian Andes straight into the 1990s whole villages clung to a Maoism from long ago, and in the big American universities and a few other places that had gotten stuck in the past still other people clung to a variety of antique doctrines about U.S. imperialism and bourgeois democracy and the evils of Western civilization. And to everyone who still adhered to the leftist fundamentals, the fading away of the old revolutionary aspiration was a dismal thing to behold, and the entire trajectory from leftist to liberal was pathetic, and events have gone steadily downhill since 1968.

But then, what does it mean—"revolutionary"? World history is not the theater of happiness, Hegel said; yet every so often comes a joke. No sooner did the old ideas about a left-wing revolution drop away than, beginning in 1989, to universal astonishment, the forgotten genie from 1968, a world revolution, flew out from a bottle. Half of Europe was suddenly on the barricades, together with any number of countries in Asia, Africa, and Latin America. Everyone watched with intense interest to discover if the old left-wing radicalism was by any chance going to revive, and the new kind of socialism appear, and the workers' councils make their bid for power. But, no. In one insurrectionary country after another in 1989 and for a few years after, the vanguard of the late-twentieth-century revolution turned out to be adventurous persons who called themselves (sometimes sincerely!) liberal and democratic and seemed to be, some of them, moderately fond of the United States, too. In the modern age, nothing is more revolutionary than what only yesterday seemed the height of reaction. And in the bright light of the democratic revolutions, the student uprisings of the years around 1968 began suddenly to look, in retrospect, a little different than they had in the past.

Suddenly it was obvious that those long-ago utopian efforts to change the shape of the world were a young people's rehearsal, preparatory to adult events that only came later. Suddenly it was obvious that the authentic political revolution of our era was now, not then; liberal and democratic, not radical leftist in the '68 style; real, not imaginary. Here and there the leaders of the revolutions of '89—a Václav Havel in Czechoslovakia, an Adam Michnik in Poland—turned out to be the same heroic persons, now adult liberals, who as young radicals had helped lead the movements of '68, just to show the relation of one uprising to the next. And with the liberal revolutions breaking out in sundry regions from the Baltic Sea to South Africa during the entire period from 1989 to 1994, the old hope of reorganizing the world on a drastically new and infinitely more democratic basis, the universal project, the grand aspiration for the poor and the downtrodden, *that* hope, the forbidden utopian dream, once again seemed, in its newly liberal and anti-grandiose version—well, thinkable. Once again there was a feeling that all over the world several main principles of a good society (a liberal democratic political system, a functioning market, free trade unions, a commitment to open debate and rational ways of thinking—to name a few) had at last been discovered. Again history seemed to be advancing in a definite direction. And again, just as had happened after the insurrections of circa 1968 in different parts of the world, came a scarlet wave of spectacular disasters, the ethnic massacres and the gangster tyrannies.

So what are we to think—we, the twice-revolutionary, who have seen worldwide political hopes rise and fall, rise and fall, two times in a short generation? Are we to conclude that the idea of progress is the enemy of progress and that revolutionary exhilaration is drunkenness and folly, to be avoided at all cost? Or are we to conclude that better societies do sometimes arise, and are arising even now because of the liberal passions that spread around the world in 1989 (sometimes with a remoter origin in the student movements of the past), and that a confidence in historical progress may have its justifications still, even if no one can feel too cheery about it? Or should we merely conclude that an endless oscillation from one of those views to the other is our modern fate?

The radical exhilarations of circa 1968; the awkward modulation from revolutionary leftism to liberal democracy on the part of rebellious-minded people around the world; the outbreak of a new and different revolutionary exhilaration in 1989; finally the unresolvable debate about world history and the idea of progress: those have been the four main stations in the political journey of the generation that came of age in the student rebellions of the past. It is a tale of two utopias—and of two reconsiderations.

The Moral History of the Baby Boom Generation

I

Every few decades, a pure flame of political rebellion shoots up somewhere and with amazing speed spreads in all directions, until half the countries on earth have been scorched.

The first time such a thing happened was in the American Revolution of 1776, though in that instance the flame, spreading with less than amazing speed, took thirteen years before reaching as far away as France. But then, yes, the main ideas of the American and French revolutions went leaping fairly quickly across whole regions of Europe and even into the distant exotic zones of colonial Latin America, until a good many countries on three continents were undergoing republican agitations and experiments with constitutional government, which was a wildly revolutionary thing to have happen. A clearer example of the same phenomenon took place in 1848. An insurrection broke out in Paris. That time the uprising invoked the ideals of liberal nationalism and hinted at socialism, too—and within a few months, powerful movements affirming those same ideas swept across Germany, the Austrian Empire, Italy, Spain, and several other countries, not always with the same heat or intensity. A few radical sparks spread all the way to the United States. A republican uprising shook the Seneca nation of America in 1848, which is odd to consider. The first convention for women's rights assembled in upstate New York.

The uprisings that broke out in 1917 showed the same pattern. There was an idea of constructing a new socialist society on the basis of locally organized workers' councils. The workers' councils arose in St. Petersburg under the name of "soviets." Then, when the First World War came to an end, the councils spread to Germany, Hungary, Italy, Spain, and several other countries. The faraway city of Seattle, Washington, underwent a general strike in 1919, and even there, in Wild West America, the strikers took over the management of the town, as if in distant lunar reflection of St. Petersburg's insurrectionary events. Still another example took place in 1936–38, that time in the form of trade union movements and factory takeovers. The union takeovers spread across France (the Popular Front agitations), Spain (the anarchosyndicalist revolution), the American Midwest (the rise of the CIO), and a few other places, too. And if you keep in mind the historical pattern of those several revolutionary upheavals, it's obvious that student rebellions in the years around 1968 should count as one more instance of the same mysterious phenomenon, except on a bigger geographical scale than ever before.

The student movements rose up all over Western Europe and in parts of Central and Eastern Europe, parts of North and West Africa, all over the United States, Mexico, Central and South America, the Caribbean, Japan, and the Philippines. You could point to China, where student insurrections played a big role in the Great Proletarian Cultural Revolution during the entire period from 1966 to 1976. Yet in the case of 1968, as in every instance back to 1848 and even back to 1776, it's hard to understand how so many rebellions could have taken place at the same time. There were some obvious causes of tension around the world: the Vietnam War and the anti-colonial revolutions, the theological reforms within the Catholic Church, the rise of the hippies, new styles in pop music, the civil rights movement and the race riots in the United States, a few eye-opening indications of discontent in the Soviet empire.

Each of those events created a pressure, which made for excitement, which sometimes was exhilarating. But it's hard to see what turned the excitement into rebellion, or what could have caused the rebellion to spread around the world. In 1968 no single, great trauma was devastating the world economy or putting an unbearable strain on the young. Social conditions were entirely different from one country to the next. It's hard even to identify a common ideology or doctrine in the '68 rebellions. We had our own beliefs in the student movement in the United States, but in the Eastern Bloc the students clung to beliefs that were quite different. In some places the student movement leaned toward Communism, and in other places, leaned away. In France the students managed to lean in both directions at once.

How to explain those many simultaneous uprisings, then? You could argue (A) that student rebellions broke out around the world circa 1968 for reasons of pure coincidence, and in each country the causes were local, and no larger phenomenon needs to be explained. But that was not how it felt in 1968. The student rebels in different parts of the world definitely recognized one another, felt themselves to be part of a worldwide movement, adopted one another's slogans. Alternatively, you could argue (B) that a desire for freedom is deeply rooted, and when desire turns to rebellion in any part of the world, people in other places will look at the rebels and recognize their own feelings and will feel prompted to stage uprisings of their own—even if freedom in one country is pictured as Communism and in another country as anti-Communism. Hannah Arendt devoted several moving passages of her book *On Revolution* to expounding a version of that idea. You could argue (C) that a desire to wreak havoc is just as deeply rooted, and may spread in exactly the same way. Unfortunately, both (B) and (C), the desire for freedom and the desire for havoc, are exceedingly vague as explanations of human behavior. And so the best way to understand what occurred would seem to be (D) to look for common features among the separate movements, in the hope that common features will point to a common motive.

What were the common features in the rebellions

of circa 1968? Everyone will agree that in each country the students followed their own national traditions, and one country's uprising was never exactly like another's. And yet, in quite a few places there was, as everyone recognized at the time, a common theme. It was the split between the young and the old. In the Great Proletarian Cultural Revolution of China, the generational split was not quite genuine, and behind the rampaging young Red Guards stood some very old Reds from the Communist leadership. But in other places the split between the young and the old was exactly what it seemed to be—a sharp split in the United States and Western Europe, less sharp in other regions, yet clear enough for the young people to identify with one another across the borders. And if you look a little closer, still another common trait looms into focus.

It is the story of how the split between the generations, taken as a political disagreement, got its earliest start. In one country after another, the split made its first appearance in the early and mid-1960s, as a fairly obscure argument deep within the ranks of the old working-class parties of the left. No more than a handful of people were ever involved. The brightest young people in the old left-wing parties or in their youth affiliates somehow got into a dispute with the adult leaders of their own organization. The arguments grew testy. Finally the irritated adults grabbed a few of the uncooperative young people by the hair and grandly expelled them from the organized ranks of the international left—only to gaze out the window a few years later, circa 1968, to see those same uncooperative young troublemakers marching through the street with fists in the air and several hundred thousand followers marching behind.

In West Germany in 1961, the student wing of the Social Democratic Party, the Sozialistische Deutsche Studentenbund (whose abbreviation happened to be SDS, just like the American student movement of the 1960s), fell out with the adult Social Democrats and was expelled. And by 1967 and '68, that same German SDS ended up leading the mass radical youth movement in West Germany. The split in France took place mostly within the French Communist Party. The party's student wing, the Communist Student Union, was led in Paris by young people from the Sorbonne. The young activists met with the Communist adults, and the meetings went so badly that by 1965 the adults felt they had no choice but to drive the uncooperative students out of the Communist movement altogether. A similar argument took place in the French Socialist Party. Then came 1968 and popular uprisings broke out in Paris and all over France, and the leaders were young people who had learned their politics in the little Parisian student world of the expelled Communists and the ex-Socialists.

Social and political conditions in Latin America— to leap across the hemispheres for a moment—were nothing like those in Western Europe. Yet in Mexico, where the most important of Latin America's 1968 movements took place, the split between young and old came about in exactly the same way. The semi-clandestine Mexican Communist Party stood at the center of the Mexican left, and at the center of the party's student organization, the Communist Youth, stood some very talented young people, including Gilberto Guevara Niebla and Raúl Alvarez Garín. The young people quarreled with their elders over the importance of student issues, which the adults were reluctant to acknowledge, and beginning in 1964 the young leaders either were expelled from the party or drifted away. Then came the uprisings of 1968, and three hundred thousand people were parading along the boulevards of Mexico City under the leadership of a National Strike Council based in the universities. And the two people who had founded that council and who figured throughout the uprising among its most prominent and revered leaders happened to be the ex-Communists Gilberto Guevara and Raúl Alvarez.

In other Latin American countries the split within the Communist movement took place earlier in the sixties and pitted pro-Cuban or pro-Chinese supermilitants against the traditional pro-Moscow leadership, who were more conservative. Generational issues were not so prominent; yet neither were they missing. There was the example of Nicaragua. The old-fashioned working-class party of the left was the Nicaraguan Socialist Party, which despite its name was Marxist-Leninist and pro-Moscow. In the 1950s a handful of middle-class students joined the party but couldn't get along with the traditional leaders, and in the early sixties the students—Carlos Fonseca, Tomás Borge, and a couple of others—put together their own organization. The year 1968 came and went in Nicaragua without a major rebellion by the student population. Yet the news from Mexico, France, and the United States had its effect on the Nicaraguan universities, and the tiny group that had broken away from the Nicaraguan Socialist Party began to flourish, and in 1970 the breakaway group—by then it was called the Sandinista National Liberation Front—succeeded, through its campus wing, in taking over the national student organization, and the 1968 phenomenon (a couple of years late) had taken place in Nicaragua, too.

The specific controversies or debates that led to the divisions between young and old in the traditional left-wing parties were different in each of these countries, as you would expect. And yet, if you peer still closer into the story of those splits, a single point of contention pops up over and over. The young people were eager for risk; the elders, not. Ultra-radicalism versus left-wing caution was the crucial division. Why were the young people so enamored of risky radicalism? Now, on this point it would make no sense to look for a single explanation, applicable to all countries. In a place like Nicaragua, risky radicalism was a logical political gamble, and people who took that gamble and threw themselves into guerrilla war had reason to think that, with perseverance and luck, they might win, and a revolution might break out, and they might end up as the new government—which in Nicaragua is exactly what happened, by 1979. But what could

radical action expect to achieve in the stable, democratic, industrial countries? Neither patience nor impa-
tience was going to make a revolution there. Whatever
pushed the students into radical action could not have
been political calculation in any ordinary sense.

Were the students pressured into radicalism by the
special anxieties of university life in those days? All over
the world during the sixties, the universities swelled in
population but not necessarily in resources, which led
to unhappy feelings and a lot of talk of "alienation."
To cite the three countries where the '68 student
movements were largest: In France, the student population increased by nearly 50 percent between 1960
and 1963. In Mexico, the student population tripled
between 1964 and 1970. In the United States, the
student population of the universities tripled between
1955 and 1970. But then, it's not immediately obvious
why crowded lecture halls and feelings of impersonal-
ity on campus (those were the fashionable complaints)
would necessarily lead the students into left-wing
adventures. Conceivably, the ever-increasing gap
between the students and the faraway world of their
professors and deans made it easier for the students
to picture themselves as a distinct generation, and in
that respect the growth of the student population may
very well have contributed to the new political attitude.
Yet the growth of the student population had little
or nothing to do with the squabbles that broke out
within the organizations of the traditional left. *Those*
squabbles, the tiny left-wing disputes between young
and old that anticipated the big student uprisings by

a few years, can only be understood with a sympathetic glance at what it was like to be a student leftist in the early or middle 1960s and to find yourself sitting across the room from the adult leaders of the left-wing parties.

Exactly who were those student leftists, the ones who got the student movement under way? In Paris, for instance? The pioneers of the student movement there were not necessarily typical of the French university population. France is a Catholic country with a small Protestant minority and a Jewish population that has never risen above 1 percent of the total. Yet of the students who quarreled with their left-wing elders and who would later turn up as leaders of their own generation, a very high number came from Jewish backgrounds. These were people with not very pleasant family histories. The parents of those students, some of them, had spent the Nazi era living like hunted animals, fleeing from place to place, taking part in guerrilla actions when they could. Some of them had ended up in the Nazi camps; others, fleeing eastward from Poland, had ended up in the Soviet camps. The oldest among the children were born under extremely grim circumstances. André Glucksmann, who as a young philosopher played a notable role in the uprisings of 1968 and after, was born in 1937 to immigrant parents who spent the war years as part of the Comintern's nucleus within the Resistance.

Jeanette Pienkny, the Trotskyist leader, born the year after Glucksmann, was seven years old by the time her father came home from a German prison. Another important Trotskyist student leader, Henri

Weber, was born during the war in a Soviet camp. Pierre Goldman—the young man who, among the '68 generation in France, came to symbolize dedication to revolutionary action—was born during the war to immigrant parents who fought in a Jewish shock brigade of the Lyons-region Resistance. And so forth. Children with backgrounds like those were brought up during the postwar years in the kind of atmosphere that used to be called "militant." For most of those children, that meant the youth groups of the French Communist Party; for others, the Zionist-socialist youth movement Hashomer Hatzair (the Young Guard); in a handful of cases, the anarchist groups.

The children sang the songs and attended the festivals. They listened to the stories of what their parents had done during the war. They knew themselves to be the children of heroes and of people who had suffered. Their own childish lives, on the other hand, were singularly free of suffering or heroism, at least after their earliest years. They grew up during the greatest prolonged boom in the history of capitalism. Everything that the parents had lacked, the children came to possess: comfort, peace, security, democracy, education, opportunity. And as the children got older, the contrast between Marxist memories of the war and the comforts of the present was bound to cast a disagreeable light on their own young lives. For who were they, these children, compared to who their parents had been? For that matter, who were these parents by the 1960s? The old guerrilla heroes of the wartime Resistance who kept prattling to their children about

Marxism and courage and the coming revolution and the feats of the past—these people had become, thanks to their own successes and the capitalist boom, middle-aged bourgeois who no longer meant a single word about revolutionary Marxism but did think the children ought to be grateful to have things so easy.

Not every young person growing up in circumstances like those would feel especially tortured by moral self-doubt or self-contempt. But there is a certain kind of young person for whom moral tortures are unavoidable, and the natural place for people like that is in a left-wing youth group. So the students who doubted themselves and worried about their own moral worth, once they had left home for school in Paris, drew together. They browsed at the Communist Party's bookstore and hung out at the editorial office of *Clarté*, the party's youth magazine. They drank coffee at Le Champo café, near the Sorbonne. And they said to themselves, as their elders would never have thought to say: I am privileged, therefore I am nothing. The chief chroniclers of the French student movement, Hervé Hamon and Patrick Rotman, the authors of *Génération*, have coined a phrase to describe what afflicted those anguished students. Some people suffer from an inferiority complex; these people suffered, on moral grounds, from an "illegitimacy complex."

The complex made them wonder if their own privileges weren't based on a lie. Their parents and the elders whom they met in the Communist Party (or in some of the other left-wing organizations) kept saying that life had become better and progress was at hand and, in the future, social conditions would continue to improve. The young people knew that, in regard to their own Parisian student lives, those statements were true. On the other hand, France in the 1960s was fighting an ugly colonial war against the Algerian nationalists, was it not? Soon enough the United States was fighting an exceedingly nasty anti-Communist war against the Vietnamese. Was life any better for the Algerians or the Vietnamese under the bombs of the Western Allies? Was the exploitation of Arab and African immigrant workers in France or of the black proletariat in the United States any different from the racist exploitation that had thrived in earlier times? Things *were* better; but only for oneself.

So the young people embarked on a reverse passion for the "other"—not a hatred for people who are different but a love for them, in eager acknowledgment of their very difference. Faraway solidarity became their religion. They said, in effect: I struggle on behalf of others, therefore I am. They conceived an idea of identity through action. It was a grand idea, morally. They imagined that, through radical action, they were going to revive the heroism and moral clarity of the old Resistance struggle against the Nazis. Pierre Goldman, in his memoirs, was explicit about it: "I think I was trying to recapture the time of my father, the time of my mother." But as soon as they tried to recapture the time of their parents in any kind of practical way, they ran into a terrible obstacle. It was the adult left. The grizzled leaders of the French Communist Party turned out to be people who felt not a single moral qualm about their own adult lives. On the topic of desperado actions by young leftists, the adults regarded themselves as supreme experts; and their expertise told them that in Gaullist France during the glory days of the economic boom, risk-taking adventures were a thing of the past. The young people wanted to aid the Algerian revolutionaries in their struggle against French colonialism; to lend military support to the guerrillas of Latin America; to do *something*. The adults flared their Communist nostrils, smelled petty-bourgeois adventurism, and gave the order "No." And so the young people looked at their elders and felt—contempt. They felt for their elders all the contempt that otherwise they might have felt for themselves, as the do-nothing heirs of heroes and martyrs.

The French children of Jewish Resistance heroes from the Second World War may have undergone these moral stresses with a particular intensity, which could explain why so many of them were quick to get into quarrels with the adult left. But nothing about their experience differed fundamentally from a lot of other people in the younger generation. Of the young French leftists who responded to the sixties cult of action by going to Latin America and joining the Marxist guerrillas, a couple of the better known were Jewish: there was Michelle Firk, who served with the Guatemalan guerrillas, and Goldman, who spent some time with the guerrillas in Venezuela. But the most famous of all, certainly the most talented political writer of the generation, was Régis Debray, who was not Jewish. Debray was a student of the Communist philosopher Louis Althusser at an elite school in Paris, the École normale supérieure. Debray, too, went to Venezuela to support the guerrilla revolution. By 1964 he was sending reports home to France, and his reports made it seem as if the old French Resistance were alive and well, fighting on in leafy Venezuela against U.S. imperialism (and against Venezuela's social democratic government) instead of against the Nazi occupiers from the European past. Debray expressed the worry of an entire generation in a famous remark about what would happen if the younger people did not, in fact, plunge into radical campaigns or join a revolutionary *maquis*: "After the veterans of Verdun, of Mauthausen [the Nazi death camp] and of Indochina, we will be the veterans of the cinemathèque." That was not a small fear.

So the tiny handful of left-wing French students argued with the adult leftists about the need for action, and when the adults lost patience and expelled the young truculents from the official organizations (in the case of the Communist Student Union, this took place in 1965–66, in two waves), the young people went ahead and organized their own solidarity groups to aid the Marxist guerrillas of Latin America. They made pilgrimages to the Venezuelan countryside, to Communist Cuba, to insurrectionary Algeria, and to China. They formed underground Trotskyist support channels for the Algerian nationalists. They discovered that adult backing was unnecessary. That was the fateful revelation. Students who were five or ten years younger began to follow their example. The younger students staged a thousand provocations and classroom coups d'état. Impudence became their signature. In 1967 a squad of young militants attacked the American Express office in Paris on behalf of the Vietnamese Communists. Groups of young people were soon enough engaged in disputes with the university administration at Nanterre, outside of Paris.

A Nanterre sit-in got under way, then another at the Sorbonne. And the handful of young people suddenly discovered that when they issued calls for a political demonstration tens of thousands of their peers showed up to participate. They acted, and the vibrations penetrated into the student population. For to be young and morally troubled in 1968 was to feel, at least in a small way, the same painful doubts and anxieties that the tiny handful of Jewish and non-Jewish left-wing youth activists had begun to express a few years earlier in their battles with the left-wing elders. It was to feel morally worthless in the face of what the parents' generation had gone through—or had gone along with. And it was to feel contempt for what the parents had become. The young people wanted to redeem their souls. They wanted to leave behind the privileges and comforts of middle-class student life and go fight in the street and in the universities for a better world, just the way the heroes of the Resistance had gone into the street to fight against the Nazis.

You hardly needed to be French to feel those impulses. In large parts of the world, not just in Western Europe, the twentieth century from the 1930s into the early 1950s had been an age of disaster, and the parents of the students of the sixties, the left-wing parents especially, were disaster's veterans. Those people had been the combatants in the Spanish Civil War. (The Communist Youth club in Mexico that produced Gilberto Guevara and some other future leaders of the student uprising in 1968 contained the children of refugees from Spain.) The parents had struggled through the Great Depression and the Second World War, and they had endured the repression of the Communist movements in a number of Western countries when the war was over, and now they were exhausted, and the children who were born of those parents had something in common. They were the after-the-deluge children. And in more than a few countries around the world those children, just enough of them to get a movement going, felt the same agony of conscience and idealism, naturally in a different style in every country. It was the moral crisis of the baby boom generation.

In one country after another, the way out of that crisis was to shake off the comforts of a stable bourgeois world and to take up the risks of radical solidarity. So a small vanguard of privileged students in place after place proposed risky campaigns of radical solidarity, and because the risky campaigns and the cult of danger seemed foolish or irresponsible to the adult left, the young and their elders fell into bitter arguments, and the young were expelled by the old. Everywhere the young discovered that adult support was unnecessary. And at once the newly independent radical campaigns of the young began to express the wider generational anguish with perfect fidelity. Tiny flames of pure idealism went up. Everywhere the effect was intoxicating, even among the great mass of students whose parents had been anything but left wing. And so the handful of young militants who had been expelled from the traditional left-wing parties found themselves with a large following of their own age or a few years younger, and the sparks of radical action flew from one country to the next so swiftly that no one could remember how or where or why the whole thing had gotten started, and the crowds were marching through the streets with red flags and black flags and it was 1968.

II

You might suppose that, in the United States, the story of the 1960s student generation would be different, given how small and marginal were the traditional parties of the American left. But not at all. The New Left in the United States followed the world pattern exactly, beginning with the beginning.

By the end of the 1950s, there was no shortage of left-wing youth movements in the United States, all of them modest in size, but full of capable people who entertained the slightly desperate hope of building up a mass American left. The Communist Party USA lost most of its members in 1956, when the American Communists finally came to believe the truth about

Stalin; but by the early sixties the party was still larger than all the other formal organizations of the American left, and it still managed to attract young people to its student organizations. Another group, much larger but not formally organized, gathered around the independent Marxist-Leninist publications, *Monthly Review* and the *National Guardian*, where the great ambition was to rescue American Communism from its own maladroit leaders. There were the Trotskyists of the Young Socialist Alliance and a number of smaller groups, and there was Michael Harrington's Young People's Socialist League (YPSL), which was strictly anti-Communist—or in the phrase of the time, "anti-Stalinist." Still other young radicals hung around the Catholic Worker movement and a few other Christian groups, the Student Peace Union, Student SANE, the War Resisters League, and the Libertarian League, which may have been tiny but had a noble Wobbly origin.

But among all these movements and tendencies, the one organization that was destined to play a historic role turned out to be the oldest and most conservative of all. That was the Student League for Industrial Democracy. The roots of that organization went back to 1905, when the Socialist Party of America was a vigorous enterprise and the party's leader, Eugene V. Debs, was a much-loved figure and the party prospects looked reasonably good. Upton Sinclair, the author of *The Jungle*, organized the Intercollegiate Socialist Society (ISS) in 1905 as a campus wing of the adult party. Jack London became the president, and the ISS succeeded in establishing seventy chapters at schools all over the country. Student radicals like John Reed (Harvard) and, a few years later, Sidney Hook (City College of New York) became active members. W. E. B. Du Bois served on the board. In time the ISS evolved into an adult organization called the League for Industrial Democracy (LID), which was, as we would say today, a think tank for the Socialist Party, backed financially by the various trade unions that maintained a Socialist affiliation.

The LID never did draw any attention to itself. But in its modest way it occupied the exact spot in American life where European-style reform socialism (or social democracy), American-style liberalism, and the trade unions came together. The LID was socialism without the crippling sectarianism of the Socialist Party of America; liberalism without the middle-class snobbism that looks down on labor; unionism without the me-first-ism of the conservative unions. The LID eventually reestablished the old Intercollegiate Socialist Society under a new name, the Student League for Industrial Democracy, which succeeded in training several generations of trade union leaders and human rights activists. Walter Reuther went from being president of his college chapter to being president of the United Auto Workers. Al Shanker went from the Columbia University chapter to become president of the teachers' union. Arieh Neier went from being national president of the student organization to a famous career in human rights. And courtesy of still another change of name, the Student League for Industrial Democracy—whose acronym was, all too sadly, SLID—became, by 1960, Students for a Democratic Society, or SDS.

No one would have predicted a great future for Students for a Democratic Society in 1960. The Socialist Party still maintained a proprietary relation over the LID and its student group, but the party by then, having long ago entered into irremediable decline, was more of a club or a philosophical society than a political organization in any ordinary sense. The International Ladies Garment Workers Union (ILGWU) and a few other labor groups still clung to a Socialist identity and faithfully paid the bills for the party's LID. But the unions themselves were by then no longer young and frisky, and their left-wing glamour was something no one could remember. The Socialist Party leader, Norman Thomas, enjoyed the kind of reputation among liberals that allowed people to speak kindly of him and blithely ignore his more radical ideas. The one jewel of the Socialist movement circa 1960 was its civil rights work. A. Philip Randolph of the Sleeping Car Porters Union, the ancient leader of Socialism's Harlem branch, was the elder statesman of American civil rights. Randolph's deputy, Bayard Rustin, another solid Socialist, was a key aid to Martin Luther King, Jr. These men, Randolph and Rustin, ran the northern front of the civil rights campaign, and they brought along the support of their white Socialist comrades in the unions, which gave the civil rights movement a powerful ally, and their role was immense.

But the civil rights campaign did not breathe youth and energy into the Socialist Party.

By 1960 the LID itself had degenerated into an old-timers' and pensioners' organization. The LID's Students for a Democratic Society was almost invisible. Instead of seventy chapters there were, by 1960, only three. Still, one of those three, the SDS chapter at the University of Michigan, was noticeably talented. The first person to conceive of something like a New Left student movement in America is said to have been Al Haber of the Michigan chapter. Haber was the son of an old admirer of Norman Thomas and the Socialists, which meant that SDS's family roots in the American left were reasonably solid at Michigan. And the Michigan chapter could claim Tom Hayden, whose abilities were great. Hayden came to SDS by way of the Shrine of the Little Flower school in Father Coughlin's parish in Royal Oak, Michigan, which was no kind of left-wing background at all. But what he lacked in socialism he made up for in literature. He read Kerouac, Camus, and C. Wright Mills. He quoted Ignazio Silone. He had a knack for integrating bits of Catholic humanism into his left-wing thinking.

In 1960 the civil rights movement in the South established its own student affiliate, the Student Non-Violent Coordinating Committee (SNCC), whose activists, the "field secretaries," organized the Freedom Rides and any number of other activities to overthrow Jim Crow. And with funds that came to SDS through the LID and its labor supporters, Hayden went from Ann Arbor into the South to support the SNCC activities. He worked on voter registration campaigns. He helped integrate the Georgia railroad. His twenty-second birthday was spent in a jail cell in Albany, Georgia. He was beaten in Mississippi. He was brave. He was the Michigan equivalent of the French students who went to fight in Latin America or ran underground messages for the Algerian nationalists. And if Hayden did anything that was, in addition, novel, it was mostly in the way that he began to write about these activities. He composed reports from the Deep South, which he worked on with Haber and some of the other Michigan SDSers and sent around for his fellow students to read. The reports exuded an air of personal daring and moral simplicity. He talked about young people proving themselves by undertaking "risky, shoot-for-the-moon affairs"—a slightly existentialist phrase—"based not on personal security desires but on a willingness to deal with the uncertain."

Middle-class comforts made Hayden and the SDSers fidgety. They worried about the corruptions of privilege. They were victims of an illegitimacy complex. And of all the youth organizations that came out of the classic American left in the 1950s and early '60s, Hayden's was the group that found itself embroiled in American versions of the worldwide internecine quarrel between the left-wing generations. In 1962 Hayden and Haber went to consult with their adult sponsors at the LID in New York. They quarreled. Hayden considered that the LID was venerable—but, in his word, "senile." The next year an SDS group that included Hayden, Todd Gitlin, and Steve Max

visited Irving Howe and the editors of *Dissent* magazine for a philosophical discussion. *Dissent* was the
socialist movement's principal intellectual journal in
the United States. Howe was the movement's shrewd-
est, most eloquent writer. The discussion touched on
the Cuban Revolution and the nonviolent tactics of
Mahatma Gandhi. Young Hayden and middle-aged
Howe ended up sneering at each other. And of all the
left-wing youth groups in America, the tiny social
democratic student organization that was incapable of
chatting amiably with its elders was precisely the group
that now found itself attracting the largest number of
new members in the colleges and universities of the
Midwest and the East, and sometimes in other regions,
too.

Who were these new SDS members? No one has
failed to notice that in the American student movement of the 1960s, students with a Jewish background
played a distinctive role, exactly as in the French movement. Of the white Freedom Riders who traveled to
Mississippi, two-thirds happened to be Jewish. A mass
student rebellion called the Free Speech Movement
broke out at Berkeley in the fall of 1964, and a majority
of the movement's steering committee again happened
to be Jewish. In the early days, SDS's Jewish component was not as large as that of some other organizations on the left; yet the component existed, and grew.
To cite some figures from Kenneth Heineman's *Campus Wars*, at Columbia and the University of Michigan,
SDS ended up more than half Jewish. At Kent State
University, where 5 percent of the student body was

Jewish, SDS was 19 percent Jewish. At Pennsylvania State University, it was 42 percent Jewish. At Michigan State University, where Jews were 10 percent of the student body, SDS was 24 percent Jewish. At the State University of New York at Buffalo, SDS and a couple of allied organizations were 62 percent Jewish. The family histories of the American Jewish students were not to be compared to those of the French Jews, except in a few cases where the parents had been wartime refugees. Yet the parents had gone through their own American experiences. They had participated in the American left-wing movements of the 1930s and '40s, and some of those parents had suffered in the labor wars or had been persecuted during the McCarthy era, and some of them had gone on celebrating the political culture that came out of the Old Left straight through the 1950s and into the '60s. So the parallel between the French and the Americans was plain enough. And just as in France, from that not-very-representative nucleus, the student movement went spreading in all directions across the American campuses.

Part of SDS's appeal was an air of intellectual originality. You can still feel it, ever so slightly, in reading the organization's manifesto or "Statement." Hayden wrote the first draft, then submitted his achievement for collective revision at an SDS conference in the summer of 1962. The conference took place in Port Huron, Michigan, at a summer camp run by Reuther's United Auto Workers. According to Richard Flacks, who contributed a few of the crucial passages, Norman

Thomas looked over the document on behalf of social-ism's older generation and said, "I've seen a lot of manifestos in my day, and this one's no worse, nor no better." Such was the adult incomprehension! The Statement was longer than the *Communist Manifesto*, and not as good. But there were reasons why the Port Huron Statement took on a legendary status in the circles of student radicalism and was cited and revered and even read, sometimes.

The Statement criticized social and economic inequality, racism, and unemployment, as any left-wing manifesto would do. It condemned American foreign policy—though the domestic and foreign criti-cisms alike were made in a notably gentle fashion. America in the Port Huron Statement was not irre-deemable; just in need of remediation. The Statement said, "American military response has been more effec-tive at deterring the growth of democracy than Com-munism"—in clear acknowledgment that deterring Communism would be a good idea, so long as democ-racy was encouraged. According to Lenin's theory of imperialism, America and the other rich capitalist countries, due to the pressure of their own economic systems, were intrinsically the enemy of every progres-sive development around the world. But Leninist logic was missing from the Port Huron Statement. And having criticized America's social structures and for-eign policies in those very sensible ways, the Statement went on to worry about some American attitudes and habits.

It complained about meaningless work, about the

national "malaise" (fifteen years before Jimmy Carter famously adopted the phrase), and about the "loneliness, estrangement, isolation" of American life. It worried about the irrationality that allowed people in a Gallup Poll to predict a nuclear war in the imminent future yet to cite "international relations" as fourteenth on a list of American problems. These were cultural points, the kind of thing you could have read (in adult versions) in Dwight Macdonald's *Politics* magazine in the 1940s or in *Dissent* in the fifties and sixties or in the writings of C. Wright Mills. Here again the Port Huron Statement was reasonably restrained. In the fifties and early sixties Herbert Marcuse, the Frankfurt School philosopher, from his home in Southern California, was working up all kinds of sexual theories about Eros and its insurrectionary possibilities. The Beat poets were perpetrating free-verse outrages on sexual decency. None of that at Port Huron! Yet even the blandest cultural points made SDS look fresh and original in comparison to some of the other left-wing student groups, the supersquares, with their proletarian style and their mania for hard economic facts.

The Statement advocated a synthesis of liberalism and socialism, as was proper for the student wing of the League for Industrial Democracy. And in the liberal socialist spirit the Statement spoke of "participatory democracy," a nice phrase—though its meaning, as Hawthorne once said of America, was deep and varied. The Statement's most famous passage said, "We seek the establishment of a democracy of individual participation, governed by two central aims: that the individual share in those social decisions determining the quality and direction of his life; that society be organized to encourage independence in men and provide the media for their common participation." The idea was a society of self-government at the grass roots. And in that way, too, SDS found itself oddly resembling the student movement in other countries. For almost everywhere the radical students came up with a distinctive way to describe the superior society that they hoped to build, and almost everywhere the description contained some common features.

The libertarian factions of the French student left, the Situationists and anarchists, imagined a system of superdemocratic "workers' councils" to replace the bureaucratic modern state and the capitalist corporations and the bureaucratic unions. The best known of all the French student leaders in 1968, Dany Cohn-Bendit (still another child with hard Jewish family memories of the war, by the way), was the voice of that idea. In France even the Maoists, hardly libertarians, pictured Mao-style Communism as a variation on the same concept, which was an error on their part, but they seemed to believe it. The Italian students talked about "workers' autonomy," which was the identical idea with a different spin. The best-known leader of German SDS, Rudi Dutschke, spoke about re-creating the Paris Commune of 1871, which suggested the same notion yet again, given that, in the imagination of the left, the Paris Commune was a revolutionary workers' council on a municipal basis.

In the Netherlands, where the student movement was strong, the leader of the radical "provos," Roel Van Duyn, proposed to revive the old idea of libertarian communes as described in the nineteenth-century anarchist pamphlets of Peter Kropotkin. A Kropotkinite commune was a town or city with a collective economy and grass-roots self-government. The Mexican students, less doctrinaire, emphasized the ordinary features of a modern political democracy—which were not so ordinary in authoritarian Mexico. Yet in Mexico, too, when the student strike of 1968 finally broke out, the students instinctively organized themselves into local assemblies representing the different schools and universities of Mexico City, and they linked the assemblies together in the National Strike Council, and the result was a day-to-day demonstration of how democratic grass-roots self-government ought to work, exactly as the Western European radicals would have advised. In Czechoslovakia (to wander into the Eastern Bloc for a moment), the main idea from 1968 was "socialism with a human face," which was mostly a pluralist version of Communism and could hardly count as a vision of grass-roots self-management; yet in Czechoslovakia, too, factory committees began to appear, and bits and pieces of the same libertarian idea could be detected.

The SDS proposal for "participatory democracy" in the United States differed from those other ideas mostly on one tiny point, owing to a discrepancy in the way that democracy is understood in the United States and elsewhere. In Europe during most of the twentieth century (here come a few shameless generalizations), the political thinkers of the right and the left have pictured the best of all societies as something other than democracy. The better world of their fancy might have been (depending on party affiliation) feudal, fascist, Communist, or revolutionary socialist in one of several versions—but it was not likely to be democratic in any ordinary sense. In the European imagination, democracy was a politics of compromise and truce. It evoked a spirit of tolerance, moderation, caution, sobriety, rationality, and fatigue, which might amount to wisdom, but also to mediocrity. Democracy was something to arrive at only when the bright dream of exterminating one's enemies no longer seemed within reach and the notion of a truly superior society had been abandoned. It was a "secondary love derived from a primary hatred," in André Glucksmann's phrase. That was why, when the European students of the sixties wanted to conjure a hope for freedom and social change, they plucked off the shelf something more glamorous and exciting than mere democracy and came up with their notions of workers' councils or the Paris Commune or some other wonderful bit of imagination from the nineteenth-century workers' movement.

Naturally, in America, too, democracy has always been understood as a politics of compromise or truce, loved in a "secondary" way, as is wise to do. But in America there has always been an additional idea, not always well defined, which pictures democracy as an *activity*, not merely an arrangement—the best of activities, at that. It is a very old idea. You can find it discussed in one of Jefferson's letters (dated February 2, 1816), where he specifies that, under a properly decentralized democracy, everyone ought to feel "that he is a participator"—that same word—"in the government of affairs, not merely at an election one day in the year, but every day." Walt Whitman gave the same notion a more extravagant twist. Whitman didn't dismiss the importance of laws and political parties and the ordinary structures of a constitutional government; but democracy for him was always more. It was a society where people actively did things and fulfilled themselves, which meant that democracy, for him, was a project for the future. A utopia, not a compromise. A love that was primary, not secondary. Or more radical still: an incitement. "*Resist much, obey little*," was Whitman's maxim (italics and all), tendered as an incendiary guiding principle for civic affairs.

The people who founded the long organizational family tree that led to SDS tended to think about democracy along those same radical and utopian lines. One of the original signers of the call to organize the Intercollegiate Socialist Society (whence the LID, whence SDS) was a turn-of-the-century Socialist theoretician named William English Walling, who wrote a book called *Whitman and Traubel* on the radical democratic theme. Walling had the idea of combining Whitman's notion of revolutionary democracy with the socialist hope for a cooperative society and equality of opportunity. John Dewey, the Vermont sage—to cite still another Whitman reader—came up with his own variations on the same democratic thought. Dewey imagined democracy as a society of individuals achieving themselves through creative labor and community action, and when he thought about how to organize something like that, sometimes he pictured New England town meetings, and sometimes he pictured a libertarian socialism along European lines.

Dewey took an interest in guild socialism, which was the English version of those same workers' councils and anarchist communes that so excited the French Situationists and Dutch provos in the 1960s. He pictured "a federation of self-governing industries with the government acting as adjustor and arbitor rather than as direct owner or manager." These ideas never led Dewey to join Walling in the Socialist Party itself. But the LID, with its emphasis on education and social reform and its deemphasis on socialist rhetoric, fit his style. In 1939–40 Dewey served as president of the LID, and until his death, in 1952, he stayed on as honorary president. Through Dewey, the whole line of thinking that descended from Jefferson to Whitman to figures like Walling entered the particular wing of American socialism that eventually produced SDS. The greatest of the professional philosophers who played any role in the Socialist Party was Dewey's disciple, Sidney Hook (another member of the LID board), and when Hook defined socialism's goal as, among other things, "a sense of genuine participation among individuals," the Deweyan touch was unmistakable.

In 1960, SDS's other two chapters, after Hayden's

at Michigan, were at Columbia, where Dewey spent his last years, and at Yale; and both of those chapters were officially called "John Dewey Discussion Clubs." Even in the Michigan chapter, where Dewey's name wasn't formally invoked, his legacy was large, partly through his own writings, partly through his influence on Mills and other authors and professors who in turn influenced the student organization. The phrase about "participatory democracy" was coined by one of those Michigan professors, Arnold Kaufman, a Deweyan who taught in the philosophy department and was sufficiently active in the LID to attend SDS's conference at Port Huron in 1962. The discussion of participatory democracy in the Port Huron Statement, because of its civics-class windiness, even managed to sound like Dewey. Dewey's biographer Robert Westbrook has dug up an essay from the 1930s where Dewey discussed the "keynote of democracy," which is defined as "the participation of every mature human being in the formation of the values that regulate the living of men together." Dewey wrote, "All those who are affected by social institutions must have a share in producing and managing them." Those phrases reemerged nearly intact in the Port Huron Statement.

Since Dewey's intellectual roots lay in Whitman and in the nineteenth-century American Hegelians and transcendentalists or even in Jefferson, you could argue that participatory democracy, as SDS conceived it, was no less antique than any of the European student ideas about workers' councils or the Paris Commune. But participatory democracy had one important difference, due to the way that democracy is understood in the United States. The workers' councils and the Paris Commune always implied, as part of the basic idea, that before anything so radical could be instituted, a proletarian revolution would have to take place. There was no such suggestion in participatory democracy. The millenarian dreaminess of the nineteenth-century workers' movement and the demagogy, too, were absent from that idea. You could shake it with both hands, and no exclamation point would come tumbling out. The phrase was calm and rational and, even so, reasonably inspiring. The 1960s student movement around the world popularized a lot of ideas and phrases for a better society—not just "workers' councils" and the "Paris Commune" but also the "New Man" of the Fidelistas, the guerrilla "focos" that Régis Debray described, the "people's justice" of the French *gauchistes*, the countercultural "tribes" that would soon enough pop up among the California hippies and would spread all over the United States and into Italy and a few other places.

But of all these concepts and phrases, "participatory democracy" was, I think, the only one to survive a generation later, at least without causing major embarrassment. It was a good idea (mostly). That rarity! And beyond those several virtues, in its quiet way participatory democracy articulated the existential drama of moral activism. For who was going to be the Jeffersonian participant in the SDS ideal, the Whitmanesque singer of the song of occupations, the Deweyan achiever of self-realization? It was going to be you, the member of SDS, the runner of risks. And if anyone in the early and middle sixties still wondered what risks or activities those might be, Hayden was there to spell it out with his own example and his feats of integrationist activism and the beatings and jailings that he underwent for the cause of civil rights. Moral activism was finally what drew people to SDS. Activism showed the wider population of privileged American students that their own cozy life did not have to be a prison, and nothing could prevent them from going out into the world and fighting for a juster society, and the choice to be a democratic participant was theirs to make.

The historian of SDS's grand democratic idea, James Miller, in his book "*Democracy Is in the Streets,*" has shown that participatory democracy went through different phases. It began as a strictly ethical ideal of citizenship. Hayden and his comrades didn't intend to get rid of representative democracy, or to abolish the idea of leadership or any of the other attributes of a normal organization. But normal organizations were soon enough a thing of the past. A Quaker-like cult of consensus stole across the world of student radicalism, as if to hold votes or to build an organization with rules and regulations and leaders and followers was to impose some kind of horrible dictatorship over the rank and file. From a civic ideal, participatory democracy swiftly evolved into a call for a movement without offices or officers—a call, in short, for marathon mass meetings. Miller cites some hilarious records of SDS meetings to show what that was like. A 1965 report from SDS's group in Newark solemnly observed, "Although many of us regard voting as undemocratic, there is a real question about whether we can afford to take eight hours to attain consensus on every issue." The members of an SDS organizing project in Cleveland once held a twenty-four-hour meeting to decide whether to take a day off and go to the beach.

Suspicion of leaders became so intense that after a while Hayden and other people who were, in fact, leaders began to pretend that they weren't, and took to sitting among the rank and file instead of at the head of the room. In that way the leaders became unaccountable, and a bit of demagogy was introduced into the anti-demagogic cause. The obsession with formlessness and consensus had the further debilitating effect of erasing any institutional memory, which is always the weak spot in student movements. Activists came along, learned some lessons, graduated from campus life—and every lesson learned was gone. There were genuine politicos in SDS who would have liked to turn their popular student organization into something solid and lasting, and earnestly tried to tame the anti-institutional madness. But participatory democracy had a logic of its own. And that was not SDS's only problem.

The "illegitimacy complex" meant that any time SDS succeeded in organizing its own world of the students, the inner core of true-blue activists entered into yet another paroxysm of moral anguish and accused themselves of having lapsed again into self-serving egotism. And instantly they took steps to restore the organization's dedication to the oppressed in neighborhoods other than their own. This habit led to a bizarre record of successes and failures. The Berkeley Free Speech Movement in 1964 (not an SDS enterprise, but close enough in spirit) showed that campus radicalism was a cause with a future. And at precisely that moment, the national leaders of SDS, under the lash of "authenticity," chose to withdraw from campus to organize poor people in the ghettos. Lewis Feuer, one of the American socialists on the older side of the generational split, wrote a fascinating and very learned (and crabby) book in 1969, *The Conflict of Generations*, in which he demonstrated that virtually every serious left-wing student movement since the early nineteenth century has gone through a similar stage, sending students out from the university "to the people" as revolutionary agitators. Under that inspiration students all over Latin America exited their law schools beginning in the early 1960s to go to the mountains and organize the peasants. In the mid-sixties the French Maoists went from the elite academies to "establish" themselves (that was their phrase) in the factories. The Mexican '68ers formed "brigades" to bring the news of the student movement to the workers. SDS merely did the same.

Its version was called "community organizing." With funding from the UAW, the SDSers moved into down-and-out neighborhoods in nine cities. Hayden went to Newark. The organizers worked patiently, and in Newark and Cleveland their work may have given a small helpful boost to the mobilizing of black political power. But bigger successes, something comparable to the Free Speech Movement, were always out of reach. In early 1965 the war in Vietnam began to draw in large numbers of American troops, and SDS issued a call for the first national demonstration against America's participation. A small phalanx of anti-militarist and left-wing organizations lined up in support. Buses poured into Washington, D.C., bearing thousands of college students and a few from high school, too (my own wide-eyed self among them), along with the memberships of those many peace and left-wing organizations. Norman Thomas spoke. Joan Baez sang. It was a glorious April afternoon. The speeches and rally set the style for the anti-war movement to come. That was a big success—bigger, in potential, even than the uprising at Berkeley. And having put itself at the head of something vast and energetic, SDS decided at once to withdraw yet again because in local organizing was virtue (which left the national anti-war leadership in the hands of the adults, who were not necessarily any improvement over the students).

Three years later, as part of the wave of 1968 uprisings around the world, the old John Dewey Discussion Club at Columbia University—now renamed simply Students for a Democratic Society—agitated against the war and the racial injustices of uptown Manhattan, which were grotesque, and several hundred white and black university students rose in rebellion. They were joined by several thousand other students, then by politicians from Harlem, and SDS and its allies led a colorful strike that closed the university. Indignant crowds marched through the streets of uptown Manhattan and police vans roared around the avenues and the atmosphere of insurrection lasted through the spring. And SDS's main leaders, having turned their organization into a genuine power in New York City, outdid themselves not only by withdrawing from the Columbia campus but, soon enough, by dismantling the organization itself. There was neurosis in that pattern.

Yet such was SDS's relation to the age that achievements sprung even from retreats. I think that on each of the campuses where the organization had any strength, SDS managed to be a walking challenge to the other students to do something more than mumble complaints about the war and the old story of American racism and poverty. The war was participatory democracy's perfect enemy. For the United States had gotten into Vietnam through the decisions of elites, not through any democratic debate and popular analysis, and the way to counter an elite was to establish an anti-elite, a grass-roots ultra-democracy of direct action. In this SDS succeeded. Even the special nuttiness of SDS's organizational style had its uses. Some of the historians and veterans of SDS don't remember it that way, but in my own experience of those days, anarchy in SDS was precisely how the movement delivered on its deepest promise, which was to take young people who felt empty of identity and give them a sense of control over their own destiny. The marathon mass meeting was typically held in an illegally occupied university building at three in the morning for the purpose of trying to decide how to react when the police arrived, and you sat through one of those assemblies knowing full well that at any moment you could quietly get up and tiptoe out the door.

Then the meeting was over, and you hadn't tiptoed out, and you gazed at the receding ivy walls of your university through the grilled back window of a paddy wagon, and you knew that no one but yourself was to blame, and off you went to jail, where for once you felt morally at peace. In this way SDS addressed not only immediate issues like the war and the civil rights revolution (which would have been quite enough) but also the moral quandary of the young people who, after the horrors of the Great Depression and the war against fascism and the chilly McCarthy years and everything else that had been experienced by the parents' generation, felt offended by the soft life that was their own. Or maybe the achievement was more than generational and SDS succeeded for a tiny fugitive moment in speaking to the moral quandary that afflicts the reasonably prosperous population everywhere in the democratic world, or ought to afflict it—the feeling of ethical emptiness that now and then descends upon people as they go about their private lives.

One of the historians of the 1968 uprising in Mexico, César Gilabert, has argued that, for a few months at the height of the movement there, a rare mood of utopian exhilaration took hold of the students. Every aspect of the Mexican revolt—its spirit of impudence, the spectacular marches through the capital city streets, the graffiti on the buildings, the leaflets, the cultural festivals every weekend, the student assemblies—led the participants to picture their own movement as a countersociety at war with the authoritarian state. The new democratic society that everyone in the movement so ardently desired seemed to have already come into existence. It was a "utopian moment," in Gilabert's phrase. The French had the same experience. The French equivalent of the Port Huron Statement was a famous pamphlet called "On the Poverty of Student Life," written in 1966 by a little group of Situationists, who described the phenomenon even before it had taken place. "Proletarian revolutions"—in Situationist eyes, any revolution worth discussing had to be proletarian—"will be *festivals* or nothing, for festivity is the very keynote of the life they announce." And that same feeling began to emerge in the American universities. By holding daily demonstrations, by doing something outrageous or impudent against the war or American racism, by disrupting an occasional class or heckling a professor (preferably a good liberal whose sin was to stand one inch to the right of the student left), by dressing slightly differently from the other students, in short by "resisting much, obeying little," SDS (and the other organizations of the student left) generated an atmosphere of confrontation, which turned giddy and hot, which created a festival atmosphere, which got hotter.

And at last, like a little curl of smoke, from out of

the festival came a few tiny indications that a new society, organized on novel principles, might at any moment burst into view. There was a feeling that every aspect of the existing society had been discovered to be wrong, and could be opposed; that in the splendid carnival of the student demonstrations and rock concerts and hippie neighborhoods and the continual insurrections of individuals a revolution had *already occurred*; that the new society and the newer ways of living already existed, in embryo. All you had to do was join. The marches, the building takeovers, the amphetamine activism that went on night and day, the agit-prop meetings in the dorms, the theatrical clothes, the music, and the strange new political rhetoric were signs of that new society. But the absolutely crucial component was the mass meeting. It was the meeting where everyone and anyone could get up and say the craziest things, where the ordinary rules about who has power and who does not were suspended. Sheer madness, those meetings were. Yet they took place, and the superdemocratic utopia flickered into reality before your eyes.

Freedom—what seemed like freedom, anyway—became visible. That was the excitement that went leaping from school to school, continent to continent, in 1968, exactly as had happened in each of the international revolutions from earlier times, all the way back to 1848 and even before.

III

The 1968-era student movements arose more or less the same way in at least several countries around the world; and from country to country they fell the same way.

Almost everywhere the movements began by promising to construct a new kind of democratic or libertarian socialism. And almost everywhere (except in the Communist world, where the student movements followed a path all their own), the democratic and libertarian aspects dropped away, in part or in whole, by the end of the sixties or the early seventies, and the protests and merry carnivals degenerated into guerrilla mayhem and Dostoyevskian persecutions, and the specter of left-wing dictatorship arose, and instead of freedom there was havoc. And in these matters, too, the American New Left—at any rate, its SDS contingent—stayed in line with the other movements around the world. The worldwide rebellion went down, and SDS went down exactly the same way. You might even argue that SDS's plunge at the end was more pitiable than most of the other movements', if only because the New Left in America, despite what is usually said about leftism in America, started at a relatively high level of political sophistication.

By political sophistication I mean an appreciation of democracy, and of democracy's difference from Marxism-Leninism. That particular understanding came out of the long and somewhat unusual history of the American left. All over the world in the years after 1917 and the Bolshevik Revolution, Communist movements were formed in order to follow the Bolshevik model, and in quite a few places the new Communist organizations overwhelmed the socialists and the older factions of the left, and Communism and the left became nearly synonymous. Some of those developments took place in America, too. Beginning in 1919, a Bolshevik faction split away from the Socialist Party of America and formed a Communist movement, and in the 1930s and '40s the Communist Party won a good deal of support and shaped the political imagination of any number of liberals and radicals who would never have acknowledged being under a Communist influence. But in America, Communism's rivals on the left fought back with a special intensity.

Partly that was because of America's ties to the Eastern Bloc. Of all the countries on earth, the United States might appear to be the furthest removed from the Soviet Union, the least capable of understanding Soviet thinking or perceiving the Soviet reality. But, on the contrary, in the twentieth century, a large part of the American working class has consisted of immigrants from Central and Eastern Europe and their descendants, who had some inkling of Communism's reality in the Soviet zone. In Western Europe or in Latin America or in other places around the world the traditional organizations of the working-class left might indulge the wildest fantasies about the workers' paradise in the Soviet Union, and the student movements that emerged from the traditional left might look for ever more clever ways to update those fantasies or to move them to exotic locales in Communist China or the revolutionary Third World. But in the United States the traditional organizations of the working-class left were filled with people who had cousins and friends in the Eastern Bloc, who kept the fantasies in check. And so, while a large portion of the American left embraced the Communist cause or, at any rate, came to look on it with a kind eye, another portion, sometimes larger and sometimes not, looked on Communism with an absolute hatred.

The battles between those two halves of the American left continued straight into the 1950s and even after, nowhere more violently than in New York. The biggest and strongest of the New York needle trades unions, the ILGWU, was built by the Socialists, but the Communists fought their way into power in the 1920s, and the Socialists and their allies among the labor anarchists fought their way back, and it was civil war on Seventh Avenue. The Communists filled Yankee Stadium for a rally; the Socialists, Madison Square Garden; and the wounds from those battles did not heal. On the topic of anti-Communism, the Socialists in a union like the ILGWU ended up strictly diehard. Outside New York, in the auto workers and several other unions where Socialism had any strength, the feeling was the same. And since it was the old Socialist unions that kept the LID alive and paid the bills for its student affiliate, the labor tradition that descended from the Intercollegiate Socialist Society to the LID to SDS could not have been sterner on the topic of Communism and its horrors.

The intellectuals who affiliated with the LID came to the same anti-Communist conclusions. Dewey was active in the teachers' union, where the battle to keep the Communist Party from taking over during the 1930s and '40s was pretty rough, and he came out loathing everything about Communists: their ideals, their style of argument, their threat to intellectual honesty, their threat to democracy. "Extremely repugnant" was Dewey's description of Communism. Sidney Hook, whose journey from the Intercollegiate Socialist Society to a seat on the LID board involved a short embarrassing detour into Communism itself, was (once he had corrected his error) fiercer than anyone, which meant that America's leading Socialist philosopher was also America's leading philosopher of anti-Communism. In 1958 Max Shachtman's wing of American Trotskyism joined the Socialist Party and came to play its own part in the LID and brought still more hostility to the Soviet Union and to Communism's supporters in America. Anti-Communism in SDS's parent organization drew, as a result, on every possible experience: on the knowledge of the immigrant workers, on the hard-won experiences of the New York labor movement, on the reasoning of the philosophers, and on the ferocity of the sectarian battlers.

The Port Huron Statement was a student flower at the end of that very long vine. "As democrats we are in basic opposition to the Communist system," the SDSers wrote. "The Soviet Union, as a system, rests on the total suppression of organized opposition, as well as a vision of the future in the name of which much human life has been sacrificed, and numerous small and large denials of human dignity rationalized." You couldn't ask for a clearer expression of anti-Communist principles. The Statement went on to specify that "an unreasoning anti-Communism has become a major social problem for those who want to construct a more democratic America." That was all too true. The Statement criticized the uncanny way that American foreign policy, devoted to its anti-Communist crusade, kept producing results that were anything but democratic. That, too, was reasonable enough.

The Statement expressed solidarity for the oppressed people of the Eastern Bloc. It condemned America's tendency to pay lip service to Eastern Bloc liberation without achieving anything practical on those people's behalf. The Statement worried about the insanities of America's nuclear armament—yet left no suggestion that Soviet policy was any more rational. The Vietnam War was not yet a major issue in 1962, but in SDS's Statement you could already detect the beginnings of a very sensible position: the criticism that saw a value in keeping the people of South Vietnam free from Communist control, but recognized that even the noblest of anti-Communist intentions could end up in calamity. That kind of reasoning in the Port Huron Statement, the combination of a principled anti-Communism with a radical skepticism about the rationality and good judgment of the American government, showed everything that was viable and attractive in the liberal-socialist-labor tradition.

The truth about the Port Huron Statement is a little more complicated, however. A lot of arguments went into drawing up the Statement, and not all of them were equally lucid. One of the Socialist elders who came to Port Huron to proffer advice on behalf of the LID was Michael Harrington, the author of *The Other America*, which came out in that same 1962, a good year for American social criticism. Harrington was thirty-four, not so elder after all, but with an intuitive political memory that seemed to bespeak three hundred years of left-wing wisdom. He noticed at once that, in its original draft, the Statement waxed less than enthusiastic about the virtues and importance of trade unions in America. That was a bad failing in the student affiliate of an organization whose paychecks originated in the ILGWU and the UAW. But the Statement's worst failing touched on Communism. Not everything that you can see in the Statement today appeared in the original draft. Harrington sat up into the night arguing with the students over the importance of anti-Communist principles. The students were unimpressed. "My notion of a progressive, leftist anti-Communism," he recalled many years later, "made as much existential sense to them as a purple cow." So he threw a tantrum (in his own description). Then he had to leave Port Huron with the conference still in session, and he never knew, until it was too late, that his tantrum had produced the desired effect.

Instead he returned to New York full of irritation at the unreliable students. According to James Miller's detailed history of these events, Harrington might have been misled by one of his own allies about what happened after he left the conference, perhaps as part of a Byzantine plot to damage SDS in favor of a rival organization, the Young People's Socialist League, which was led by Harrington himself. YPSL came out of Shachtman's Trotskyism, and Byzantinism was the Shachtmanite ideology. In any event, Harrington reported back to the anxious New York adults of the LID about the young SDSers in the Middle West, and his report was not flattering. The anxious adults called in the SDSers to make their own examination. That was the occasion in which Hayden and Al Haber presented themselves to the New York office for the first of those famously disastrous meetings between the young and the old. The room was full of ideologues from the ILGWU and the Jewish Labor Committee and other pooh-bahs of New York Socialism. The two young men found themselves roundly denounced—by Harrington himself, no less—for "united frontism." That meant consorting with Communists, a terrible crime. And the LID swung into action. The SDS leaders discovered that the lock on their national New York office had been changed. Such was, in America, the exact content of the mid-sixties split between the left-wing generations that made the New Left new. Three years later, in 1965, the break between SDS and the LID became official.

Simply on human terms, when you look back on that squabble it's easy to sympathize with the young people. I think that every one of the historians who has written about the dispute between SDS and the

LID has sided with SDS, not just because to line up with youth against age is always more pleasant. Harrington himself was filled with remorse in later years, as shown by that remark about a tantrum. He was a wonderfully sweet man under most circumstances, but his comrades in the LID and the Socialist Party and YPSL were sandpapery individuals, and the rough style may have rubbed off on him. He and the other adults treated the young people like hardbitten faction fighters from the New York wars, which they weren't. SDS's elected field secretary, Steve Max, happened to come from a family with a history in the Communist Party. In the past, Field Secretary Max's father had worked as an editor of the party's *Daily Worker*.

Yet the father had quit the *Worker* out of political disagreement with the Communist Party, which was the best of reasons. The son had belonged to the party's youth group, the Labor Youth League. But he, too, freed himself of those ties before going over, first, to the civil rights movement and then to SDS, which ought to have pleased the elders of the LID. But they were unpleasable. The elders looked at the Communist background and refused to pay young Max's salary at SDS. That was cruel, and stupid. Did the elders honestly think that SDS's other members were going to shrug their youthful left-wing shoulders while a good friend was fired on account of his father's repudiated past? You could worry about those adults. They had achieved wonders in the past, and in the civil rights movement they were still achieving. But they had contracted a touch of fanaticism. They were visionaries, and haters. The hammer and sickle made their eyes twitch. Steve Max, as it happened, stood closer to their own view of liberal socialism than did any number of other people in SDS. A few years later the LID recognized its error and hired him, energetic organizer that he was, for a different job. But the reconsideration took time. And if the elders of the LID were slow to see the talent in someone as young and uncomplicated as SDS's field secretary, how would they know when to call off their anti-Communism in more complicated circumstances? Vietnam was simmering, simmering. Would those old-time Socialists know a true disaster when it stared them in the face? Some of them would know. The others didn't have a prayer. The whole tragedy of the liberal left in Vietnam-era America was already inscribed in their gnarly hearts, and somehow the students saw the disaster even before it had occurred.

Still, there is a word to be said on behalf of those old Socialists. The ten thousand New York battles of the past between Socialism and Communism may have curdled their souls but, at the same time, left them with a useful knowledge of idealism in America and its peculiar weaknesses. Exactly how the elders expressed that knowledge I cannot say; it's easy to imagine that sectarian crabbiness prevented them from expressing it at all, except in the wooden language of the labor movement and the cold war. But this they knew: they had fought the Communist Party from 1919 straight into the 1950s, and they had triumphed.

America was a different place because of what they had done. But the victory came harder than anyone who stood outside of those battles could ever know. The old Socialists had learned that democratic leftism in America contained a potentially fatal weakness. The democratic leftists, with their alliance of intellectuals and labor and their scholarly heritage, could make persuasive social criticisms and propose reforms and move liberals to the left. But they could raise their voices only so far. They could condemn the basic principles of American capitalism, but not of the American political system. And their enemies among the Communists—not just the Communist Party but the larger circle of authoritarian leftists and Marxist-Leninists and fellow travelers—were under no such restriction. In times of calm the Communists and other authoritarians in America might run into obstacles of their own, America's democratic culture to begin with, followed by government repression (i.e., America's undemocratic culture). But with a sharp enough social crisis those same Communists and authoritarians would stumble upon a crucial advantage. They could speak the language of the democratic left, except louder. They could say the wildest things. And wildness would do them no harm.

The bitter old New York Socialists had learned that deep streaks of naïveté run through the liberal heart in America. They had learned that, during a social crisis, the liberals may move leftward, but not in any reliable way. The liberals needed to be instructed first in the difference between socialism and Communism;

needed to know that socialism and Communism were opposites, not twins; needed to know that social democratic words take on completely different meanings in the mouth of a Communist; needed to know the difference between democrats and dictators. And if the liberals lacked any of those skills or understandings, the poor stupid things would be all but guaranteed to conclude that Marxist-Leninists were social democrats with courage. Let a few thunderbolts of social rage and political distress fall across the country, and the naive liberals would make their fatal leftward lurch, and the disaster would occur. They would look at the many solid achievements of America's socialists and trade unions and reformers and civil rights leaders, and the naïfs would curl their lips in scorn at the paltriness of democratic progress, and they would declare that only the authoritarian revolutionaries could achieve anything worth doing. And the naive liberals would out-Stalin the Stalinists—while imagining themselves to be sweetly untainted by any ideology at all. They would go on binges of posturing and ultra-radicalism until every last achievement the social democrats had built over the years lay in shambles, and the whole business of organizing a left-wing democratic movement in America would have to be started up anew.

How many times the elders of the LID had seen that happen! The story of socialist student movements in America was a tale of repeated efforts by the Communists to take over the movement, and repeated Communist successes, and then ashes and ruins. The

Intercollegiate Socialist Society fell apart after the First World War because of defections to the Communist Party. In the 1930s its successor organization, the Student LID, was seduced into allying with the Communist Party in something called the American Student Union. Then the Communist allies pushed the American Student Union into endorsing Stalin's pact with Hitler in 1939, and the student movement was destroyed. It was the same among the younger people in a number of socialist unions over the decades: first the seduction into a Communist alliance, then ruin. If you took the position that America stood in need of a socialist influence, if you felt that socialist notions of rights for working people and socialist proposals for better unions and a generous welfare state and a warmer sense of community were precisely what America most required, if you believed that socialist reforms were the answer to America's singular callousness to the poor and that only a socialist movement could provide the puzzle piece missing from American democracy—if that was your position, who were these American Communists? They were the stick that beat down the American left, decade after decade. That was what the elders of the LID knew. And burdened with those many appreciations and piled-up experiences, the sour New York elders of the LID gazed into the fresh young midwestern faces of SDS, and worried.

The young radicals, prodded by Harrington, did say they were clear about Communism. The final draft of their Statement was admirable. But the enthusiasm was missing. Nor were the SDSers especially eager to discuss the issue. Knowing too much about Communism struck them as a kind of illness. Hayden wanted to avoid "the morbid traditions of the left centered in New York City," which meant, boiled down, that he wanted to avoid getting caught in New York's left-wing civil war. And in those circumstances, though it's a delicate issue to raise, maybe the elders did have a point in fretting over the family backgrounds of some of the SDSers, even if they were wrong about Max. The students who came pouring into SDS in the early and middle sixties, the Jewish ones especially, included a number of people with family backgrounds in the socialist movement. But there were many more, the red diaper babies, whose backgrounds lay in the Communist Party. In the movements of the sixties those people played a hugely positive role. Energy and courage were their family traits. They had grown up in the McCarthy era and were alive to an unpleasant reality about the FBI and the local police and an American spirit of intolerance that dreamier students could scarcely bring themselves to acknowledge. The red diaper babies possessed as a personal quality the one great achievement of their parents' party, which was a bristly hostility to race prejudice. They may have been the first reasonably large generation of white children in America to be brought up to regard as shameful even the slightest display of racism against blacks.

With only a very few exceptions, they weren't Communists themselves, those red diaper babies. On the contrary! By the time they came pouring into SDS they had conducted their living room rebellions against their own parents. The parents themselves, most of them, had begun to entertain doubts about the virtues of the Soviet Union. And yet, the political culture of the American Communist Party was exceedingly strong, and bits and pieces of that culture sometimes clung even to the disillusioned militants who had always meant to leave it behind. Among some of the red diaper babies, there was a fondness for drawing a distinction between big-C Communism (meaning the Soviet Bloc and the official Communist Party USA of Gus Hall) and small-c communism (meaning the larger political tradition that was founded by Lenin and the Bolsheviks). Big-C Communism was deplorable, everybody conceded; but was small-c communism entirely to be rejected? Maybe Marxism-Leninism was the truest democracy of all, if only it would keep to its own ideals. Maybe the left in America needed a real Lenin, not the fake Lenins of Gus Hall's ridiculous little organization. Those thoughts passed for wisdom in the student left. Even at the Port Huron conference there was talk of Hayden as "the next Lenin," as if a Lenin, and not, say, "the next Eugene V. Debs" or "the next Norman Thomas," was to be desired. And in those ways, the ancient Leninist gods were slipping into the social democratic church, carried there by young people who would never for a moment have regarded themselves as anything but democrats.

The next Lenin himself was one of the culprits. Hayden never really liked the idea of an anti-Communist plank in the SDS Statement. He thought that Communism in the Third World was going to be progressive and admirable. Maybe some of the big-C Communists in America weren't so bad, either; he admired their stand on civil rights. But finally he agreed to keep those thoughts to himself. Which is to say, the anti-Communist sophistication that can be seen today in the Statement was less than it seemed. The phrases appeared, but for some people the language was merely tactical, meaning insincere, inscribed for the purpose of mollifying Michael Harrington and the bill-paying elders of the LID. Or the anti-Communist phrases may have represented a genuine confusion, based on the belief that John Dewey was admirable, and so was the world of *Monthly Review* and the *National Guardian*. Either way, Harrington and the LID elders sniffed out something in those talented young radicals that cannot be detected merely by reading the grand manifesto of the American New Left. It was a faint odor of an anti-democratic idea. And having detected that whiff, those grizzled adult survivors of ten thousand faction fights of the past were going to draw on every possible weapon to prevent their own student affiliate from getting entangled one more time with socialism's worst and most devastating enemy in America, the Communists. It was only too bad that, in coming down so harshly on the erring students, Harrington and the pooh-bahs of the LID managed to encourage the very thing they were trying to prevent.

IV

SDS's backsliding into left-wing authoritarianism went in stages, beginning with insincere anti-Communism, sinking to anti–anti-Communism, then arriving at what ought to be called democratico-Stalinism. It was the belief, not exactly new on the American left, that Communism might well be a dictatorship, which was too bad; but the dictatorship was in some respect a democracy, too. Dictatorship at the top, democracy at the grass roots—that was the idea. C. Wright Mills, SDS's intellectual hero, was at times inclined to view Communism in that very strange light. Mills was a fan of the Wobblies and, like any good Wobbly, an advocate of workers' control, anarchosyndicalist style. His leftism was libertarian, in principle, which explains his appeal to the New Left. Yet in the 1950s he had not been especially outraged by big-C Communism in the Eastern Bloc, even if the anarchosyndicalists there were suppressed and exterminated. Fidel Castro came to power in Cuba at the end of the fifties, and the Cuban anarchosyndicalists, the fraternal comrades of the American Wobblies, fled for their lives to Venezuela and Florida. Yet Mills, the Wobblies' fan, gazed in Cuba's direction and was filled with happy enthusiasm. And opinions like his, naive and self-contradictory and a little blind to suffering, became popular in SDS.

The first wave of SDSers, the people who joined the organization in the early sixties, found it impossible to imagine that SDS was slipping into Communist habits of thought. Suggestions to the contrary struck them as insanity. Bob Ross, one of the early leaders, told Jack Newfield, who wrote a book on the early New Left, that the LID's fear of Communism in SDS was "Kafkaesque." At the SDS convention in 1964, someone offered a motion to emulate Red China and Cuba, and the motion failed to carry. The organization was definitely drifting leftward, but less toward Communism than toward the radical pacifism of A. J. Muste's *Liberation* magazine, which was Christian and pacifist and not at all interested in Communism. Yet *Liberation* had its quirks. Some of the radicals around the magazine were already speaking of making a revolution in the United States—a nonviolent revolution, to be sure, but a full-scale overthrow of institutions nonetheless. A picture of the world as a stark battle between the forces of good and evil was already visible in that radical pacifist idea; and from there, it became ever easier to imagine that, in distant parts of the world, the forces of good were, in fact, Communist.

Dave Dellinger, one of the founders of *Liberation* (and by the late sixties a main national leader of the anti-war movement), tended toward that view. Dellinger visited Ho Chi Minh in North Vietnam and, as he describes in his memoirs, felt right away a bond of Christian identification. Dellinger pictured himself and the Communist ruler as "members of the same Beloved Community." Sometimes the Communist influence on SDS was direct. In 1965 Herbert Aptheker, one of the leaders of the Communist Party, invited Hayden and Staughton Lynd to visit North

Vietnam—which was an invitation that would have caused heart attacks at the LID, if SDS and the LID weren't already at the point of breaking relations. So the radicals arrived in North Vietnam, and they noticed the selflessness and egalitarianism that arise in any popular war and in the first stages of any revolution, and they took these things as essential qualities of Vietnamese Communism, and they came away convinced that "rice-roots democracy" was growing under Communist rule.

The SDS national office began mailing out song lyrics like: "And before I'll be fenced in, / I'll vote for Ho Chi Minh, / and go back to the North and be free." Muste, the old pacifist at *Liberation*, who knew better (on some days), remonstrated with the students. Likewise Norman Thomas, who always knew better. North Vietnam—free? One of Hayden's comrades from civil rights days in Mississippi was Paul Potter, the SDS president in 1964–65, who had gone with Hayden and the others to pay that disastrous early visit to the editors of *Dissent*. Potter, too, put up a fight against identifying too closely with the Vietnamese Communists. But those arguments became ever harder to sustain. The United States armed forces were raining decimation on the Communist fighters of Vietnam, and the fighters were showing a lot of bravery in return, and it was easy to feel a twinge of admiration for the bravery; and once you had felt the admiring twinge, it became ever easier, absent any detailed knowledge of Communism and its inner quality, to accept the many silly and extravagant ideas that now came floating into view.

Sometimes the idea cropped up that non-white populations were spiritually superior to the whites, and since the Communist movements in a variety of Third World countries were distinctly non-white, didn't that suggest a spiritual superiority in Communism as well? The spiritual loftiness of Ho himself—he wrote poetry, he looked like a Buddhist sage—was accepted as a given. And the Chinese Communists, weren't they, too, wonders of soulfulness? Those earthy peasant maxims of Mao Zedong, didn't they bespeak a humble heart? Even if you suspected otherwise, it became harder and harder to suppose that any virtue at all inhered to the cause of anti-Communism. For it was anti-Communism that had brought the United States to Indochina, and it was fanaticism, anti-Communist style, that pushed America ever deeper into the idiotic war. By 1966, as Miller's history recounts, a new edition of the Port Huron Statement quietly dropped the sections on "anti-Communism" and "Communism and Foreign Policy"—which changed the meaning of everything that remained, since the blame for every confrontation between Communism and the West was left with the United States. SDS's professed commitment to participatory democracy endured almost to the end. But if participatory democracy could no longer define itself against something as obvious as a Communist dictatorship, what did that wonderful phrase mean anymore—apart from endless meetings?

The final pathetic stage in SDS's decline occurred as a result of still another decision made at Port Huron. It was the decision, adopted in the face of American socialism's every experience, to permit a member of an explicitly Communist organization to attend the SDS conference. A clause in SDS's statutes, dating from 1947, when the organization was still called the Student League for Industrial Democracy, forbade any such thing. The clause was written by Harry Laidler, a Socialist Party eminence who, during his long-ago student days back in 1905, had been one of the founders of the Intercollegiate Socialist Society. The clause forbade participation in the organization to anyone who advocated racism, dictatorship, or totalitarianism, which shut the door mostly on Communists and Trotskyists—given that racists and fascists were not too likely to throng into a socialist student movement. The logic of that clause was not closemindedness; it was self-preservation. The purpose was to shield the liberal lambs.

As Al Haber explained to Miller years later, the elders insisted on that clause out of a worry that horrible calamities would otherwise occur: "Because any Communist could come into a meeting and plant his seed. And these Communists would be in every meeting in every chapter, coordinated from headquarters—and we would all be just little nebishes out in Podunkland subject to their disciplined infiltration." Which seemed unimaginable, to the students. The mockery in Haber's language expressed the incredulity. In Hayden's view at the time, as he recalls in his autobiography, secretive infiltrators from the Communist Party did perhaps make trouble for democratic organizations back in the 1930s and '40s. He would concede such a thing, in regard to the past. But the Communist Party was moribund by the sixties, no? Killed off—wasn't it?—by McCarthyism and by its own doctrinal inanities? The question of excluding Communists from the student movement seemed to him "totally irrelevant," in his own words.

Such was the reasoning of the young. On that basis the SDSers at the Port Huron conference voted to seat, as a non-voting observer, a lone high school student from New York, an old friend of one of the ex-Communist SDSers, who was attending the conference as the representative of the Communist Party's official youth group. It was an innocent decision. Three years later, in 1965, on the instigation of SDS's president that year, Clark Kissinger, and with only the smallest opposition, the organization took the further step of formally dropping the anti-totalitarian exclusion clause from the statutes and from the membership card. Dropping that clause seemed so harmless, so refreshing, so liberating! The decision brought on the final rupture with the LID, but, in the minds of the students, that was just as well. It was the moment of generational emancipation. Good riddance to the senile Socialists! And then every last Kafkaesque nightmare that was dreamed by the senile Socialists slowly came to pass.

The red diaper babies who flocked into SDS in the early sixties were, in several cases, the reformed, democratic-minded veterans of the old "right wing" of the Communist Party's youth affiliate from the 1950s, the Labor Youth League, who had recognized that Soviet Communism and the American Communist Party had lost their credibility. But the Labor Youth League had a "left wing," too. In the same year as the Port Huron conference, some of the veterans of the "left wing," having likewise come to fret over the Communist Party's lost credit, made their own belated exit from the party and organized a splinter group of fifty intrepid people called the Progressive Labor Movement, later the Progressive Labor Party, which was more Communist than the Communists. Progressive Labor was pro-Beijing, admired Stalin, worshipped Mao. And in the same year, 1965, that SDS dropped its anti-totalitarian exclusion clause, the crafty Communists of Progressive Labor launched their campaign to infiltrate the organization, or, at any rate, SDS's East Coast and Midwest chapters. (Maoism on the West Coast followed a slightly different history.)

Looking at those Progressive Labor people, you could have easily shared the disbelief that any kind of Communist infiltration could get anywhere at all. Progressive Labor was the antithesis of every rebellious instinct in SDS. The PLers struck genuine SDSers as robots. They wore anti-hippie short haircuts, which made them look like marines (except with the flabby muscles and pale complexions of bookish personalities), and they maintained a marine-like discipline, too. Their manner at meetings was notoriously patient and manipulative. They raised their hands and quoted Stalin or Mao in flat tones that were oddly remote from American English. Yet something about the PL spirit was in keeping with the era. Maybe there was, after all, a link, faint though it had to be, between the faraway young Red Guards of Mao's Cultural Revolution and the young rebels of the Western world. In Paris a group that was quite similar to Progressive Labor broke away from the French Communist Party in 1965 and established a political base at the École normale supérieure, where Althusser was the professor and Debray had been a student. The École normale was a prestigious school, and its students were famously brilliant, and it made a perfect place to begin influencing the French student movement as a whole. And in America Maoism followed the same strategy.

The PLers established their base at Harvard. Soon enough student Maoists (and the occasional assistant professor) were attending every meeting in every chapter of SDS they could find, carrying out a disciplined infiltration that was coordinated from party headquarters—and the little nebishes out in Podunkland were in no position to resist. The deadpan Maoist rhetoric sounded weird, but weirdness was good. Many a student revolutionary who was privately frightened out of his wits by the hippie counterculture discovered with great satisfaction that PL, in its scary Chinese fashion, offered a counter-counterculture, which was exceedingly straight, yet exceedingly radical. The PLers gave up cigarettes. These were not potheads. Their look may have been androidal but at least they weren't fashionable. Their attitude toward ordinary working people was laughably paternalistic, but they did at least pretend to sympathy, which was better than some of the anti-PLers managed to do. And because of the machine-gun efficiency of their Leninist discipline, plus the allure of their ghastly Chinese rhetoric and the reassurance that came from their stodgy cultural ideas, the Maoists in chapter after chapter were able to rope in a handful of students long enough to get them to vote at one or two meetings, which was sufficient to take over a committee, then to influence the chapter, sometimes to take over entirely.

The PLers managed to confuse the SDS rank and file with their accusations of anti-Communism directed at anyone who spoke against them—since by the time of their challenge, 1967–69, it had become impossible for true SDSers to affirm anti-Communism as the movement's proper doctrine. Almost five decades of left-wing repudiation of Communism lay in SDS's past, but the break between generations had performed a kind of lobotomy on the collective student brain, and the whole previous experience of the American left had disappeared from memory, except for the history that was passed along through family tradition. And since, in no small number of cases, family tradition among the SDSers contained a fond nostalgia for the Communist Party of the 1930s and '40s and a keen appreciation of the non-party Communism that flowered at *Monthly Review* and the *National Guardian* during the 1950s, living memory tended to become, for SDS, a celebration of American Communism and of everything that accorded with the Communist past, and of nothing that did not. In SDS the phrase "social democrat" came to mean "the left wing of imperialism," exactly as in the writings of Lenin.

So the crew-cut robots stood up and quoted Stalin. No one among the ordinary SDSers knew what was wrong with Stalin, except maybe that he went too far, or that Trotsky was vaguely preferable. Lenin was declared a saint. No one knew how to explain that Lenin was a dictator. The short-hairs chanted, "Smash red-baiting!" The long-hairs, speechless, adopted the fateful strategy of opposition by imitation. They went thumbing through the handsome little pamphlets published by China's Foreign Languages Press, looking for Maoist quotations to hurl back at the Maoists. They read North Vietnamese pamphlets and speeches by Fidel Castro. The Little Lenin Library became a common possession. Stalin's theory of nationalism was everyone's favorite reading. And by provoking those several responses the robots of Progressive Labor did more damage to SDS than a thousand secret police agents—who, to be sure, were also, by the late sixties, active everywhere you looked.

By 1968 the national membership of SDS was well up into the tens of thousands, perhaps as high as a hundred thousand. SDS had become America's largest left-wing organization since the Great Depression, even if SDS membership tended to be loosely conceived, established more often than not simply by showing up at a few meetings and cheating on your dues. I think that, among those tens of thousands, a great majority, the non-leaders, still thought of participatory democracy as their cause and goal, though they might not have been able to expound the idea too clearly. But at the top of the SDS hierarchy, the leaders, by the autumn of 1968, were rolling the phrase "revolutionary Communist" around their tongues with delicious glee. They were either straight-out Maoists from Progressive Labor (along with one or two other pro-Chinese factions), or else, in a much vaguer way, countercultural Maoists, half freak and half Commie, which was an impossible amalgam but popular enough, for a while. Mao and Lenin pins sprouted like fungi on black wool Che berets. SDS was Students for a Dictatorial Society now (though of course the leaders would have said that Communism in its Chinese and Cuban versions was participatory and democratic enough). The same disaster that had befallen the idealistic young socialist tailors and seamstresses of the ILGWU in the 1920s and the Student LID in the 1930s had happened yet again. American Communism—this time in the form of the Communist Party's pro-Chinese splinter group—had scored yet another historic triumph over the democratic left. And the peculiar invaluable current of libertarian radicalism that had descended from Whitman and the nineteenth-century democrats through Dewey and the Socialist Party to the students at Port Huron was at an end.

In 1969 the organization finally went mad. The PLers never did have a lot of popularity, outside of Harvard. But their institutional shrewdness allowed them to take over the national leadership of SDS, without much opposition, either. The main leaders from the anti-PL faction were by then no longer interested in student organizations, anyway. It was guerrilla war that had their attention. They set about organizing America's brand-new Red Army, in the shape of Weatherman (later called the Weather Underground Organization), which enjoyed a real popularity in the student movement and the hippie neighborhoods, for a few months. My own Podunkland chapter of SDS, the former John Dewey Discussion Club at Columbia University, consisted in 1969 of a couple of hundred students, among whom sixty formed the inner "cadre," among whom eighteen, by my count at the time, left the chapter and the university to join the Weather adventure. Naturally most of the adventurers came to their senses quickly enough and tiptoed back into ordinary student life (with a look of terror on their faces). But guerrilla armies were cropping up everywhere you looked in those years. Weatherman was mostly an East Coast and Midwest phenomenon. The West Coast could claim the New World Liberation Front, the George Jackson Brigade (named after a Black Panther who was killed in a courtroom shootout during an escape attempt), the Symbionese Liberation Army, and the Red Guerrilla Family, plus a few others. From out of the Black Panther Party (and the black student movement at New York's City College and other schools) came the Black Liberation Army. There was the Puerto Rican independence group, the Fuerzas Armadas de Liberación Nacional Puertorriqueña

(FALN). And the effect of those many guerrilla mini-organizations was devastating—not on American imperialism, which survived, or on any other of the declared enemies of the movement, but on the left.

The irony was that, by the time of those several hapless guerrilla campaigns, the American New Left in its non-guerrilla version was nothing mini at all. In 1969 some five hundred underground newspapers were carrying the New Left and countercultural message to perhaps two million readers (according to a *Newsweek* estimate), or in other estimates to many more. Another five hundred radical or alternative newspapers brought the message to a vast high school population. Every university town had its smattering of New Left groups. There were formal organizations, radio stations, research units, informal affinity groups, leagues of apartment house communes, political-minded food co-ops, and radical bookstores. The first humble building-block organizations of the academic left were coming into being, mostly as radical caucuses in the social science departments. And all of those groups were united by at least a few warm sentiments of community and shared purpose. At the end of April 1970, the United States Army, supporting the South Vietnamese, invaded Cambodia, which was American lunacy incarnate, and those many groups and organizations acted as one.

During a demonstration at Yale on behalf of the Black Panthers, a couple of thousand people held a typically enormous meeting and ended up calling a national protest strike, and Hayden brought the call to a waiting throng on the lawn outside, and the response was spectacular. Protests took place at 1,350 colleges and universities, 500 of which were shut down completely, 51 of them for the rest of the academic year. More than ten thousand young men pledged to turn in their draft cards. The police or the National Guard were called out at more than a hundred schools, and some of the confrontations were rough, and, by the end, four anti-war protesters at Kent State and two more at Jackson State had been shot to death, and still other students had been shot and wounded at Kent and at SUNY-Buffalo, which sent new ripples of outrage and protest around the country. More than four million students took part, in one way or another. It was one of the biggest protests in American history.

According to poll statistics from the Harris organization, America's student population by then was more than 40 percent "liberal," and 11 percent "radical"—which are large figures in the American context, especially if you keep in mind that student radicalism was concentrated in some regions more than others, and that "liberalism" can refer to all sorts of democratic and peaceful positions pretty far to the left. Yet by that moment, SDS had disappeared, except for a few local chapters and a small-scale PL front that never did attract many members, and nothing had come to replace it. Many a radicalized young insurrectionist felt an attachment to Dave Dellinger and his Mobe (that is, the National Mobilization Committee to End the War in Vietnam, which kept changing its name) and to Abbie Hoffman and some other national anti-war leaders. Any number of smaller and regional organizations had sprung up. But to undo the organizational shambles that had been caused by Maoism and the Weather Underground, to reassemble a membership organization with any kind of national following among the young—that was impossible.

It was because the madness in SDS and, by then, in a wide swathe of the left was much too strongly rooted to allow for any other outcome. The New Left had been founded by students who felt a revulsion for the softness of their own student life; and the guerrilla leap at the end of the decade was made by students who felt a revulsion for the softness of their own revolt against student softness. Guerrilla leftism was in that respect merely New Leftism, intensified. It was hardness, hardened. In the circles of SDS, even the people who knew quite clearly that guerrilla war was insanity tended to feel that a few basic particles of the guerrilla motivation remained admirable in spite of everything—which was an attitude that undid any possibility of arguing effectively for a more intelligent position. Some of the arguments that did prove effective were merely variants on the cult of the hard. There was the variant of crime. Around the edges of the guerrilla movement in New York, Cambridge, Berkeley, and a few other places, wherever the Weather Underground or one of the other Red Armies enjoyed some support, a culture of criminal leftism (to call it that) grew up.

Mostly it was based on a network of marijuana concessioners with a halo of utopianism above their long hair, who could feel that crime was in the eye of the beholder; yet beyond the marijuana dealers lay a penumbra of bank frauds and shoplifting and the inevitable diversifications into cocaine and beyond. Criminal leftism was a desperate idea, but compared to guerrilla war it was, in a certain fashion, a model of realism, and it attracted no small number of people. It had a literary side. Abbie Hoffman's *Steal This Book* was the light classic of the movement. The heavy classics were by the prison authors from the Black Panther Party, Eldridge Cleaver and George Jackson. And just as the books were light and heavy, the crimes, too, were light and heavy, and among the Panthers in California and New York and perhaps among a few other people, too, there were rackets and rubouts and murderous purges, all of them conducted under a haze of sinister-sounding slogans. The fist salute and "Power to the People!" took on creepy overtones, to anyone who knew what was going on.

The other alternative was ascetic Leninism in a non-guerrilla version, which drew on the same revulsion for the softness of the student world. Several thousand people went in that direction, though nothing in their own impulses or in the atmosphere of the moment obliged them to coordinate their many efforts. And so the 1970s became the golden age of the micro-parties. There were the Maoist sects: not only Progressive Labor but also the Revolutionary Union, the October League, the Communist Labor Party, Workers' Viewpoint, and some others, too. There were the Trotskyist sects: the Socialist Workers (which dominated one wing of the national peace movement), the Workers' World (with its Youth Against War and Fascism, strong in Buffalo), the Workers' League, the Independent Socialists, the Spartacist League. Plus the *truly* small Trotskyist groups. There was talent in those parties, which would have produced a powerful movement, if only the many militants could have figured out what to do. But as Lennon and McCartney took the occasion to observe, "If you go carrying pictures of Chairman Mao/ You ain't gonna make it with anyone anyhow." As was true of Trotsky, too. The Communist Party enjoyed a bit of a revival itself. The Communists established some influence over the West Coast Black Panthers, which might have led to big results, if only the Panthers hadn't been so intent on killing one another. Angela Davis made loyalty to the party of Comrade Brezhnev seem—well, not exactly fashionable, but not unfashionable, either. And between the guerrillas, the dope dealers, the criminals, and the Leninists, what chance was there, really, to reassemble any kind of normal organization?

All kinds of people made the effort, far more than ever flirted with the "hard" alternatives. A trickle of decent souls slowly wended their way back to Michael Harrington and into what eventually became the Democratic Socialists of America, in an effort to pick up the old severed thread of the democratic left. Some of the community-organizing enterprises managed to thrive, usually by putting away their left-wing posters and slogans. There were the academic radicals, who had a lot of success in the humanities departments and a few other places, and there were the journalists of the weekly radical press, which flourished in cities around the country. But there was nothing to bring those different people together. And beyond the guerrillas, the outlaws, the Leninists, the democratic socialists, the levelheaded organizers, the academics, and the weekly scribblers, the vast majority of people who had once felt a loyalty to the world that had come out of SDS and its fraternal organizations simply slipped away. They took up tomato farming, or Buddhism, or the *I Ching*. Or they threw themselves into political causes of a different sort, something post–New Left. By 1972 or '73 the movement was gone. Nothing remained but ashes and embers and several million people in a daze. And in this way, too, the American student movement followed a pattern that, outside of the Communist countries, was strangely universal.

There was the version in France. The self-destruction of the French student movement was fairly orderly, by world standards. The Maoists from Althusser's school, mad as hatters every one, ended up as the most dynamic of France's micro-parties, and they brought their movement ever closer to guerrilla war, and they worked up a cult of criminals and prisoners, too, exactly as in the United States. But in 1974 the Maoists came to their senses and the criminal-leftist atmosphere of gangsterism and underground cells and bravura terrorist manifestos was gone. The Dutch version was not too terrible. Anarchist "provos" gave birth to violent "desperados," which was no favor to anyone; but desperado violence remained limited, and a useful municipal radicalism with a libertarian flavor lingered on. The story was uglier in Italy and Germany, the old centers of the Fascist Axis. In Italy the student movement produced the Red Brigades and other guerrilla groups, who killed a lot of people and kept on fighting straight into the nineties. Out of the German SDS came the Red Army Faction (Baader-Meinhof), a group called June 2nd, and the Red Cells, the last of which combined its cult of violence with a touch of anti-Semitism (in the form of anti-Zionism, of course). There was a Japanese version. The student movement produced something called the Japanese Red Army, which distinguished itself with an indiscriminate terror attack in 1972 on Puerto Rican Christian pilgrims visiting Israel; and something called the United Red Army, which massacred fourteen members of its own group in a bit of sectarian insanity.

But the classic decline was Mexico's, if only because, among the student movements around the world, Mexico's surely held the greatest promise at the start. The mass movement there arose in July 1968 almost exactly the way it had arisen in France, three months earlier. In Mexico City, the police cracked down on a political demonstration and on an unrelated gang fight, which led to student protests, which led to a police attack on the autonomy of the university, which led to a student rebellion. The students drew up a list of strictly democratic demands—for the abolition of the much-hated police Grenadiers, for the freeing of political prisoners, for the abrogation of some repressive laws. General assemblies sprang up in each of the seventy schools that were on strike in Mexico City, and out of the general assemblies came delegates to the National Strike Council, which was organized as a model of democracy itself, and in the '68 style: ten-hour meetings, turmoil, the fading of differences between the leaders and the rank and file.

Along with the democratic ex-Communists who founded the Strike Council were activists and leaders who never did leave the Mexican Communist Party, plus some Spartacists and other champions of the Bolshevik idea. Even so, the talk was of a "democratic spring," and the phrase was intended to evoke Prague Spring in Czechoslovakia. Marxists in the National Strike Council did not make the movement Marxist, at least not in any conventionally political way. The exalted feeling that came out of the mass marches and the acts of militant irreverence and the new informal ways of speaking and the new music was democratic, above all. But as the months wore on the participatory egalitarianism of the student strike somehow tilted in a top-down direction, and the cultural radicalism took on ever more of a Marxist-Leninist tinge. By September 1968 a Central Committee became dominant within the National Strike Council, and the dominant group within the Council's Central Committee came to be (according to some interpretations, though not others) the Communist Party, through its youth organization and through student Communists who always kept their political identity secret. By the end the students themselves began describing their own

National Strike Council as a "Supreme Soviet," not with any sense of irony or disapproval, either.

In October the Mexican army went into action in the Plaza of the Three Cultures at Tlatelolco, Mexico City, and even today no one knows how many students were killed—a few dozen? more than three hundred? And the horror of that event, the killings themselves and the concealment of the bodies and the dictatorial cloak of secrecy that fell across the massacre, the subsequent arrests of the student leaders, the jailings and beatings, finally the prison sentences that stretched into the early 1970s—all of that pushed the movement into a moral free-fall, not in every corner of the student left, but in some corners, definitely. In Mexico, too, the micro-parties had their golden age. The wave of academic Marxism proved far stronger in Mexico than in the United States, and more Leninist and doctrinaire. And above the micro-parties and the academic Marxism and the dream of a Supreme Soviet came a foam of tiny doomed guerrilla groups whose emotional home was either Havana or (via Althusser and the Maoism of Paris) Beijing.

There was the Armed Brigade of Workers Struggle of Chihuahua, the National Liberation Front (or alternatively, Armed Forces of National Liberation), the Armed Commando of the People, the Revolutionary Action Movement, the Revolutionary National Civic Association, the September 23rd Communist League (which some people suspected was the police), the Zapatista Urban Front, the People's Union, the Revolutionary Student Committee of Monterrey, the Revolutionary Armed Forces of the People, the Nuevo León Group, the Revolutionary Student Front of Guadalajara, the Spartacist Leninist League—and even that doesn't exhaust the list. Those groups fought on until about 1972 and in some cases longer, with no success at all (apart from one very long fuse that led from the Armed Forces of National Liberation to a 1994 peasant uprising in the southern state of Chiapas, under the leadership of the Zapatista Army of National Liberation).

At the end the Mexican government was as despotic as ever, the poor and the oppressed were no less poor and oppressed. But the guerrilla groups had succeeded all too well at stamping out whatever democratic sentiments lingered on from the original radical impulse. Gilberto Guevara, the '68 democratic leader (who spent the next years in prison along with so many others), recalled of the period after the original student uprising, "In three years the student movement adopted a discourse that had nothing to do with what was upheld in 1968. It was the inverse discourse: democracy was persecuted." Not just with snubs or denunciations, either. "Whoever demanded elections was satanized." The guerrillas took to assassinating student leaders and teachers—a Communist professor here, a Trotskyist teacher there—whose crime was to belong to the wrong faction. Students sometimes cheered the killings. It was a reign of terror. Yet on the left, Guevara said, "You couldn't speak ill of the guerrillas."

Even in poor and backward Nicaragua (where the

student left did succeed in making a revolution, eventually), the movement followed something of the same trajectory. The Sandinistas got started in the middle sixties with a vaguely democratic leftism (having broken away from orthodox Communism without entirely establishing a distinct ideological position of their own), only to move on, by the late sixties, to a renewed identification with Marxism-Leninism along the same Cuban and Maoist lines as the guerrillas in Mexico. And because of the universality of this pattern in the non-Communist world, it seems plausible to suppose that, just as a grand generational factor contributed to the rise of at least several of the student movements earlier in the decade, some other factor, applicable to one movement after another around the world, must have contributed to the decline and disintegration at the end.

V

After the American and French revolutions of the eighteenth century, the first classic instance of a worldwide simultaneous insurrection took place, as I say, in 1848. Today it should be obvious that New Leftism's decline and disintegration around the world had something to do with 1848 and with the peculiarities of what was born that year.

From a certain point of view, the left-wing idea, defined a bit vaguely, is a permanent feature of any reasonably modern society, and leftism's origins must lie deep in the past. But 1848 (to be precise, December

1847) was the time of the *Communist Manifesto*. That was the moment when a large number of people began for the first time to identify the labor movement as a new force, capable of reorganizing all of society for the general good. Out of the revolutions of 1848 came the organizations that, after innumerable twists and turns, would become the mass left-wing movements of the twentieth century. Never was a year more fecund than 1848; but the fecundity was slightly disturbing to the shrewder participants even at the time. The new left-wing idea was stout and sturdy; but didn't bend. The leftists of the 1840s invoked modernity and change; but (we are allowed to speculate) an obscure portion of their revolutionary souls may have shrank at their own radicalism. P.-J. Proudhon worried about the new rigidity in a letter to Marx as early as 1846: "For God's sake, after we have demolished all the dogmatisms *a priori*, let us not of all things attempt in our turn to instill another kind of dogma into the people." But dogma was the left wing disease.

The entire inner history of the left from 1848 to 1968 was a story of repeated efforts to break out of the old rigidity and adapt and evolve; and repeated countercalls to remain forever unbending. Lenin claimed to be more unbending in his fidelity to the mid-nineteenth century than were Kautsky or Bernstein or the social democrats; Trotsky, in the years after Lenin died, claimed to be more unbendingly faithful to Lenin than the official Communists, who claimed to be more unbending than Trotsky. And so it went. The year 1848 and some aspect of leftism's connection to reality thus receded at an identical rate. In the mind of many an intelligent person a classic working-class revolution along Marx's nineteenth-century lines seemed possible in Western Europe and elsewhere, too, as late as the end of the Second World War—either because the Great Depression was going to resume and set off a revolution or because the fall of fascism was going to open a door to the revolutionary left. Instead came the capitalist boom and some considerable non-revolutionary reforms. And at that point the predicament of left-wing orthodoxy and its mid-nineteenth-century expectations became disastrously acute.

Each of the main political tendencies that claimed a root in the old workers' movement looked for its own way to cope with the unexpected direction that modern society had taken. In the Third World from the end of the Second World War straight into the 1970s and '80s, it was possible to reinterpret dogmatic Marxism along anti-colonial lines and to suppose that nineteenth-century ideas about a class struggle and a decisive revolution and a break with capitalism still made sense (so long as you gave the old terminology a few new definitions and "workers" meant "peasants"). But how to solve Marxism's difficulties in the industrial democracies? The Communists in France and some other countries after the war chose to go on affirming the ancient dogma about the proletarian upheaval and the revolutionary society to come, as if 1848 were now and forever; and meanwhile adapted to modern life by tacitly agreeing to ignore their own dogma in everyday practice. That was a feeble thing to do, but at least it got them through the day. The Italian Communists went a little further by splitting their loyalties down the middle between modern society and the ancient doctrine.

The postwar Social Democrats in West Germany and northern Europe were infinitely bolder. In 1959 the German Social Democrats went so far as formally to abandon the Marxist label altogether, which brought theory and practice into alignment, more or less. The American Socialists after the Second World War were barely a faction, let alone a mass party. But the Americans, some of them, took the same steps. You could see it in the LID and its marriage of liberalism and socialism, or in Hook's philosophy of Deweyan socialism, or in the political and cultural criticism that came out of *Dissent* magazine. And in those several ways, the left-wing parties and movements in quite a few countries made the effort to adapt to modern life, sometimes in a straightforward way, other times by accepting a ludicrous disjunction between doctrine and action.

The rebellion of the New Left students against their elders in the early and middle 1960s seemed, at first, to be one more lurch in the modernizing direction. SDS's philosophy, as outlined at Port Huron, conformed entirely to the LID's ideas about social progress and liberal democracy, except that SDS wanted to loosen the old bureaucratic rigidities of the American labor movement and to shake off the glum rhetoric of the traditional left, and in those ways to accept what the LID had done, and outdo it. In some countries where the adult parties had not yet turned democratic, the students, some of them, made the turn on their own. That was the case in Mexico. Or at least the students gestured in that direction, even if, in certain countries, they didn't go all the way. The young rebels of the French Communist Student Union enraged the Communist elders by trying to publish documents of Italian Communism, which was scandalous precisely because the Italians were inching their way toward liberal democracy. So the modernizing campaign seemed to be moving ahead, and in one country after another the students seemed to take the lead, as you would expect.

Even so, the atmosphere that surrounded the student movement was thick with a certain kind of pining for the past. Among the philosophers and theoreticians who ended up as gurus of the student left around the world, modernity was not necessarily the consistent theme. Marcuse and Sartre celebrated the Young Marx of the 1840s; Althusser, the Old Marx of the 1870s. Such was the debate! Ernst Mandel, the Trotskyist economist, took Marx's *Capital* as gospel. The little factions that buzzed like flies around all of the big student movements were agog with one or another ancient intoxication. The Trotskyists lived and breathed for the days of Lenin and the St. Petersburg revolutionaries of 1917 (who themselves had been lost in dreams of the Paris Commune of 1871). The Maoists and Fidelistas dreamed of fielding primitive peasant armies from the pre-industrial world. The anarchist

groups always seemed to me more creative and appealing, not to mention liberty-loving, than everyone else
among the radical sects; but the anarchists, to be honest, were lost in the red-and-black glories of Barcelona
in the 1930s and the Wobbly songs from 1910. When
the hippies and freaks happened along, their vision,
too—the backcountry communes and food coopera-
tives, the new-style Buddhist-Hindu religious impulse
—came dressed in costumes taken from nineteenth-
century daguerreotypes of the American frontier. A
sod hut and Daniel and Mrs. Boone were the hippie
vision of the future. And the seductiveness in those
yellowed images from the past proved irresistible.

Why was that? Let us not forget that the student
movements went through some fairly grim experiences
here and there—the killings that kept recurring during
the civil rights campaign in the American South, the
police attacks on Columbia University in April 1968,
on the Sorbonne in May, on the demonstrators outside
the Democratic Party convention in Chicago in
August, and on the demonstrators in Mexico City in
October (that was the worst, obviously), not to mention the violence at People's Park in Berkeley in 1969,
the killings during the Cambodia strike in the United
States in May 1970, and so forth around the world.
When it came to expressing a fury and frustration at
those events, the modernizing adults, those masters
of the well-modulated tone of voice, proved to be no
help at all. But the dogmas from the past turned out
to be oddly articulate. The ancient texts of Marxism
and anarchism, if you studied them correctly, con-

tained a series of very powerful tales—"legendary narratives," in Alain Finkielkraut's phrase (himself one of the '68ers from Paris)—about heroes and champions whose names were Che, Mao, Ho, Trotsky, and Bakunin. Within those legends was a vision of right and wrong as stark and dazzling as anything to be found in the medieval tales of El Cid and Roland. Suffering, martyrdom, the meaning of history and humanity—all were lavishly expressed.

Did the ancient left-wing texts sound strange when discussed in public? Were they incomprehensible to a great mass of uninitiates? Incomprehensibility was virtue. The sheer irrationality of standing up in the late 1960s or early '70s and speaking in the tones of a barricade fighter from the mid-nineteenth century or a Third World peasant guerrilla vented deliriums of rage with every phrase (which, incidentally, was exactly what the old anti-Communists of the LID had always feared). And the archaic rhetoric was good at one thing more. The phrases evoked the kind of utopian expectations that kept popping up in the mass marches and the communal life of the university uprisings. So the young people pulled away from their elders, and willy-nilly the pulling led into bizarre political languages from the remote past and the Third World countryside. And when the bizarre rhetorics came blaring outward from the loudspeakers at a public rally, and the posters of Mao and Che and other heroes and champions covered the university walls, and the red-blue-and-gold banners of the South Vietnamese National Liberation Front and the black-and-red flags of Barcelona syndicalism snapped briskly in the tear-gassy breeze—at those utopian moments the here-and-now of modern times was gone, and the excitement was almost unbearable.

The turn away from modern ideas helps explain the crazy choices that people made at the end of the 1960s and in the early '70s. Almost everywhere the students were taking up theories and dogmas whose relation to the society around them was archeological and nothing more. The students were, almost everywhere, militantly anti-intellectual; yet they had outfitted themselves with a worldview that existed nowhere but in books. They were energetic; and blind. They had aimed for the future and had hit the nineteenth century, and nothing was left to guide them except the cult of the will, which sent them careening from sensible reformism to lunatic ultra-radicalism, from thrilling idealism to thrilling cynicism. In the end, bizarre unpredictability became the signature of the New Left's most prominent personalities. The most celebrated example in France was Serge July, who helped found the movement at the beginning of the sixties as one of the rebel leaders within the Communist Student Union. It was July and a few others at the Communist student magazine *Clarté* who enraged the adult party with their "Italian" sympathies, which meant that, relatively speaking, he was a liberal leftist.

Then came the '68 uprising, and the emotion was unbearable, and the "Italian" flip-flopped to Mao. July and his comrades got together to write a book called *Toward the Civil War*. He lined up with

Glucksmann and the other red-hots in the super-revo-
lutionary groupuscule, the Proletarian Left. Dutifully
he trekked into northern France to conduct a clandestine Maoist agitation among the oppressed miners.
He was a young man living out the plot of Zola's
Germinal. He spent 1971 and '72 at that task, and the
proletarian insurrection failed to occur. He edited the
Maoist newspaper *Libération* (under the titular direc-
torship of Sartre). Only now, once he had come to
grips with Maoism's failure to start the revolution, he
steered his newspaper in a new direction, toward rock
and roll, business reporting, French slang, and liberal
values, which was a formula that elevated *Libération*
into one of France's principal dailies, quite a good
paper, everyone agrees—but nothing to do with Maoism. The man was a zigzag.

Hayden was our American version. He, too, was a
liberal leftist at the start. He, too, flip-flopped into a
kind of Maoism, hippie style, only without any of the
highbrow rigmarole. He was close to the Weather
Underground for a while. He moved to Berkeley and
joined something called the Red Family, which in a
half-serious way celebrated a cult of North Korea's
Kim Il Sung. The cult of Kim was briefly a fad in the
American New Left (and, not so briefly, in Latin
America, where the North Korean Communists
offered guerrilla training). The Weathermen and their
sympathizers used to sing, to the tune of "Maria"
from *West Side Story*: "The most beautiful sound I ever
heard/ Kim Il Sung, Kim Il Sung, Kim Il Sung. . . ."
Eldridge Cleaver preached the virtues of Kim. In that

spirit, Hayden and the Red Family prepared for guerrilla war. Yet all the while he kept his ties to the reform wing of the Democratic Party, and when Kim Il Sung proved to be of no possible use and the revolutionary civil war failed to break out, Hayden took to running for office in California first as a liberal reformer, then as a mainstream figure of the Democratic Party, backed by big money from Hollywood. Someone once said of Hayden that he gave opportunism a bad name, which is the sort of insult that in France was flung at July, too. But opportunism and zigzagging are not necessarily the same.

Young men like Hayden and July had energy, talent, ideals, ambition, social indignation. They were their generation's natural leaders. But by rebelling against the adults they ended up with nothing more than a rusty old compass from 1848 in their hands. So they went lurching across the field—now as democratic leftists, now as champions of totalitarian violence, now as crafty analysts of what the market could bear, improvising at every step, always good for a ringing phrase and an inspiring call to action, until the accumulated lurches had torn the youth movement to pieces.

VI

Anybody who watched the collapse from outside may have figured that New Leftism, having gone mad, shortly after did the decent thing and quietly faded away. But that was not how it felt inside the movement. Inside, nothing faded; everything exploded. A million fights of indescribable intensity broke out, which destroyed or badly damaged almost every group and organization within the movement and succeeded in being hugely destructive to individual personalities, too. But then again, as Bakunin said, the destructive urge is a creative urge.

The exact way that destructive urges turned out to be creative had something to do with the movement's origins. The arguments between the left-wing generations back in the early and middle sixties mostly revolved, as I say, around the young people's desire to embark on risky moral crusades. But one other issue intruded into those quarrels. There was a dispute over cultural style, very minor at first, sometimes merely over taste. Around the world, the left-wing adults tended to be fairly prim, and the young people, not so prim. The young people were fascinated by movies and pop music, sometimes by literary rebellions, in ways the older people couldn't share. In Paris, the earnest members of the Communist Student Union were excited about New Wave French cinema. The French adults preferred films from the Soviet Union. Incredible—but true. Arguments over America broke out. Politically, the young people in France and in the left-wing parties everywhere tended to be more, not less, hostile to the United States than their elders; more enraged at the genuine instances of U.S. imperialism, and against the instances that were somewhat debatable; more prone to accept the analogy between the United States and Nazi Germany that figured so prominently in the political analyses of the far left in those years.

But on questions that were literary, musical, or cinematic, the antipathies of the young turned into sympathies. At *Clarté*, the editors ran articles about John Ford and *Catcher in the Rye*, which was nearly as unnerving to the Communist elders as running translations from the Italian. Sometimes the flirtation with American culture was too hip for words. There was the case of the French Situationists, who promoted a theory about the super-oppressiveness of popular culture, especially the kind that is beamed from Hollywood to the world. Yet the Situationists seemed to take a perverse pleasure in everything they denounced. Their tracts were turgid, and they lightened them up with comic strips, Roy Lichtenstein style, in order to look down their noses at the comic book mentality of "Americanized" culture. But because the comics were amusing, you could sneer at American culture and enjoy it at the same time. That was a curious ambiguity in the student movement, not just in France.

The radical student magazine in Nicaragua during the early and middle sixties was a journal called *Ventana*. It was edited by (among others) Sergio Ramírez, who went on to become Nicaragua's vice-president during the Sandinista People's Revolution of 1979–90—an anti-Yankee revolution if ever there was one. Yet *Ventana* was the journal that brought Allen Ginsberg's *Howl* to Nicaragua, quite as if the United States, imperialism's home, was also rebellion's. In Mexico the ambiguity was probably sharper than anywhere else. During the '68 uprising the chants were anti-American; and the songs were American (some of them, anyway). Fidel Castro, Bob Dylan, and Joan Baez were local gods. Beatlemania (which was not exactly American, but was close enough, from a far-away Mexican perspective) played no small part in the radical mood. There was a cult of California. The first hippies showed up in Mexico City shortly before the student uprising, on their way from San Francisco to seek magic mushrooms (of course) in the mountains of Oaxaca and bringing news of the "San Francisco sound." And no one could mistake the subversive implications of those several cultural novelties. People who were old and conservative and powerful in Mexico hated the student movement because the young people were making democratic demands, and because they were paradoxically flirting with Communism, but also because they were listening to music with English-language lyrics.

It was always hard to say what the new interest around the world in English-language pop culture was intended to mean, or what ideas or anti-ideas lay buried within the new styles and tastes, or what the unintended consequences of those ideas would be. A worldwide victory for liberal principles? A defeat for cultures far richer than America's? But on one point everyone can agree. The music and movies were spreading new ideas about sex and the relations of men and women. Those ideas were not peripheral to the student insurrections. At Columbia University in New York, one of the little incidents that prepared the way for the student strike in April 1968 was the university administration's attempt to punish a girl student who had moved in with her boyfriend. It was the same in France. The first fateful spark of the 1968 uprising there was a student takeover of a university building at Nanterre to demand sexual integration of the dormitories.

The new ideas provoked an argument everywhere they went; but what everyone forgets is that the earliest and perhaps the bitterest of those arguments took place within the movement itself. The New Left in America in the early and middle sixties was notorious for its old-fashioned sexual division of labor, which made men leaders and relegated women to the rank and filing cabinet, to borrow a phrase from Robin Morgan. But as the years advanced, the division of labor blossomed into a division of political opinion, until by the movement's final days, New Left thinking came in two versions, one for straight men, the other for women (and soon enough for homosexuals). The retreat into left-wing antiquity, the turn toward Marxism-Leninism, the celebrating of totalitarian leaders around the world, the lurch toward guerrilla war— those impulses were primarily the business of the men, though with enough female participation to refute any latent suspicions about the inherent masculinity of the Marxist-Leninist imagination. The new ideas about sex roles were not, however, the business of the males, anyway not the straight ones. By the early 1970s (in some circles, even earlier) the straight males would talk about the Young Marx and the Old Marx and the coming crisis of capitalism and that sort of thing; and the women and the gays would talk about elitism and male chauvinism and the division of responsibilities within the organization. It was leftist antiquity on one side, gender-role ultra-modernity on the other. And between the antique and the ultra-modern, a strictly domestic war broke out, invisible to the outside world, devastating to the inside world.

In his memoirs, Hayden describes what that was like in Berkeley in the early seventies. The preparations for guerrilla violence and the celebration of Kim Il Sung were apparently fine and good, at any rate provoked no hair-raising debates that he reports; but regarding personal relations within his own Red Family, a series of hideous inquisitions got under way. The Red Family demanded an end to "male power plays, self-centered jealousies, and wounded egos," and set out to enforce the demand by engaging in accusatory discussions—"torture sessions" is Hayden's phrase—designed to correct the erring comrades. "The discussions took the form of self-criticism, a group psychotherapy in which it was assumed that anything said in one's own defense—whether about washing dishes, exhibiting macho attitudes, or being attracted to a woman—was probably a self-serving and defensive alibi." The atmosphere came straight out of the French Revolution—not because anyone was wheeling up a guillotine but because the cardinal threat to the revolutionary movement was thought to be a bad attitude whose name was *hypocrisy*, as in the days of Robespierre. And since disguise is hypocrisy's essence, there was no way to ferret out the dangerous deception except by gouging ever deeper into the sinner's psyche, which made the hearings and inquisitions a matter of revolutionary duty.

University readers of a later generation may recognize in those ultra-left torture sessions from the early 1970s the ancestor of the infamous "political correctness" of the college dormitories in the eighties and nineties. Only the original version was conducted with great solemnity by groups of earnest revolutionaries sitting on a floor littered with marijuana ash, hoping to get through the rebuking of comrades as quickly as possible in order to return to pistol practice. Every one of the later New Left's thousand little organizations embarked on those "discussions" in the early seventies. And soon enough the rattled brothers and sisters of the struggle were running for the door, hands clutched to heads, hoping to hurl themselves as soon as possible into a regimen of brown rice or any conceivable thing except membership in a left-wing political movement. It was not (or not merely) that people lost interest in politics or grew cynical. They fled.

Why did those intramural discussions take such a nasty turn? You could point to external pressures: to the age itself, to the national paranoia that radiated outward from the Nixon White House, to the hysterias that wafted back to America from distant Indochina. You could point to the moral concerns that had given rise to the movement at its start, which led to a style of argument based on assertions of moral superiority, which was always hard to bear and became altogether too much when the political thinking turned dog-matic. The two sides in the argument over sexual hierarchies were oddly mismatched in debating style, which exacerbated the mutual irritation even more. The (mostly) straight male champions of archaic Marxist revolution were sometimes more forceful (at first) and better read in the left-wing classics, which made them feel outraged when their critics failed to acknowledge defeat; yet the antiquated Marxism of the straight males made no sense at all, which was infuriating even to themselves. The (mostly) female and gay champions of anti-sexist anti-elitism felt put down and insulted by every patronizing word directed against them, which likewise was infuriating, and dou-bly so because the women and gays were on to some-thing, and knew they were. And both sides knew that on the results of their debate rested the future and even the existence of the movement.

Anti-sexism presented itself as more radical even than the wildest radicalism; and meanwhile opened a way to criticize the wildest radicalism. You could see the power of that criticism as early as the last loony convention of SDS in June 1969. A Black Panther Minister of Information got up to speak. The scary nature of the Panther movement was easy enough to detect. The paramilitary leather uniforms, the titles like "Minister of Information" and "Minister of Defense," the jailhouse tone, the apology for rape in Cleaver's writings, the lapses into anti-Semitism, the assassination campaigns against the police—every-thing advertised the terror and dictatorship that were bound to spring from Panther power, if the party ever had the bad luck to acquire any. None of which, not one word, could be said—not in the New Left student circles of 1969, except by the members of the little sects. But when the Minister of Information stood up at the SDS convention and let loose with wisecracks about feminism—"pussy power!" the man said—a vein of legitimate criticism opened at once. From the seats of outraged students arose the wooden Maoist chant, "Smash male chauvinism!" A phrase like that offered a less than thorough criticism of Panther politics, left-wing gangsterism, vanguard Leninism, and Third Worldist fantasies of universal dictatorship. But it was a start.

Anti-sexism shed a few beams of light on life in revolutionary Cuba. To worry in public about the humble Cuban refugees who kept fleeing the island or the fate of the Cuban poets or generally the state of liberty in Cuba *libre* was out of the question in the later sixties, except among a few anarchists and social democrats who were not especially popular. But gay oppression was a legitimate issue to raise, and from that single issue a larger analysis of Communist society was bound to emerge, given time and reflection. Something similar happened in the course of the discussions of guerrilla war. You could see it in the pamphlets and journals that began to argue for an armed struggle. In California in the early seventies a small organization called the Bay Area Research Collective produced the journal *Dragon* as a discussion organ of the revolutionary campaign, and the pages were full of reports of bombings of supermarkets and corporate headquarters, none of which seemed to excite any controversy among the readers or editors.

But when a question about feminism or gay liberation appeared, all hell broke loose in those pro-guerrilla pages. And if, in those pages and in the university towns and bohemian neighborhoods all over the country, the arguments over sexism and elitism became superheated, if the pointing fingers trembled, if voices rose and the vapors of anti-sexist terror filled the room, finally you can understand why. For the anti-sexist criticisms that seemed quite narrow and peculiar when they were first raised turned out to have ever-widening implications, until the New Left as a whole was under attack. For what was New Leftism's deepest purpose? The entire project of building a new kind of left-wing movement had begun with a moral worry about being privileged in a world of suffering. The idea had been to take privileged young people and put them on the side of the oppressed. On someone else's side, not their own. On the side of people who needed help. But the argument for feminism and gay liberation said, in effect, that in the student world everybody was not, on closer inspection, so wonderfully privileged. On the contrary!

Whole groups of the comfortable middle class—the women, the homosexuals, and by extension anybody at all who suffered from historic prejudices—were suddenly revealed to have grievances of their own. Naturally the newly understood grievances were announced with a rhetoric that borrowed from the

New Left itself. It was the language of "oppression," "colonization," "occupation," "resistance"—the language that had come originally from the French Resistance and the anti-colonial revolution. But once the anti-sexist argument had been raised, those terms took on extravagant new definitions. The language of oppression and resistance, in its feminist and gay version, was now employed to mean: the despised middle class has legitimate problems of its own. The language meant: there is more to student life than afternoons at the cinemathèque. It meant: the illegitimacy complex of the New Left was delusionary. For the radical left that had come out of the baby boom generation could now see itself as a group with privileges, but also with problems; a group that was morally not so different from the rest of the world.

The new arguments meant that you no longer had to go out and undertake "risky, shoot-for-the-moon" political actions to establish who you were. Action and identity were no longer the same. Doing was no longer being. The moral crisis was over. You were already yourself merely by being a woman, or a homosexual, or a member of an ethnic group. Of all the methods that have ever been proposed for discovering a personal identity, the affirmation of womanhood, homosexuality, or ethnicity was not one of the grandest; but it sufficed. It brought the moral tensions of the after-the-deluge generation to an end. It opened a vast new terrain of social criticism and reform for the future, even if the full implications of what had been begun were not always understood at the start.

The new criticisms made the New Left suddenly look old. And if any of us who had the misfortune to be straight white males took it all a little hard, if the new mania for analyzing personal relations seemed to lead away from anything that would normally have been called politics (never mind that revolutionary fantasies were not exactly politics, either), if the whole process of disbanding the radical left was "torture," that was too bad. But the New Left was finished, and the age of feminism and gay rights and a variety of other movements whose ideas and aspirations would define the next few decades had already gotten under way.

The creative self-destruction in America offered one more example, by the way, of how the '68 student movements followed the same pattern in different countries. For all over the Western world, the uprisings proved amazingly unproductive in regard to conventional political or economic change. Several years of radical agitation and street fighting and university uprisings came and went, and the Atlantic Alliance was still in place, capitalism was not especially transformed, the poor were no less poor, the republic of workers' councils had never been formed. The Vietnam War was ended, but that was mostly a feat of the North Vietnamese army. You could argue that, as a result of the student uprisings, the larger culture had come to think about individual rights in a more expansive way. In the United States the civil rights movement was strengthened, and in France and perhaps in other countries the rights of minority populations were likewise given a boost, ever so slightly.

But the main effect of the insurrections was on the insurrectionists themselves and on people of their own age—and younger. César Gilabert writes about Mexico, "If the '68 movement revolutionized anything, it was its own rank and file." That was certainly the case in the United States, where the movements that came after the New Left wanted most of all to revolutionize the self. In France it was not much different. The feminist and gay challenges during the early 1970s, the "torture sessions," and the pop culture celebrations followed a road that was almost perfectly parallel to the American New Left, even if in France the feminist and gay movements were never quite as lively and strong; and, at the end, you could see something of the same result. There was a new kind of individualism and a loosening of the old cultural constraints within the younger generation. That was the main consequence of the '68 uprisings almost everywhere, in varying degrees in different places. And along with the cultural transformations came, almost everywhere, a feeling of bafflement.

There was bafflement that a movement so grand and touching in its motives as the student leftism of the 1960s could have degenerated and disappeared so quickly. And beyond the bafflement there was—I think there still is—a tremor of anxiety about what those worldwide events might mean for the future. It was because the student movements of circa 1968 were a weird phenomenon, but not an unprecedented one. A political or industrial or moral crisis followed by the spirited rebellion of a handful of people; the outbreak of sympathetic uprisings by larger numbers of people in a surprising number of places; a movement that sends up a pure flame of idealism, and is unable to preserve the purity of its idea; a radical ebullience that turns into radical ugliness; a movement for freedom and solidarity that turns into a movement for tyranny and violence, then produces rebellions against itself—that is not a novel pattern. Nothing is so old as a wave of the new. Similar sequences played out in 1848–49, in 1917–21, in 1936–38. Should we be surprised if bits and pieces of that same pattern reappear in the future? Spontaneous international insurrectionary movements are mysterious; but not unusual. Economics has its cycles; so does rebellion.

The Gay Awakening

The symbolic high point of the '68-era rebellions all over the world was reached on May 10, 1968, "The Night of the Barricades," in Paris. Some twenty thousand students paraded through the Latin Quarter threatening vague unimaginable revolutions against the prejudices, power, practices, and hierarchies of every conceivable thing that could be labeled a yoke on the neck of mankind. Activists from the old-fashioned Marxist youth groups and the official student organizations paraded along with everyone else, dreaming of keeping order among the demonstrators and providing marshals, leaders, and slogans of their own, as had always been done in the left-wing demonstrations of the past. But Marxist youth movements and official student organizations were themselves a yoke on the neck of mankind. Dany Cohn-Bendit, the *enragé* from the university at Nanterre, stood on a bench with a bullhorn shouting his own slogans: "There are no marshals and no leaders today! Nobody is responsible for you! You are responsible for yourselves, each row

of you responsible for itself! *You* are the marshals!"
And the youth of France marched by in a tizzy of
utopian aspiration.

Exactly how do you write the history of insurrectionary events like that? The first impulse of any sensible historian might be to trace the footsteps of the
influential leaders and the doings of powerful institutions, and generally to bring to bear the gray categories
of ordinary political analysis. But there were nights of
the barricades all over the world between the spring
of 1968 and the spring of 1970, and the young generation filled the streets, and the leaders of ordinary political organizations ran around influencing nobody (for
the moment), and the hipper firebrands shouted weird
anti-leader slogans of their own. And if you took the
ordinary political categories and applied them in a
spirit of scholarly zeal, uprisings that once lived and
breathed would drag themselves across your page and
expire on the spot. For the '68-era movements were
political insurrections; but also cultural and moral
insurrections. Leaders and institutions played their
roles; but a history of leaders and institutions would
be the history of everything except the spirit of revolt.
And how would those conventional political categories
help you explain that slogans about making love
instead of war and forbidding to forbid stood at the
mysterious heart and not on the freaky sidelines of
the many curious events?

The leftism of the sixties staged its uprisings in any
number of fields, and one of those uprisings, as it
happens, was intended to overthrow the conventional

habits and styles of writing history. In one country after another, the groups and individuals who would eventually form the New Left broke away from the old working-class parties of the left during the early and middle sixties. But in England the crucial break took place a bit earlier, in the middle fifties, and among its leaders were a number of scholarly historians who had finally lost patience with the British Communist Party. The historians made use of some well-known ideas from their academic predecessors, added some new impulses that were strictly of the New Left, and came up with the project that E. P. Thompson described in 1966 as "history from below," which meant writing about the past from the viewpoint of the downtrodden.

History from below was always supremely difficult to write, either because the research was hard to do, or because the narrative was likely to end up dreary, or because the historians had no sure way to avoid getting sidetracked into marginal and unimportant topics. But history from below could always claim some virtues, too, and the grandest of those, anyway the cleverest from a literary perspective, was the ability to tell two stories at once, while seeming to be telling only one. The apparent story, the tale that sometimes seemed a little slow and tedious, was typically a minutely documented account of, say, riotous crowds in the eighteenth-century streets, or of drinkers in the taverns of long ago and how they spent their idle, boozy hours, or of rural people with quaint and unusual customs, or of some other ungainly topic whose drama and purpose were hard to see. But beneath those many arcane details you were supposed to glimpse a few glittering hints of something huger and deeper, and when you put those hints together, what you half-detected was a buried epic of freedom and history.

You saw, in a fragmented version, the great drama of the left: the story of people who have long been exploited or persecuted coming to understand their true condition, and painfully thinking their way through to an idea that life can be better, and rousing themselves at last to fight for a juster world, not only for themselves. At *those* moments, history from below was anything but dreary. For a brief second, the historians themselves, in the course of their own narratives, seemed to be up on a bench, shouting: "Leaders and marshals and powerful institutions do not, in fact, count for much! Humble individuals and lowly despised corners of society make their own history—at least they can, and someday soon they will, and the tiniest details of the forgotten past show their capacity to do so!" Then the half-uncovered epic slipped once more beneath the surface, and you were back to poring over obscure documents and forgotten events, and you could almost forget that anything had taken place.

The classic themes for the historians-from-below were topics like the French Revolution of 1789 and the rise of the labor movement, which lent themselves naturally to the up-from-below idea. But as the years have passed, one other field of scholarly investigation has similarly lent itself, namely, the story of the 1968-

era movements themselves—the most natural topic of all, you might suppose, for a style of writing whose every page exudes a remnant scent of the sixties left. No one seems to have noticed the achievement, but writers in a number of countries, not just academic historians and not just in English, have worked up something that could be called, with a bit of exaggeration, an international style for writing the history of those several uprisings.

The style has two main methods or approaches that derive from the academic school as well as from documentary filmmaking and the "roman vrai" and Latin American "testimonial" literature. By now each of the two main approaches has managed to generate, in one country or another, a history of the period that, because of its vividness and authenticity, can be regarded as more or less classic. There is the method of braiding together a collective biography of innumerable big-shots and small-shots in the style of a Victorian novel, to show that events come about because of a large number of modest personal histories and not because of impersonal forces and giant institutions. The classic example is the two-volume history of the '68 movement in France, *Génération*, by Hervé Hamon and Patrick Rotman, whose 1,311 pages offer the most grandiosely thorough account in any country of the student insurrection. And there is the "micro-history" method of reconstructing in hyper-detail the story of a single representative event, in order to demonstrate that crowds and mass protests consist of individuals responding to personal promptings in understandable ways. The classic example is Mexican. It is *La noche de Tlatelolco* by Elena Poniatowska, the chief chronicler of the '68 generation in Mexico, who weaves together a huge number of "oral history" testimonies with crowd chants and newspaper clippings to reconstruct the student movement up to the final gruesome massacre in Mexico City in October 1968.

I don't know why, but writers who have set out to compose full-scale surveys of the 1968-era movements in the United States have mostly shied away from these two techniques (though some excellent books have been written). Still, here and there you do find the international 1968 style applied, on a small scale, to American themes. Some years ago the English historian Ronald Fraser and a small phalanx of colleagues set out to compose an ambitious oral history overview of '68 movements in several of the Western democracies under the title *1968: A Student Generation in Revolt*, and the American students were accorded their portion, with vivid results. But the sharpest and most vivid of the small-scale American studies is, I would say, a volume by Martin Duberman called *Stonewall*, a modest book, written in a manner closer to popular history than to a full-sized Thompson-like academic study, yet with a perfect focus, from the viewpoint of the international style.

For if the single violent incident that Duberman has reconstructed was, in comparison to the Latin Quarter uprising or the massacre in Mexico, small and almost peaceable, no one can say that public memory of the event has faded, any more than memory has faded of the French May or the Mexican October. And if Duberman's strand of 1968-era radicalism could never be confused with the uprising of an entire generation, if his chosen strand was in fact so marginal and idiosyncratic in its early days that most of the historians of the era have passed it by entirely or have recorded its existence with only a handful of squeamish and embarrassed sentences—even so, no one can say that humble origins have meant a humble future. Not at all! The marginal has expanded and will undoubtedly keep on expanding, until one day this single radical strand will probably end up looking like the hardiest of all the products of the '68-era upsurge, and the truest: '68ness itself, in leafy bloom. For what Duberman's book has so tenderly brought to life is the political tendency that announced its existence to the world on June 28, 1969, thirteen months after the uprising in the Latin Quarter, when New York's Greenwich Village went through its own Night of the Barricades in the odd-angled eighteenth-century streets outside the Stonewall Inn at Sheridan Square, and the modern international movement for gay liberation was born.

Duberman's method is to recount the biographies, beginning with childhood, of only six people instead of the dozens that you find in Hamon and Rotman's chronicle of the '68 generation in France. Yet six life stories are enough to beam a clarifying light on the uprising that finally took place in Greenwich Village and on quite a bit that has happened to the gay movement later on. The purpose in writing a group portrait, as he explains it, is to affirm a democratic belief in "the importance of the individual" and the "commonality of life," which gives his book the mark of the international school. But in the case of *Stonewall* collective biography permits the historian to accomplish something else, too, which is to lower us, by a ladder of intimate details, into realms of psychological reflection and sexual motivation that, until the '68 era, had always been considered too murky or remote from public events to be taken into serious consideration. And so we find ourselves reading that, of the two women in this group of six, both went through a youthful phase of having boyfriends, and both had early lesbian relations, too—even back to summer camp at age seven, if you count childhood crushes. As for the men, none of them seems to have experienced any appreciable longings at all for the opposite sex. In the old Kinsey system for grading homosexuality and heterosexuality, grade one meant pure heterosexuality and grade six pure homosexuality; and with Duberman's males, sex is six or nothing.

Foster Gunnison, Jr., the most conservative of Duberman's personalities, recognized himself as homosexual at the advanced age of twenty, and followed this recognition with a life of near-perfect chastity. The sexual orientation of the three other men was entirely clear in childhood. Craig Rodwell attended a Christian Science boarding school for "problem" boys in Chicago and found himself having some sort of pre-pubescent sex with fully half of the other "problems" in his class. Ray "Sylvia" Rivera had sex with his cousin at the age of seven. And each of the males, Gunnison apart, had sex either as children or as early teenagers with adults. Jim Fouratt traded sex for car rides during his teenage years in Providence, Rhode Island. In high school, young Rodwell used to cruise for gay men in Chicago. Rivera's experience was altogether extreme. His long-suffering Venezuelan grandmother brought him up in the New York-area Spanish-speaking working class and did her best to keep him on a reasonably normal track. But by fourth grade the boy was wearing makeup. In fifth grade he was seduced by one of his teachers and was having sex with other men, too. At the age of eleven, he ran away to live as a transvestite prostitute under the name "Sylvia" on Times Square, where his poor old granny used to hunt him down and one time even frightened off one of his johns, not that hounding the boy brought him home again.

We are not in the land of the bourgeois sexual ideal. Duberman keeps studiously cool in the face of these tales, even if he knows that a percentage of readers are clutching the walls. Sex between youngsters and adults? We non–Ancient Greeks draw the line. But though Duberman normally feels no reluctance to wave his fist and declare positions on the most contentious of issues, on this delicate topic he merely reports without judging, and his reporting shows that simple codes of morality never seem quite adequate to the human complexities of sex. The men whose childhood stories these are look back on their precocious experiences, and wistfulness suffuses them, the way it suffuses anyone whose early sexual experiences were halfway agreeable. The life that Craig Rodwell led at fourteen or fifteen, cruising for men at the Chicago ballpark and in department stores and having sex in the toilet stalls of public men's rooms, strikes Rodwell the adult as "high adventure." Even about Sylvia Rivera, Duberman says that prostitution at Times Square made him feel "elated" and "euphoric"—though it's true that on another page, Rivera appears to have expressed a hope in his adult years that other boys won't have to go through what he endured—or rather, "she," in the pronoun that his biographer considerately chooses to employ.

The bad part for these men wasn't the sex, it was the circumstances. Jim Fouratt was one time taken by a group of men and raped and beaten. Rodwell's early experiences were especially awful. One of his adult lovers was arrested for having sex with boys and committed suicide. Another of his adult lovers was sentenced to five years for the crime of consorting with Rodwell himself, who was likewise arrested, though not prosecuted. When he got to be eighteen, in 1958, Rodwell moved to New York, and soon enough was arrested once again, this time for wearing too small a bikini at the Riis Park beach in Queens, and arrest led to a beating and three days in jail. He went cruising for a lover in Washington Square, was arrested again, and again ended up beaten. He took a summer job at the elite gay men's resort at Fire Island, and the shadow of official repression fell there, too. From time to time the police raided the resort and chained the men one to another and to a telephone pole in gangs as large as thirty or forty, until a police launch brought them to be booked and fined on the mainland. And over these ugly and humiliating scenes in Chicago, Providence, New York, and Fire Island hovered clouds of anguish, sometimes of mental imbalance. Rodwell tried to kill himself twice and spent a month at the psychiatric ward at Bellevue. Rivera spent two months there and tried to commit suicide at least once. Fouratt attempted suicide. Whether or not suicide figures as a larger factor among homosexuals than among other people (which is one of the many unresolved issues that continue to surround the debate over homosexuality), the urge to die does pop up often enough in these bitter tales.

The pioneers of the modern gay movement had to ask themselves some very hard questions about the inner anguish and the suicidal impulses. For what if the predicament of homosexuals was, finally, a function of their own mental illness—of the "psychopathic personality disorders" that military psychiatrists began to warn of back in 1942? What if homosexuality was an insanity? The modern gay movement was founded in a small way in 1950 in Los Angeles by perhaps a dozen men, some of them with Communist Party connections (along with Rudi Gernreich, the fashion designer whose own contribution to the radicalism of the sixties was the famously funny-looking topless swimsuit for women). These men put together a semi-clandestine organization with a name drawn from a medieval secret fraternity, the Mattachine Society, to advance the rights of homosexuals, and the Mattachine addressed the psychological question at once. The members proposed that, in Duberman's summary, "most gays had internalized the society's negative judgment of them as 'sick,'" but in reality they weren't crazy at all and were, instead, "a legitimate minority living within a hostile mainstream culture." Those were advanced views for the 1950s.

But the Mattachine fell into an internal squabble, the Communist sympathizers were driven out, some of the early glamour wore off, and things went from bad to pathetic when the Mattachine's national center got converted into a front for a San Francisco businessman's gay sex club and porno theater. Elsewhere the Mattachine settled into cautious placidity. Typical meetings of the Mattachine's entirely proper and legitimate New York section in, say, 1960 featured middle-aged men in business suits filing into a room provided by Freedom House, the human rights group, to listen respectfully to psychiatric experts, "who pontificated at length about the entitlement of homosexuals to civil rights *even though* their sexual development might have been distorted."

Yet if gays were not only persecuted by police and condemned by the great religions but in addition were, even in their own eyes, mentally ill, how were they going to organize themselves to press for civil rights? They needed reservoirs of self-confidence and had not a drop. They could hardly turn to the American Psychiatric Association. As late as 1973 the organized psychiatrists insisted formally on seeing homosexuality as a psychological disorder. A leader of the far-from-placid Mattachine Society of Washington, D.C., Frank Kameny, drew the unavoidable conclusion as early as 1964. "The entire movement," he said, "is going to stand or fall upon the question of whether homosexuality is a sickness, and upon our taking a firm stand on it." Among the people Duberman describes at length, Foster Gunnison in particular set out during the middle sixties to prepare the ground for that kind of rigorous stand in the years to come.

Gunnison had a sophisticated business background, derived from his years working for his father's prefabricated construction company, and he drew on that background in trying to unite the several tiny and scattered gay organizations: the Mattachine, the Daughters of Bilitis, which was the Mattachine's slightly younger lesbian sister, and a number of regional groups. Together with Rodwell, Gunnison was one of the very few who went each year, beginning in 1965, to picket the White House for "Equal Rights for Homosexuals" and to endure the contempt of the public and the snickering of the press. But organizing came hard. The leaders of gay groups in the early and middle sixties tended to be, for easily imagined reasons, hardbitten individualists. No particular style or outlook drew them together. Gunnison himself, in matters of dress, was a Brooks Brothers man. His political ideas were strictly conservative, apart from his militant advocacy of what was still called the "homophile" cause. He wanted full acceptance of homosexuality by conventional society, but he hoped that society, once it took that radical step, would in all other ways remain conventional still. He had no use for Communists, and as for "beatniks and other professional noncon-formists," he worried that if people like that ever got hold of the movement, all was lost.

To go plunging into the beatnik and left-wing depths of downtown New York was, however, the gay movement's inescapable destiny. New York's theater world has probably always had a gay tinge. Clever and mordant drag shows have been a staple in the downtown Manhattan streets for as long as anyone can remember. But in the course of the 1960s the old downtown tinge took on a fatefully deeper hue, and the deeper the hue, the more people seem to have been drawn to it from around the country. Jim Fouratt left his home in Providence and in 1961 found his way, via a doomed effort at joining the Catholic priest-hood, to the New York theater. He hung out at places like the Caffè Cino in the Village, where the atmo-sphere was such that Joe Cino himself, the proprietor (and soon enough another suicide), used to call out, "Get real, Mary," to any shy gay performer who kept his gayness under wraps. And as this sort of avant-garde marched steadily avant, its population and even its geography tended to grow, until whole city blocks in Greenwich Village and on the Lower East Side and in San Francisco took on the freaky theater quality of exhibition and provocation.

Not everything in the new countercultural neigh-borhoods meant new and exemplary attitudes toward homosexuality. Even on the extreme left, in the young people's oases that lay somewhere beyond the hidebound downtown Communists and Trotskyists (whose principal party, the Socialist Workers, retained a ban against homosexuals until 1970), you couldn't count on enlightened behavior. Fouratt went from the theater to the theatrical politics of the group around Abbie Hoffman, who was the Pan of St. Mark's Place in the mid-1960s. It was Fouratt—the "original flower child," in Hoffman's appreciative phrase—who thought up the stunt of dropping dollar bills on the New York Stock Exchange, which made Hoffman famous. Fouratt helped put together the Central Park Be-In of 1967 and a few other trippy efforts to raise political protest to the plane of the Zen surreal, where the sexual atmosphere was supposed to be open to every sensual possibility, closed to none, in a spirit that might be called the polymorphous transcendental.

But the truth about polymorphous transcendentalism was sometimes disappointing. Hoffman used to drop in on his buddy Fouratt and snub his buddy's lover, as if a homosexual couple was too much for even Pan to abide. (At least that was Fouratt's impression. Hoffman himself, in his autobiography, makes it sound as if Fouratt's gayness was one more admirable trait of an admirable guy.) One of Duberman's women, Karla Jay, was a student at Columbia University's Barnard College in the late sixties, on her way to a career as an academic literary scholar, and had similar unhappy experiences in an uptown student version. The Columbia uprising took place, and she was in the crowd. Yet there, too, on the uptown barricades, the revolution against sexual convention kept ending up in outbreaks of male hetero-inanity, and the radicalized young women gagged in unison and raced off to organize the consciousness-raising groups of the early New York feminist movement. Jay made her way into the influential little group called Redstockings, which was the epitome of every radical feminist idea; and even there felt less than perfectly at home.

Yet for all these left-wing failings, it's easy enough to see that, via the hippie sensual ideal (which helped overthrow the rule of tradition in sexual customs), then via the feminist challenge (which overthrew the overthrow), then via an unexpected shimmer of the homoerotic that began to run through some of the new women's organizations, the question of homosexuality was creeping up on every side. Already in the hippie sensibility, bisexuality glowed with special prestige, roughly the way that taking ever stronger drugs was seen as evidence of spiritual superiority. In the pre-guerrilla revolutionary cells of SDS's Weatherman, bisexuality became, by the early months of 1969, positively mandatory, enforced on all the prospective warriors of the impending armed revolt. Every month that passed seemed to bring crashing to the ground some taboo or inhibition that used to be regarded as basic to civilization. And to raise a few modest questions about homosexuality in that kind of environment became ever easier, ever less avoidable.

Any number of challenges began cropping up within the already existing semi-underground world of gay society—within, for instance, the world of New

York lesbianism. This was not a very ancient world. According to the historians of lesbianism, the first more or less modern lesbian circles in the United States arose only in the late nineteenth and early twentieth centuries, and the custom in those early circles was to re-create lesbian versions of the him-and-her distinctions of the larger world. In the old-fashioned lesbian bars, women regarded themselves either as "butches" (alternatively, "lesbians," "stud broads," "diesel dykes," and "truck drivers") or as "femmes" (alternatively, "girlfriends" and "ladies"). Everyone knew her proper place and dressed accordingly and made love either "actively" as butches or "passively" as femmes. And the attitude toward this sort of homosexual convention on the part of the new young generation of hippie-minded radical young women circa 1968 can be pictured in an instant. Karla Jay, having been dismayed first by the swaggering machos of the student left, then by the radical feminists, wandered into the Manhattan lesbian bars and was immediately asked: Which are you, butch or femme? Neither, obviously. She was something new, a young woman who was attracted to women (as well as, in those days, to men) yet not at all attracted to the idea of playing a single fixed sexual role that might be defined by anyone but herself. By the late 1960s personalities like that were becoming so common as practically to be a sociological category.

A different kind of challenge to homosexual tradition turned up in the old-line homophile groups. As early as 1961, young Rodwell, the Mattachine firebrand, arrived with six other rebellious souls to demonstrate at Manhattan's Whitehall Street draft board against the army's anti-gay policy—which was the kind of action that made the business-suit rank and file squirm with dread. In 1967 Rodwell opened the Oscar Wilde Memorial Bookshop in the Village as a movement center—which upset some of the older-style homosexuals still again, if only because the store claimed to be gay yet failed to carry the pornography that gay bookshops had always carried before. And while these several historic changes worked their way through the mostly underground New York gay world, one other factor, having nothing to do with homosexuality per se, has to be taken into account in order to understand what happened next.

The uptown student radicals and the downtown freaks—the two wings of the New York countercul-ture—kept bumping up against the police depart-ment, and the bumps were getting sharper. Something very close to rioting, mounted cops versus SDS action squads, broke out on Sixth Avenue and in Times Square in November 1967 when Lyndon Johnson's secretary of state, Dean Rusk, came to speak at the New York Hilton. Anti-draft marchers went roaming around downtown and midtown Manhattan in December, and the conflicts with the police were not always gentle. In March 1968 fighting broke out at Grand Central Terminal during one of Abbie Hoff-man's demonstrations—with Fouratt in faithful atten-dance, half-disgusted at Hoffman's cynical willingness to conjure up violent situations. A month later, when the Columbia insurrection took place, battles between students and police were such that, on a single miserable day, 712 people were arrested and 148 got themselves clobbered by police billy clubs and blackjacks badly enough to count as injured, and some of the police were injured, too, and it was a wonder that no one was killed. In the fall came a new uprising at City College, farther uptown, then another near-riot in midtown when Governor George Wallace of Alabama visited New York, then a bigger and more violent student strike at City in the spring of 1969, led by City's black students.

The New York Black Panther Party had gotten organized by then and was hard at work in Brooklyn and the Bronx, preaching a line that within a couple of years would lead to Panther assassinations of policemen. Demonstrations went on throughout the spring on behalf of twenty-one Panthers who had been accused of a hair-raising conspiracy to blow up sites around the city, and the demonstrations sometimes drifted into scenes of mass vandalism with a lot of broken windows and scuffling with the police. As early as 1968, the downtown underground newspaper *Rat* adopted a gun-toting rodent as its logo and printed such headlines as "THE YEAR OF THE HEROIC GUERRILLA FIGHTER." Groups like the East Village Motherfuckers—more or less a street gang, loosely affiliated with SDS—decided that "Armed Love" made a better slogan than "Flower Power." Such was the atmosphere. And so, by June 1969, when the fateful incident at the Stonewall Inn finally occurred, these many events guaranteed that in a neighborhood like

Sheridan Square, the sidewalks would at any time of night or day be filled with the impossibly hip young veterans of who knows how many nasty scuffles with the police, and any number of those people were bound to have mused at length over what looked like an impending citywide black-Latino-freak-student insurrection—the uprising that was supposed to take place along the uptown-downtown double axes of East and West 116th Street, East and West 8th Street. The New York Commune, it was going to be.

The Stonewall Inn on Christopher Street, just west of West 8th, stood on the downtown axis, next door to the Lion's Head, the writers' bar. Duberman—to return to his account—describes the place in loving detail. The Stonewall catered to male gays, but not exactly to the Fire Island elite. Fouratt and Rodwell would never have been caught dead there. They regarded the Stonewall as a hangout for unsavory "chickenhawks," or older men on the prowl for boy prostitutes—though Duberman, no stranger to the bar, is reluctant to accept that description. Nobody disputes the filthiness of the place. The liquor was bootleg or hijacked, and in either event, watered down. The glasses were rinsed in the kind of water that will sooner or later give you hepatitis. But the Stonewall was not lacking in color. The bar was one of the gnarly marvels that only great cities can produce. The classic nineteenth-century novelists lived and breathed to write about such places. Mafia guys from the neighborhood were the owners and managers—though the guys in question were, it turns out, fairly queer themselves.

A gangster named Petey used to hang out at the bar wearing a black shirt and a tie, like any movie hoodlum, except that he kept falling in love with drag queens like "the beautiful Desiree" and "blond Harlow." The Stonewall was not a drag queen bar (the Washington Square Bar on Third Street and Broadway was the drag queen bar), which meant that, at the Stonewall, only a few full-time transvestites might be hanging around, though others were camped out across the street in the little park. But drag queening has its degrees. At the Stonewall, there were "scare drag queens"—these were "boys who looked like girls but who you knew were boys"—and there were "flame" queens, who wore makeup and teased their hair but dressed in male clothes, sort of.

A chubby queen named Maggie Jiggs stood behind the bar and poured the drinks and dealt acid and uppers. The chinos-and-penny-loafers crowd stood around listening to Motown on the jukebox. And regularly, as just another dab of color, blue-uniformed police from the Sixth Precinct—known not quite fondly as "Alice Blue Gown" and other names—staged their raids. New York State statute required that everyone wear at least three pieces of clothing "appropriate to one's gender," which was a require-ment aimed precisely at bars like the Stonewall Inn, where clothing and gender kept wandering off in sepa-rate directions. Alice Blue Gown would round up the cross-dressers along with some of the employees and anyone who lacked ID, and the bar would be pad-locked for the night—though never for good, since

the queer Mafia kept the crooked precinct well sup-
plied with bribes, and locking the doors forever would
have impoverished all and sundry.

Duberman leads us with poker-faced affection
through the historic evening by following the single
one of his people who happened to be drinking at the
bar on the historic night. That person was Sylvia
Rivera, the drag queen. By June 1969 Sylvia was an
upstanding citizen, almost, living in New Jersey with
her lover, Gary. She had been invited to a birthday
party for another transvestite, Marsha P. Johnson, who
him/herself went on to play a significant role in the
early super-radical moments of the gay liberation
movement. Sylvia decided to pass up Marsha's party.
But the whole detailed cityscape portrait of the Stonewall Inn is Duberman's moment of narrative glory,
and I will let him escort Sylvia to the bar:

> It wasn't that she was mad at Marsha; she simply
> felt strung out. She had been working as an
> accounting clerk in a Jersey City chain-store ware-
> house, keeping tally sheets of what the truckers
> took out—a good job with a good boss who let
> her wear face makeup whenever she felt like it. But
> it was an eleven-to-seven shift, Sundays through
> Thursdays, all-night stints that kept her away from
> her friends on the street and decidedly short of the
> cash she had made from hustling.
>
> Yes, she wanted to clean up her act and start
> leading a "normal" life. But she hadn't counted
> on missing the money so much, or on her drug

habit persisting—and sixty-seven dollars a week in take-home pay just wasn't doing it. So she and her lover, Gary, decided to piece out their income with a side gig—passing bad checks—and on June 27, a Friday, they had just gotten back from papering Washington, D.C. The first news they heard on returning was about Judy Garland's funeral that very day, how twenty thousand people had waited up to four hours in the blistering heat to view her body at Frank E. Campbell's funeral home on Madison Avenue and Eighty-first Street. The news sent a melodramatic shiver up Sylvia's spine, and she decided to become "completely hysterical." "It's the end of an era," she tearfully announced. "The greatest singer, the greatest actress of my childhood is no more. Never again 'Over the Rainbow'"—here Sylvia sobbed loudly—"no one left to look up to."

No, she was not going to Marsha's party. She would stay home, light her consoling religious candles. . . . But then the phone rang and her buddy Tammy Novak—who sounded more stoned than usual—*insisted* that Sylvia and Gary join her later that night at the Stonewall. Sylvia hesitated. If she was going out at all—"Was it all right to dance with the martyred Judy not cold in her grave?"— she would go to the Washington Square. She had never been crazy about the Stonewall, she reminded Tammy: men in makeup were tolerated there, but not exactly cherished. And if she was going to go out, she wanted to *vent*—to be just as outrageous, as grief-stricken, as makeup would allow. But

Tammy absolutely *refused* to take no for an answer and so Sylvia, moaning theatrically, gave in. She popped a black beauty and she and Gary headed downtown.

It got to be 1:20 A.M., prime time at Sheridan Square. Eight officers of the Sixth Precinct burst into the bar, as they had always burst before. Except the great mystery of historical change had already occurred, and because of the slow work of the old-fashioned homophile political organizations, or because of the hippie piety about an all-accepting sexual spirituality, or because of the winds of insurrection and impudence that were blowing around the world, or because the feminists had succeeded in making everyone skeptical about traditional sexual relations, or for all of these reasons, the roomful of drinkers who should have gulped and blinked in fear and humiliation at the sight of Alice Blue Gown instead grew cold and mocking.

The police checked IDs and told some of the people that they could leave. The lucky persons emerged from the bar to Christopher Street. A crowd had gathered on the sidewalk, and the campier types from the bar struck starlet poses as they exited the door, and the crowd cheered. A paddy wagon pulled up. The cheers turned to boos. Who was that random nighttime crowd? The exact social makeup of riotous crowds (we partisans of history from below disdain the tainted word "mob") was always the most central of questions for the historians. Not everybody pouring out of the bar or walking down Christopher Street at that instant came from Rivera's world of the stoned-out petty hoods and homeless prostitutes. Nor were they all of them the chinos-and-penny-loafers homosexuals of the timid middle class.

Craig Rodwell was, by June 1969, nicely established as a Greenwich Village storeowner, and here by chance he happened to come, strolling down the sidewalk, a distinguished member of the riotous assemblage. By happy coincidence here came Jim Fouratt, who was not only fairly well known as an actor and as a mover in the permanent Yippie revolution but had taken a job high up at CBS, promoting rock music. In books by other historians—Eric Marcus, Randy Shilts—I notice still other well-known faces in the crowd. Walking down the street was Vito Russo, a prominent film historian in the years ahead. Stumbling up from the bar was Morty Manford, a famous figure from the Columbia student left in those days, soon to become a notorious gay rights "zap" heckler of Mayor John Lindsay. Here briefly was Martha Shelley, a secretary at Columbia who played a major role in the Daughters of Bilitis, giving a late-night street tour to a couple of visiting lesbians. ("What's going on here?" her visitors asked. "Oh, it's a riot. These things happen in New York all the time.") One of the future personalities in the gay-rights-for-service-people movement happened by (though it's not clear exactly when), dressed in his bell-bottoms and love beads and not looking like the former air force sergeant that he actually was. So there were political skills and famous careers in that random late-night crowd. This was Manhattan!

Exactly what set off the riot has never been established. But we know that the police were loading the wagon with transvestites when somebody saw, in Duberman's description, "a leg, poured into nylons and sporting a high heel, shoot out of the back of the paddy wagon into the chest of a cop, throwing him backwards." Transvestites came leaping out of the wagon. Somebody was shouting, "Nobody's gonna fuck with me!" Stones, bottles, and coins flew through the air. The police fled into the bar. By then the crowd was feeling its power. The bar window broke. Some fool in the crowd poured lighter fluid and tried to set the place on fire.

Inside the bar, the police called for reinforcements from the Tactical Patrol Force, who were, among all the units of the New York Police Department, the most widely feared by everyone with experience in the political demonstrations of the time. TPFers were beefy men, bristly with clubs, guns, and tear gas canisters. They wore helmets and visors, and when two dozen of them showed up on Christopher Street, they linked arms and marched in formation up the block, looking like what anyone in 1969 would have instantly called scary motherfuckers. But as this force moved forward, the crowd merely doubled back and regrouped. A few people circled around the block to harass the marching formation from the rear, shouting and throwing things. And so Alice Blue Gown, the beefy TPF "mothers," the drugged-out transvestites, the chinos-and-loafers types, the lesbians, the queer Mafia, the flame queens, the scare drag queens, the gay Yippies, the resentful discharged veterans of the United States armed forces, the beatniks, the intellectuals, the student activists, the guitar pickers and the homeless riffraff of the little downtown park—this explosive crowd, living testimony to the sexual chaos of humble humanity, squared off in the Village street, and fumes of scorn and joy and sexual titillation went mixing with the smoke from the burning trash cans.

The TPFers whirled around. They found themselves face-to-face with what Duberman describes as "a chorus line of mocking queens, their arms clasped around each other, kicking their heels in the air Rockettes-style." And the chorus line thundered:

> *We are the Stonewall girls*
> *We wear our hair in curls*
> *We wear no underwear*
> *We show our pubic hair . . .*
> *We wear our dungarees*
> *Above our nelly knees!*

Talk about weird revolutionary slogans! People were hurling rocks and bricks. The police grabbed someone off the sidewalk and beat him, though the poor victim turned out to be Dave Van Ronk, the folk singer and not a homosexual, who had been drinking at the Lion's Head. Fouratt and maybe a few others in the crowd tried to cool things down, which was a decent thing to do—though Fouratt was also calling in his own reinforcements from among the city's radical left (some of whom responded, others did not), which must have kept the tensions high. Rodwell was calling in the press. And though the fighting died off after a couple of hours, on the next day and for two more days after that, the confrontations resumed, along with the derisory singing and the kick-lines. Then it rained and there was peace—only to break out into angry standoffs once again, when the rains cleared and the good old *Village Voice* came out with a suitably incendiary issue.

The actual amount of violence from either side doesn't seem to have been especially high after the initial moment—not compared to what happened to the civil rights movement in the South, or to the Tlatelolco massacre in Mexico, or to the May 1968 fighting at the Sorbonne, or even to the Columbia strike a little more than a year earlier, where that same TPF had pretty much gone on a rampage. Yet those June and July 1969 crowds in Greenwich Village were furious even so. And their fury had an odd quality: it didn't fade.

II

Exactly why that was, why the noise from the Stonewall riot went on resonating during the months after Sheridan Square was finally cleared, why those days of street scuffling afterward ascended into zones of legend and myth, why in later years the annual June commemorations under the name of "Gay Pride" or

"Gay Freedom" (as proposed by Rodwell) gradually became, in Randy Shilts's phrase, "the high holy day of the national gay movement," why the history of homosexuality neatly divides into pre-Stonewall and post-Stonewall eras, not just in the United States but in a variety of countries—that is easy enough to see, if you let yourself look through empathetic eyes.

The riot at Sheridan Square was not the first bit of trouble on the street between gays and police. In San Francisco as early as 1966, three days of fighting followed a police raid on a gay hangout called Compton's Cafeteria, and there had been other incidents, and the West Coast marched several steps ahead of the East. Only those early West Coast developments took place in too staid a time, and the noise from those protests did not penetrate beyond a few small California precincts. That was not a problem in the summer of 1969. Life was a loudspeaker that year. And what everyone—some people, anyway—heard at the riot on Christopher Street was distinctly new. It was the sound of voices tuned to a different pitch, airing emotions that had never been aired publicly before. In response to that sound, around the country any number of homosexuals who for so long had lived in secrecy or in self-repression seem to have begun undergoing, one by one, their own personal Stonewall insurrections—released by public events into an individual "no" that by the intensity of its tone and the novelty of its cry tended then and tends even now to make anyone standing nearby gape with astonishment. For who outside of the world of the homosexuals could have known, until that moment, how much unhappiness and despair were woven into that clandestine world, or how big that world would turn out to be?

Where precisely to channel the newly released energies once the six days of fighting had ended was a bit of a problem. Ideas went into the riot, but were shattered there, and did not come out again. The old homophile notion of achieving rights for gays along the dignified lines of the old pre–Black Power civil rights movement was discredited in a nanosecond. During the nights and the days of Christopher Street agitation, the Mattachine Society posted leaflets in the Village telling gay people to cool it. But cooling it was exactly what whole crowds on the sidewalk no longer wished to do. That most mysterious of social changes, a mass instantaneous radicalization, had taken place. Civil rights liberalism was already a speck receding into the distance, and the only remaining question was which among several varieties of radical leftism those suddenly fired-up young people would sieze on for their own. Looking back on those times, you might think the new gay militants would naturally have lined up with the libertarian left and found some way of saying, along with Cohn-Bendit, "Nobody is responsible for you! *You* are responsible for yourselves!" The old-line anarchists had their little foothold in the downtown theater avant-garde. The Living Theater was anarchist, and around it was a penumbra of hardboiled Wobbly proletarians. Even the French Situationists, with their vision of a libertarian future and their highly appropriate call for a "revolution of everyday life," had a Lower East Side branch, minuscule though it was. To go in one of those directions would not have been inconceivable.

But in the history of the American youth movement, June 1969 was precisely the month in which the libertarian and radical democratic ideas went down to their miserable final defeat. Students for a Democratic Society fell apart that month in a convention at Chicago, and over the spot where SDS once reigned arose a newer impulse that was dominated by the round enigmatic face of Mao Zedong and the idea of joining, in Mao's phrase, "the raging tide of the people of the world against the U.S. aggressors." And if the proposed new raging tide seemed, at first glance, to leave very little room for Americans of any sort, on second glance there was, in fact, an honored place, so long as the Americans could show themselves to be the victims, not the beneficiaries, of the imperialist system.

The Chicago SDS convention and a second convention a few days later in Oakland, hosted by the Panthers, set out to identify the several elements of American life that could plausibly claim to stand outside the golden circle of imperialist privilege and prosperity, and to group these elements into an "American Liberation Front" under the leadership of Fidel Castro, Ho Chi Minh, and Mao (though in Oakland, where the Communist Party was not without influence, some discreetly preferred Leonid Brezhnev). The new idea was a national version of the New York insurrection that so many people kept expecting to take place. It pictured a network of semi-Bolshevized ethnic street gangs headed by the Panthers, and behind them the Young Lords Party among Puerto Ricans, the Brown Berets among Mexican-Americans, the Young Patriots of Chicago among working-class whites, the Chinese-American Maoists, and any number of other groups reaching all the way to the extreme left of the not yet ethnically divided student movement and the dope-smoking Yippie outlaws. And with these very peculiar ideas in the air, Fouratt and Martha Shelley and some of the other faces from the crowd at Sheridan Square broke off from the strait-laced old homophile organizations to put together their own gay wing of the revolutionary alliance in the form of the Gay Liberation Front, which was a spectacularly novel idea.

Needless to say, not everyone in the older homophile circles burst into applause at the notion of enlisting the gay movement in the world crusade led by Mao Zedong. Poor old Foster Gunnison, the conservative nuts-and-bolts hero of the older homophile movement, had to stand back and watch as his own worst nightmares about Commies and nonconformists materialized into real-life packed auditoriums. Gunnison showed up at gay meetings where he wasn't known, and people took him to be some kind of police spy and saw him to the door. For among the younger people who were just now coming out as homosexuals, what was the homophile past? Brooks Brothers, what was that? The idea of forming a liberation front and aligning with Panthers, Mao, the Viet Cong, Fidel—

that was the notion of the hour, even if Shelley and some of the other participants harbored a few quiet reservations. Gay Liberation Fronts arose in all the big cities. New gay newspapers—the homosexual wing of the underground press—spread the news. And the gap that opened between the brand-new gay militance and the older stolid homophile campaign was, I suspect, even more cavernous than the gap that had opened a year or two earlier between the Negro civil rights movement of the past and the Black Power movement of what looked like the future.

Thus the gay revolution got off on a very awkward foot. The proposed international allies of the new gay movement could not have been more disastrously chosen. Mao's Red Guards were not above staging public castrations of "sexual degenerates." Castro's pathologies about homosexuality had already earned him an immortal place in the history of homophobia. Fouratt, in the same year that he helped found the GLF, also helped found the Venceremos Brigade to bring Yankee volunteers to toil in the Communist sugar fields—and when the time came to depart for the Caribbean and start cutting cane, the gay Yippie found himself forbidden to participate, out of fear that a Christopher Street ebullience might contaminate the Fidelista ethic. At home in the United States, there was the continual embarrassment about the Black Panthers, whose own sexual ideas were other than progressive.

The new vision of gay liberation was not exactly helpful from an organizational point of view, either.

The basic notion of putting together a revolutionary coalition among groups deemed to be innocent of imperialist crime implied a system of defining people by their historic grievances: the grievances of blacks, of Latin and Asian immigrants, and—by extension— of women and homosexuals. But grievance means fission, in the law of political organization. The Gay Liberation Front clung to the highly un-Bolshevik anti-elitism of the New Left in regard to conducting its meetings and shaping its organization, which guaranteed bedlam; and the shape that bedlam took was a progressive fracturing along lines of subgrievance and double-subgrievance. GLF ecumenicism included women and men both, but the women quickly split off into a Women's Caucus, and then the black and Hispanic women split off into their own group, and the Hispanic women left to form "Las Buenas Amigas," who themselves were lucky not to splinter along lines of skin tone or Latin American country of origin. That was exactly the process that was destroying the larger New Left. And soon the GLF, too, was only a memory.

Still, some inner essence of those early ideas clung to life, and adapted, and flourished. Deep within those several founding notions from 1969 you could already see, in germ, the fateful idea of ascribing everyone's personal traits and beliefs about politics and culture to the one or two ethnic and sexual factors that might constitute the basis for a historic grievance. There was already a tone of pious sympathy for the victimhood of each and all (except, of course, for the hetero-Euromales). There was already the expectation that with sufficient pity and piety all around, the many victimized ethnic-and-gender personalities would form themselves into their respective "communities" under the banner of their respective "cultures," and the communities would generate a movement for a new society that was eventually pictured not as worldwide Marxist-Leninist liberation or even as libertarian socialism but as a democracy of communities. Not liberty in the old sense but "diversity" in the new sense.

The idea that came to be known as "identity politics" had, in short, made its entrance into American life. And if this idea slowly spread outward from the left-wing world into the easy liberal assumptions of well-meaning Americans on campuses everywhere and in the Democratic Party, that was because, for all the silliness in the identity-politics idea, and for all the crippling effects of reducing everybody's personality to two or three factors, and for all the kitschiness in the new notion of "cultures" and "communities," identity politics did address some very keen modern anxieties. For look what the more radical young people, not just the gays, had gone through by the early 1970s. Huge crowds of young black people, having been catapulted by the civil rights revolution into the colleges and universities, found themselves hurtling into the blue yonder of an American middle class that their own parents had never dreamed of entering. Masses of young women were throwing aside the outdated ideas of their own mothers and were declaring themselves to be women of a bolder and more aggressive type than they or their mothers or anyone else had ever seen. These people were nervous! And in the aftermath of the Stonewall riot, the radical young gays found themselves in circumstances that were still more extreme and unprecedented.

The young post-Stonewall gays were no longer merely coping with homosexuality, as gays had always done before, with a lowered head and a guilty conscience. By proclaiming homosexuality as their right, they were bound to feel that they had overthrown Catholicism, or Protestantism, or Judaism, as the case may be. They had overthrown Mom and Dad. Ten thousand years of repression crumpled at every step they took. They were free; and freedom was terrifying. They felt supremely alienated from what they imagined to be the main currents of American life (little realizing that they themselves were a main current). In which case, who exactly were they anymore? They were American rootlessness uprooted. And to people in that alarming circumstance, identity politics offered a consolation. The new idea proclaimed itself to be a radicalism beyond all radicalisms; but its deeper message was a soothing, traditionalist reassurance. Identity politics taught that forthright radical homosexuals and other brave social pioneers did in fact dwell among the comforts of a noble community with the kind of ancient roots that flower into confident modern-day personalities. Or, at least, the homosexuals *would* dwell in such a community, if only they could demonstrate that the premises of identity politics were true both in general and in their own special case as homosexuals, and that community in the identity-politics version was real and not just a slogan.

The tremendous outpouring of gay creative energy during the quarter century after Stonewall, the sexualized artworks, the solemnity about pornography, the efforts to work up a distinctively lesbian or homosexual aesthetic, the homosexual interpretations of literature, the rise of gay and lesbian studies as academic disciplines—these many notable features of recent times show how strongly people have felt the need to build up the gay culture that identity politics said must surely exist. And if in the atmosphere of excitement and revolution it was sometimes very difficult to draw a line between the good new work that came of these efforts and the mass of bad new work, if a militant wind began to blow and accusations of bigotry and homophobia went careening around the college lawns and everyone learned to talk with the sweet unctuous decorum of diplomats and to refrain from disparaging even the wildest of claims and political pretensions on the part of individuals who might be ethnically or sexually different from oneself—who could be surprised? For in the identity-politics vision, where democracy is a matter of communities, and communities are defined by their culture, to criticize somebody else's cultural expression is to question the dignity and the rights of an entire population, which no decent person would want to do. So there was a moral intimidation in the new idea.

The intimidation spread a blanket of protection over the cheesiest renditions of old-wives' superstitions and bad poetry and silly history. And there was, in the identity-politics idea, a virtual guarantee of rejection on the part of a larger public, if only because to underline the gay identity tends to mean underlining the sexual component, and one man's turn-on is bound to be another's gross-out. Arlene Stein, the editor of a lesbian anthology, *Sisters, Sexperts, Queers: Beyond the Lesbian Nation*, has ruefully noticed part of the problem in regard to the lesbian movement. "The paradox," she writes, "is that if we don't name our difference in explicitly sexual terms, we remain invisible as lesbians—but if we do name it we're typecast as little more than sexual beings, and the vast complexity of our lives disappears." But such is the allure of the identity-politics paradox that even the author of those self-conscious and slightly embarrassed cautionary words has gone ahead and awarded herself, by the title of her own book, the honorific "sexpert," which, of course, anybody would like to be, though maybe not twenty-four hours a day.

At the "high holy day" Stonewall commemorations straight into the 1990s, the dour gay politicos would come marching by demanding civil rights. But in public demonstration of that same inbuilt paradox, next would come, row after row of them, the sexperts, naming their difference. Barechested young men danced erotically on flatbed trucks. Women marched by in masses with their blouses stripped off. Fetishists decked out in leather motorcycle caps and studded risqué leather pants came rolling along in still more trucks, followed by strangely flabby and obese sadomasochists who marched down the street literally flogging one another. Random persons paraded between floats in a pathos of individual isolation carrying placards of their own handmade construction that affirmed the strangest of all strange slogans: "Rectal Pride," "Vaginal Pride." Because of the epidemic, a warm sickly breeze of Thanatos blew across these public scenes. On the back of a flatbed truck bearing the grim banner "HIV-Positive" came yet another gaggle of handsome barechested young men with sinuous arms and gleaming chests who seemed to be, still, soaring on a cloud of sexual exaltation, dancing seductively, almost as if beckoning to the crowd and crying out "Join us!" And, yes, those marches were a political protest, but by the paradox of identity politics, the marches were an erotic festival, too—despite everything, even death. For the parading marchers were making themselves sexual on the occasion of their merry and tragic and political "holy day" in the same way that Polish-Americans don embroidered peasant costumes for the Pulaski Day parade.

A reign of terror was guaranteed to come of this, even without the pressures of an epidemic. In any movement based on building up a cultural identity, sooner or later someone will step forward to declare his own identity to be truer and more authentic than everyone else's, and will announce a grave impending threat to the collective identity, and on that basis will take into his own hands the right to make decisions for all, and to unmask traitors, and to carry out the executions. Alisa Solomon, writing in the *Sisters, Sex-*

perts, *Queers* collection, has described a fairly
depressing zealotry against "ideological contamination" in some nether portions of the lesbian movement, where AIDS has not had to be a central concern.
And if you throw in the epidemic, the threshold for
genuine hysteria was bound to slide ever downward.

One of the political responses to the disease among
gay activists—the formation of the group ACT-UP
in 1987 to stage protests against irresponsible foot-
dragging by the government and the pharmaceutical
industry—reverted as if by instinct to the same gay
world of the New York theater that had produced
so much of the gay movement's Stonewall-era noisy
activism. Larry Kramer, the author of one of the earliest
plays about AIDS, *A Normal Heart*, served as presiding
authority, and the results were good, at first. But
theatricality is an inebriant, and once a large number
of people had tasted its pleasures, there was nothing
to keep the livelier types from acting up in other ways,
too. ACT-UP gave birth at the beginning of the
1990s to a group with a broader mandate that called
itself "Queer Nation"—whose name, like "Lesbian
Nation," resurrected Abbie Hoffman's Yippie notion
of the "Woodstock Nation" (from the Woodstock
rock festival of August 1969, a few weeks after the
Stonewall riot). And with 1969 resurrected on every
side, the terror (of a nonviolent sort, of course)
announced itself at once. You could see it in the
internal campaigns against ideological contamination,
which by then were an old story in the gay movement,
and in the ferocious condemnations of the Catholic

Church and other implacable enemies of an enlightened sex education. But the terror was above all visible in public acts of retribution against the gay revolution's own inadequate partisans and ungrateful intended beneficiaries.

The "outing" of fellow homosexuals serves, in effect, to blackmail influential persons into helping the gay cause, as interpreted by the blackmailing "outer." True, there might be a personal or professional cost to the poor soul who has been "outed." The threat of getting blackmailed might discourage a timid gay person from a public career. "Outings" might succeed in "outing" individuals who were never really "in." But what is that to Robespierre? Show me a guillotine and I will show you a career ladder. There was the example of a Queer Nation activist who made himself famous by harassing one of President Bush's assistant secretaries of defense. The activist telephoned his chosen victim at home in the middle of the night and, not liking the assistant secretary's way of talking, took it on himself to reveal this man's homosexuality to the world.

According to Randy Shilts, the main authority on military homosexuality, this same assistant secretary "was not particularly circumspect about his opposition to the gay policies" of the Pentagon. He may even have used his high position to whisper liberal advice about gay issues to still higher officials in the Bush administration. But outing, as I figure it, is not really designed to advance the cause. Outing is a way of expressing what Shilts, in an irritated mood, calls "the

deeper intolerance many gay radicals held toward anyone, heterosexual or homosexual, who did not subscribe to their rigid ideology." It is an act of supreme
power, like a mob boss's power to "whack" some poor
slob who falls down in his loan payments. And as in
all reigns of terror, a fog of conspiracy theorizing drifts
across the field in order to justify the most lurid of
actions. The activist who outed the assistant secretary
wrote a book called *Queer in America*, boasting of his
achievement, and evoked the conspiracy chillingly.

"There exists in America," he announced, "what
appears to be a brilliantly orchestrated, massive conspiracy to keep all homosexuals locked in the closet"—
requiring, of course, the efforts of militants from organizations like Queer Nation to destroy it. The components of this conspiracy are, as anyone could have
guessed, "the media industry, centered in New York,"
"the political system, centered in Washington," and
"the entertainment industry, centered in Hollywood,"
all of which are full of cowardly homosexuals who are
eager to sell out the cause but who will soon enough
meet the wrath of the militant queer avengers. Phrases
from the McCarthy era pop up in this kind of conspir-
acy-mongering as if from the national id: "naming
names" (an act of virtue, in this version), "Is there
an absolute right to privacy?" (not among the gay
avengers). And what a shame it is that the great historian Richard Hofstadter did not live long enough
to add a post-sixties addendum about homosexual
militancy to *The Paranoid Style in American Politics*!

Yet how is it that none of these embarrassments

and misfortunes has managed to sink the gay movement? The organizational chaos of the Gay Liberation Front in the months after the Stonewall riot, the calamitous notion of allying at home and abroad with every pirate and tyrant who ran up a revolutionary flag, the invention of a kitschy cultural identity on the basis of sex and the ensuing campaigns to eroticize art and culture, the snarly air of intolerance radiating from the radicals, the parading fetishists, the maneuverings of the flacks and the blackmailers and the conspiracy theorists, not to mention the horrors of disease and the cold breeze of repeated Republican presidential landslides: any one of those elements would have sufficed to sink a flimsier cause, exactly as happened to the larger New Left, in no time flat. But the gay ship was unsinkable. Its reason for being was always too clear and obvious to be ruined by some idiocy or other.

It was a movement for the right to love. It was grand; nothing could pull it down. It took that other theme of the great nineteenth-century novels, after the eccentricity of city life—the theme of natural love bumping up against society's artificial laws and customs, bumping up even against death—and turned love's story into a crusade in the streets. The gay movement was the most romantic political campaign that ever existed. To prosper under the conditions of American life in the years after the Stonewall riot, all that was needed was to announce the basic concept of rights for gays—and followers were going to flock to the cause and were going to brush off the nonsense that came wafting from the daffier professors or the less scrupulous self-promoters, and still more followers were going to join the campaign, and the entire movement was going to advance in stages so plain and logical as to exude a quality of sociological permanence.

The first of these stages, in the immediate aftermath of the Stonewall riot, was a gay twist on the hippie inspiration to go build geodesic-dome communes in the Rockies, except that gay community building confined itself, in a practical spirit, to the project of colonizing big-city neighborhoods. Ever since the late nineteenth century in New York, a few gay nightclubs or bars had huddled together in the red-light and theater districts—originally on the Bowery, later in Greenwich Village, Harlem, Times Square, and most recently the East Village. But now those handful of seamy streets began to flourish into full-fledged sprightly "gay ghettos"—fixtures of modern urban geography not just in Greenwich Village or in San Francisco's Castro District but in Miami's South Beach, Seattle's Capital Hill, Houston's Montrose neighborhood, Cincinnati's Liberty Hill and Northside, Washington's Dupont Circle, and in Philadelphia, Atlanta, Los Angeles, Chicago, St. Louis, Denver, and other places, too.

An unlucky mix of factors in the seventies—the residue of hippie sensuality (except in a masculine version that had never been reigned in by indignant feminists), the old-fashioned gay orgy scenes that now went on all but freed of police raids, the slightly sinister disco tone of post-revolutionary decadence and chemically improved ebullience—produced the big delirious gay sex clubs, which proved to be a medical misfortune even before AIDS, and afterward became a catastrophe. But the view that gay communities depend on erotic extravaganzas was never quite right. The epidemic began noticeably to spread in the early 1980s, and the new neighborhoods and institutions gave the activists some modest first mechanisms to begin the dismal task of organizing against the plague—even if the anti-AIDS mobilizations were always too weak and too late and involved a lot of intramural fighting. So the gay movement turned out to have a strictly practical side, and the people whose hearts did not beat for utopia or for identity politics or for the cult of ecstasy discovered a grim sort of trade union usefulness in the new gay organizations. Some people may have discovered a moral gravity in their gay affiliations, too, and time and disaster made the bonds between individuals and the movement grow tighter, not looser.

Within six months of the Stonewall riot, the more levelheaded types split off from the GLF to form the Gay Activists Alliance, which was the GLF without the part about Fidel Castro and the Black Panthers; and from the GAA split off a still more establishment-oriented group that called itself the National Gay Task Force (with the words "and Lesbian" added later); and each of these groups proved to be more powerful than the last. Neither the National Gay and Lesbian Task Force nor any other group ever managed to dominate the field of gay politics, nor did gay politics ever generate a single widely accepted national leader—and this failure, which in the case of most political movements would signal weakness and fragility, seems to have been, in the case of the gay movement, a sign of strength. "There are no marshals and no leaders today!"

There was only the ideal model of a grass-roots insurgency, '68 style. By 1976, a quarter of the nation's campuses could claim a gay student organization—where hardly any had existed a decade earlier. Gay Democratic clubs took root in all of the biggest cities. Yet if there was a single definitive moment when the gay campaign's more-than-superficial strength became obvious and undeniable, that moment arrived when the campaign began to assert a claim to citizenship in society as a whole and not just on the bohemian margins, and the gay movement cropped up in places that were inconceivably far removed from the Greenwich Village sidewalks. And so the movement that got its start among the kick-line queens at the Stonewall Inn and the hyper-revolutionary students of 1969 began to spring up spontaneously from deep within the ranks of the U.S. armed forces.

III

How did such a thing come to pass? It is possible to trace the steps, mostly due to a titanic job of research performed by Randy Shilts, the author of *Conduct Unbecoming: Gays and Lesbians in the U.S. Military.* Shilts conducted 1,100 interviews with military people, and he worked up his research into 700 pages of stories and anecdotes, presented in the same international '68 style that you find almost everywhere among the historians of the gay movement. And by sifting carefully through Shilt's discoveries, you begin to see that, in the American armed forces, one person after another has spun a variation on a single unhappy military theme.

In its male version, this is the theme of a teenage boy or young man who is privately troubled by his attraction to other males, or else by his failure to feel much sexual urge at all. The boy or man would like to grow up in conventional masculine directions. So he does what any football coach would advise: he enlists in the service, only to discover that his adolescent doubts and worries are becoming graver by the minute and that high school was bliss compared to the miseries of life in a uniform. The young man finds himself more or less having an affair with another man, or he finds himself drawn to the bustle and comradeship of the gay bars. It is the nature of military life to encourage a bit of homoerotic foolery—at any rate, a keen sentimental affection between buddies in a unit. Yet there are buddies and there are buddies, and some of the foolery is not just foolery, and for the soldier whose homoeroticism is the real thing, deep feelings turn out to be at stake, and the depth of emotion is exactly what must be concealed. So the young man gropes his way into a circle of other people with the same experience, and his circle of friends finds its way to still other hidden circles, and the result is like the gas and cable networks under the city streets, going everywhere, visible nowhere.

But then, if Shilts's research is to be believed, what a network this turns out to be! Each of the great ships in the U.S. Navy—though I suppose we knew about the navy—seems to have had its own hidden gay subculture. Over the years, the "Connie girls" (that is, boys) flourished aboard the U.S.S. *Constellation*, the "Easy girls" aboard the U.S.S. *Enterprise*, the "Rangerettes" aboard the U.S.S. *Ranger*. The *John F. Kennedy* was at one time known to some as the "Jackie O," the *Dwight D. Eisenhower* as the "Mamie." According to Shilts's information, in the late seventies fully 60 percent of the crew was homosexual on the U.S.S. *La Salle*, "the gayest ship in the Navy," which steamed into the Persian Gulf and met up with some merry Arab oil princes, and quite a time was had by all.

The olive drab Pentagon, seen through Shilts's lens, looms as a giant pink triangle of homosexuality. There was once a men's room in corridor six of the Pentagon where "men literally stood in the line outside the stalls during the lunch hour, waiting their turn to engage in some hanky-panky." Nor is homosexuality confined to the humbler ranks. "Every service has had at least one gay person at four-star rank since 1981, and at least one gay man has served on the Joint Chiefs of Staff in that time." As for the women, according to some lesbian sources that Shilts cites, the number of lesbians in uniform has never sunk beneath a full 25 percent of the military's female population, which might seem a lot, except in comparison to the amazing days of the Second World War, when lesbians accounted for fully 80 percent of the military women, and it was the heterosexual minority that cowered in a corner.

Seven hundred pages of this! To read is to blink. You do have to wonder: How much of what Shilts reports can really be true? Maybe Shilts's movement enthusiasms ended up turning him into a gay version of Joyce's Bloom, the addled Jew, who stumbles around Dublin crowing to himself about the many distinguished persons who have been Jews. One of the gay rights pioneers told another historian of the gay movement, Eric Marcus, that the Mattachine Society back in the early fifties used to build up a mystique of power by boasting about unnamed "senators and generals" who were secret members. Maybe every uniformed gay whom Shilts wheedled into giving an interview took the opportunity to indulge in a bit of happy boasting along those reassuring Mattachine lines.

Yet how do we know who is authentically homosexual? Who counts as a true-blue lesbian is a famously tricky question, much fought over within the lesbian movement, due to unmistakable tendencies among some young women to feel an attraction now to women, now to men, then to take a few tours through the lesbian bars only to end up, androgynous butterflies that they are, in the arms of a properly heterosexual male—which is a phenomenon that drives the harder-line lesbian militants to apoplexy. Shilts himself, in reporting the statistical claims about lesbianism, carefully refrains from endorsing them.

The anecdotes nonetheless point to one more station in the gay soldier's typical progress through the military. That is the moment when, having made the sexual discovery, the unfortunate man or woman in uniform looks up and sees the steely blade of institutional repression inexorably descending. A previously hidden tale of secret interrogations, spyings, coerced confessions, mail searches, telephone tappings, and pressures on people to testify against one another suddenly reveals itself to the astonished soldier's eyes. Then come the formal charges of sodomy or committing indecent acts or fraternization with the wrong people or "conduct unbecoming an officer." Shilts cites a South Carolina lawyer who has dug up a German witch-hunters' guide from 1484, the *Malleus Maleficarum*, to show the medieval spirit of these inquisitions. And just as in the witch-hunting crazes of centuries ago, the zeal for persecuting gays seems to rise and fall according to a logic that is impossible to detect.

During the Vietnam War, gay bars, clubs, and social circles made up a "vast gay subculture" of the American military, especially in Saigon, where wildness among the friskier gays seems nearly to have rivaled wildness among the friskier straights. But that was war; peace is hell. In tranquil 1980, to pick a peacetime moment from Shilts's study almost at random, the number of persecutions was fairly amazing. An investigation at the San Diego air station zeroed in on eighteen women. A purge of military lesbians in Georgia resulted in charges against another half dozen. Thirty gay airmen were investigated at Malmstron Air Force Base in Montana and at least eight were discharged. The women's softball team at West Point was investigated, followed by the women's volleyball team at the Air Force Academy in Colorado. And so it went—Shilts's details keep piling up—until, in a mere twelve months, the ever-vigilant four services had discharged 1,966 people for homosexuality. That is an expensive way to run a military. The dollar cost to the armed services, as estimated by Congress's General Accounting Office, has been $22.5 million a year, though the true figure has got to be a lot higher—hundreds of millions of dollars a year, in Shilts's estimation—given that most of the people who come under suspicion choose to tiptoe out of the service before getting formally accused. As for the cost measured in injuries to the soul—that is beyond reckoning. It is infuriating to read about these things. And the more you read, the more you have to wonder why these military persecutions always seemed, until recently, like something less than a moral outrage. The abuses were never invisible; yet neither were they seen. Everything was public; nothing was noticed. How could that have been?

I think the explanation has to do with the extreme peculiarities of a movement that went from minuscule to mass in a very few years. In 1961, when Rodwell picketed the Manhattan induction center to protest the military's policy on homosexuality, the entire national organized homophile membership was no more than four hundred people, men and women both, who had no hope at all of bringing their issue to the public. It was only the Stonewall riot and the New Left that gave the movement strength. But the New Left also made the movement anti-militarist, therefore indifferent to questions of military reform. When the first audible protests against military policy did arise, it was only because by 1974 or '75 even the most conservative and Republican of military officers, if they happened to be gay, were inhaling the post-Stonewall cultural atmosphere, and to inhale was to be transformed, and the transformed soldiers were coming up with indignant responses of their own, one rugged individual at a time. With a sailor here and a sergeant there, by 1976 the political and legal challenges to the military policy were springing up on a weekly basis. Plainly the typical career of a homosexual in the armed forces had generated yet another phase. It was the moment when enough was enough, and the accused person got over his mortification and began to shout, in the vivid language of June 28, 1969, "Nobody's gonna fuck with me!," which might as well be the national motto. The soldiers called their lawyers. And that was the cross-over moment when the newly assertive military gays reached out to the anti-military gay movement that had created the conditions for the new assertiveness.

The anomalies were not slow in appearing. At the annual Stonewall marches around the country in the mid-seventies, people were still chanting slogans that derived from the GLF and the high tide of the New Left. Lesbians chanted, "Dare to struggle, dare to win, dare to snuggle, dare to win," which may have carried no echo in their own minds but was nonetheless a cozy, ladylike adaptation of Chapter 7, "Dare to Struggle," etc., from *Quotations from Chairman Mao* (which begins, "People of the world, unite and defeat the U.S. aggressors and all their running dogs!"). Gays chanted, "Ho ho homosexual, the status quo is ineffectual," which was a not-so-distant echo of anti-war chants in praise of the same Ho Chi Minh against whom the American military had fought with such little success. Yet in 1975 Sergeant Leonard Matlovich, the first and most celebrated of the gay soldiers to put up a public fight for his own career, arrived at one of these parades in New York and was celebrated as a hero of the movement—even if the other paraders must have scratched their left-wing heads over what to do with a U.S. Army sergeant. And this kind of anomaly, once it had cropped up in the gay demonstrations, proved to be a perennial.

You could see it in the march on Washington by several hundred thousand homosexuals in April 1993, the hugest such gathering in the history of the world. The march adopted gay rights in the U.S. military as the chief of its several demands—yet some of the 1993 nostalgics for 1969 still raced around in loincloths, and more than a few of the speakers and performers at the podium still displayed an instinctive disdain for anything connected to a uniform. The long-ago New Left could never decide whether it despised American culture as a force for imperialist oppression or loved it as a force for pop rebellion; and a generation later, clouds from that same confusion still hovered over the gay movement, and maybe gay oppression derived from the larger cruelties of the American system, which ought to be overthrown, or maybe the dream of gay liberation derived from the larger dream of American liberty, which ought to be expanded, and the uniformed military gays waving from the podium might have been the agents of imperialism, or might have been the sword and shield of American-style individual freedom, and who could say?

The level of muddle was impressive, and it was hard to see who was going to clear it up. The movement had gotten started in the wildest period of the New Left, and over the years it had slowly evolved into a novel branch of American liberalism. It had made the same transition, in an American version, that in France had been made by the left-wing intellectuals and in the Soviet empire by some of the dissident activists— the transition from 1968-era radical leftism to liberal democracy. But the gay movement in America had made that transition in the field of practical politics only, not in the field of ideas. Between the ideas of the past and the practices of the present the gap was enormous. And no one wanted to point that out. The old-time ideologues were not about to challenge the surviving bits of New Leftism that had served them well enough over the years. The shrewder political leaders could scarcely be expected to irritate and divide their own march-going and dues-paying constituents by launching a debate over basic political beliefs.

If anyone was going to work up some genuinely new thoughts and give them a sharp enough edge to command attention, it would have to be writers or thinkers of the sort who don't mind a little unpopularity. It might have to be a new generation entirely— just as, among black intellectuals, only an unpopular and sometimes conservative new wave of writers in the course of the 1980s was able to challenge the old Black Power orthodoxies from the same era of '68. And by the 1990s, something like that did seem to be under way among the gay writers. Shilts's career, brief as it was because of AIDS, suggested such a possibility, due to his habitually inconvenient choice of journalistic topics (army life, for instance) and his snappish rejoinders to radical critics (even though he had begun as a radical himself). The *New Republic* published a series of articles that counted as still another sign. And there were further indications, less visible, more astonishing.

I doubt that at the 1993 march in Washington many knapsacks carried, stuffed among the bologna sandwiches and bottled water, a rolled-up copy of the previous month's issue of *Commentary*, which has never been the gay movement's friend and comfort. Yet here were hints about a possible new direction in gay intellectual life where no one would have thought to look. Having published perhaps one fulmination too many against the evils of homosexuality over the years, the editors of *Commentary* found themselves, in their March 1993 issue, publishing no fewer than fourteen pages of letters responding to the discussion of homosexual themes, and while some of those letters stoutly defended the magazine's customary antipathy, several of the others struck a different note altogether. The authors of those letters were not the avatars of the radical left. They were the readers of *Commentary* magazine. Yet in textbook illustration of the fact that homosexuality is not ideologically determined, some of those *Commentary* loyalists happened to be gay themselves, and chose to announce it, and saw no reason to keep their indignation hidden, either. Cultural developments travel a little slowly among the right-wing intellectuals; but some things can't be stopped. For here was the Stonewall uprising at last, fourteen pages of it, angry and inflamed, pounding at the door of the neoconservative flagship journal.

Naturally the neoconservative Stonewall uprising of 1993 departed in several particulars from the 1969 original. The first and most passionate of *Commentary's* letter-writing *enragés* was, to the surprise of at least some of his occasional readers, Bruce Bawer, who for many years had served as the main literary critic at *Commentary's* sister journal in the arts, the *New Criterion*. In his letter—then in a book of his own called *A Place at the Table*—Bawer gave the new outlook a full exposition, mostly by painting a portrait of himself. The portrait is not a confirmation of every Jean Genet cliché about outlaw homosexuality that you keep stumbling on in the literature of gay studies. The pillar of Bawer's week, as he describes it, is Sunday attendance at Episcopal services. He lives quietly and monogamously with his companion, Chris. Every molecule of his existence, except one, seems to be almost insufferably straight. Yet that one small departure from the norm has brought down on his unoffending head any number of insults and injuries.

His friends invite him to a wedding that he himself, playing Cupid, had helped bring about. But when he and Chris arrive for the ceremony, the bride and groom go out of their way to look down their smug heterosexual noses at their own non-hetero guests. (At least in his own memory. The bride later on wrote a letter to the *New York Times Book Review* offering a version more flattering to herself.) He labors for four thankless years as the film critic of the neanderthal *American Spectator*, but when he declines to erase even the briefest mention of homosexuality and AIDS from one of his reviews, he is forced out of his column, if only to maintain the integrity of the magazine's commitment to its own intolerance. And the sober, un-self-pitying picture that Bawer's book paints of these humiliations, which are so typical of gay life—injuries brutal to the gay person, yet (nearly) invisible to the offending party—yields at last to a barrage of controlled anger. He is a man with a rifle and a motive. He asks: Is homosexuality immoral? Is it incompatible with ordinary decency? Is it un-Christian, un-Episcopal? Unintelligent? A threat to children? And his argument advances to a steady fire of no, no, no.

Here at last is a book-writing Foster Gunnison, full of enthusiasm for a narrow social and cultural reform, namely the one that bears on himself, and wholly indifferent to the left-wing dream of a grand radical coalition of the aggrieved. He calls for "the legal recognition of gay unions"—whether these unions go under the name of marriage or of domestic partnership. He wants gays everywhere to be able to enjoy the kind of household tranquility that he and Chris have managed to enjoy. He wants respectable gay lovers to receive the same kind of respect—the same "place at the table"—as respectable heterosexuals. The counterargument that gay companionships cannot really be a "moral equivalent" of heterosexual marriage strikes him as offensive, not to mention farcical, given the many cheating husbands and wife-beaters and bickering couples that he says he knows. Love's content, not its form, is the important thing for him. For Bawer is, in the end, a true man of the modern gay movement, which is to say, a romantic. Honesty and love are his gods.

His complaint is attractively made, and it comes burnished with a sheen of righteous rage, and I only wonder if the passionate insistence on honesty and love still leaves him in the realm of opinion that ordinary conservatives could identify as their own. For what happens to a family where love is no longer as romantic as it used to be? A good many people who wish to preserve the conventional family at nearly any cost— the advocates, that is, of "family values"—may recall that personal honesty can pose a problem from time to time; and where honesty is a problem, hypocrisy is a solution, though no one ever says so (thus proving the point). The less than happy marriages that Bawer disdains may strike the advocates of "family values" as better and safer than no family at all. When he thinks about the radical gay writers, about Allen Ginsberg and the ink-stained wretches of the *Village Voice*, he sputters with indignation. He denounces the "false dichotomy propounded by the gay subculture: out, proud, and promiscuous versus closeted, ashamed, and repressed." He says, "Sexual orientation is one issue, sexual irresponsibility another." The notion of sexuality as a kind of utopia that keeps popping up among the radicals strikes him as a lunacy. Where others see a commendable gay radical freedom-forging, he detects a pitiable gay self-hatred. Yet I wonder if the radical writers don't see more clearly than he why the gay arguments for honesty and romantic love might seem threatening to a conservative advocate of family stability.

A lot to argue about! But the striking thing is mostly the fact that such an argument is going on at all. For just when you might have counted the gay movement out, just when it seemed to have become trapped forever in its old ideas and splendid colorfulness and its unresolvable left-wing ambivalence about American life, fourteen pages of letters in *Commentary* and *A Place at the Table* came wandering down a revisionist path where only a few lonely writers had gone before. The suggestion was strong that history had not yet said its last word about the gay movement, and newer people would still be heard from. Bawer is emphatic on the point. He thinks that, among intellectuals who are gay, there are more conservatives than radicals, though the conservatives are only beginning to come out of hiding. He thinks the gay majority has not yet spoken up. And if any of that is true, the interesting possibility arises that, sooner or later, hipsterdom will have had its day, and the gay movement will move to still another stage. For here come the squares. They are men and women both, and they are adjusting their ties and arranging their skirts, and if Bawer's book and the uprising in the *Commentary* letters section are any indication, these people are slowly preparing to announce, in a polite and well-modulated tone: "Pardon the intrusion, fellow citizens, but henceforth nobody's gonna fuck with us, either."

IV

Single-issue reform campaigns and movements are so old in American life that Tocqueville was already struck by their importance and democratic role in the 1830s, as recorded in his chapter "The Usages that Americans Make of Association in Civil Life" in *Democracy in America*. But from Tocqueville's time until our own, the grandest of America's single-issue movements have tended to divide into two loosely defined categories, and the two categories have stumbled their way to different fates. If only we knew which of these categories corresponded to the highly unusual movement that sprang into life during Greenwich Village's Night of the Barricades in 1969, we might be able to predict what the fate of gay liberation, too, will eventually turn out to be.

The first category, the kind of single-issue movement that seemed so exotic and un-European to Tocqueville, has always aimed at achieving that most arrogant of goals, a moral improvement in the hearts and the practices of other people. The classic example was the temperance campaign, which made Tocqueville laugh, until he reflected that under democracy, the aristocratic elite that ought to set examples of superior behavior for the plebian mass of society has been driven into exile or has been hanged or has met some other democratic mishap; and the remaining plebian population has no alternative but to organize mass movements on behalf of whatever change in behavior seems like a good idea. So he came to respect these campaigns.

It's a little odd to suggest a comparison between the old-fashioned strait-laced campaigns for moral improvement and something as extravagant and modern as gay rights. Yet here and there in the argument for gay rights a hint of moral exhortation in the old style does crop up—and why not? The slogan "gay is good," Frank Kameny's impossibly radical 1968 variation on "black is beautiful," contains, as if in computer code, any number of buried assertions: that sexuality in general is good; that morality in sex is to be judged at least in part by its inner meaning for the individual, not by some external or religious code; that homosexuality is therefore not only tolerable but positively commendable, just as is heterosexuality. A program for moral improvement lurks unmistakably within those Freudian assertions. There is the invocation to be true to yourself, sexually and otherwise. There is the proposition that self-fulfillment is virtue—even if, under certain circumstances, self-denial might also be virtue.

Viewed from the ancient Protestant perspective that underlay the old nineteenth-century movements for better behavior, the modern arguments in homosexuality's defense add up, I'm sure, to a satanic program. But even in the nineteenth century, American Protestantism had its dissenting sects, and from sects to sex was never a distant leap. "Plural marriage" and other sexual experiments in a variety of earnest socialist communes were always an eye-catching element of nineteenth-century reform. Compared to the old Perfectionist socialism and the Fourierist phalansteries, not to mention the nineteenth-century Mormons, all of whom shared the goal of rearranging domestic sexual relations according to a higher moral idea, what really is so bizarre about the gay movement that got its start in 1969?

Still, if the gay campaign rests mostly or entirely on an argument for moral improvement, we might wonder if the movement will prove to be any stronger or longer lasting than those other, older campaigns. The Stonewall riot was followed by seven biblical years of steady advance, and the gay movement had reason to savor the likelihood of an eventual full acceptance into society. By February 1977, no fewer than nineteen states had repealed their sodomy laws and forty cities had enacted civil rights ordinances mandating gay rights, and the Democratic Party was strong, and all looked well. But later that same year, Anita Bryant, the orange juice queen, invoking "the laws of God and the cultural values of man," organized a countermovement to a gay rights ordinance in Miami, which proved successful, and the Miami phenomenon went national. The countermovement against homosexuality took its prominent place within the Reagan coalition, and the advances from 1969 to 1976 went into an extended period of hand-to-hand combat with the right-wing counter-revolution in the armed forces and everywhere else. The vehemence and unpredictability of those debates were such that, by Bill Clinton's time, the advances and retreats seemed to occur on an hourly basis, even in the calculations of the president himself. To see any kind of grand historical trend was not so easy.

For if the back and forth of argument over gay issues merely throws one movement for moral improvement up against another, nothing can guarantee that gay prospects won't keep on wavering forever, and every onrushing wave for social tolerance will spill up against an equal wave for traditional values, and the question never will get settled. One day the fervor for gay reform might even subside, as usually happens to single-issue movements that are fundamentally moral in their appeal. Prohibition, for instance, silently withdrew to a handful of "dry" towns and counties, where people today can still quietly refrain in peace and suffer the derision of the lost-soul "wets" who comprise the rest of the population. It is impossible to imagine the new ideas about homosexuality being driven out of Greenwich Village and the Castro District and a few other militant zones. But outside of those neighborhoods is the movement really so strong? There are large business corporations that have adopted formal policies establishing an admirable tolerance. Yet even in the most enlightened places the gay office workers typically go on concealing their homosexuality behind an intricate filagree of deception and disguise. Those people are a target, not a force. In the face of sustained attack you couldn't expect them to put up much of a fight.

Still, in American history, and not just in America, there is a different kind of single-issue campaign— not a campaign for moral reform, but a movement for political and cultural enfranchisement. The movement to enfranchise poor white workingmen during the 1820s that led to the presidency of Andrew Jackson, the battle for trade union rights and government protections for industrial workers that began in Jackson's time and has never ended, the abolitionist movement to free the slaves and later the civil rights movement to free the freedmen, the women's suffrage movement of earlier times and the modern feminist movement that arose a split second before gay liberation: these were never movements for moral improvement or for better behavior, except maybe in a secondary way. They were campaigns to lead one sector of society after another upward from the gloom of bottom-place

standing in the social hierarchy into the glorious mediocrity of the American middle. And with movements
like these, a question of progress and its irreversibility
arises, and at once plunges us into a deep question of
philosophy.

The idea of progress in these last days of the twentieth century has reached the point where mere mention
of the word makes people break out in the same
patronizing smile that crossed Tocqueville's lips upon
discovering a naive American phrase like "temperance." The belief in history's forward motion turns
out to be an oddly self-negating idea, such that anyone
who subscribes to the idea with any fervor is halfway
guaranteed to set mankind back a thousand years,
given the chance. And yet progress, especially in the
experience of us fellow citizens of Andrew Jackson
and Martin Luther King, Jr., has been known to take
some less alarming forms, which are neither so heated
and furious as to be millenarian and dangerous nor
so slow and cool as to be entirely undetectable. In the
introduction to his book on America, Tocqueville
talked about a progress of that middling sort—the
progress from below that he perceived over the course
of six hundred years, which he thought was surging
upward at fifty-year intervals and was leading toward
ever more equality, ever less hierarchy. The scale and
the grandeur of the upward motion seemed to him,
after so many centuries, a matter of "providence."
And if there is any ground for talking about that kind
of progress, if it still makes sense to speak of a gradual
rise into social equality of ever more downtrodden

sectors of poor unhappy mankind, if progress has not at last stumbled to an end under the hot rays of television culture and fundamentalist preachings, as some people think, and the upward motion is still somehow discernible in spite of the violent downward jolts that are perfectly capable of lasting for periods longer than Tocqueville's fifty-year intervals—if any of that is true, then the prospect for people whose desires are homosexual appears a little brighter.

Or at least the prospect would look brighter if homosexuals could reasonably be equated with the other historically oppressed sectors of society that have benefitted from irreversible emancipations. Do those equations exist? The white workingmen, the blacks, the women, and the other beneficiaries of past and present emancipatory campaigns have been around forever, and the Jews and sundry religious minorities in need of similar emancipations have been around for nearly as long. But while homosexuality itself is doubtless eternal (may even be genetically programmed, according to a much-contested theory), the antiquity of a group of people who can be called "homosexuals" is a vexed question, to which vast portions of the scholarly literature of modern gay studies have been devoted.

According to Michel Foucault, who counts as the literature's founding father, a word to describe homosexuals didn't even exist until 1870. Until then, you could talk about certain sexual pleasures or practices that people might partake in, and only later could you talk about a full-blown human type. In Foucault's formula, "The sodomite had been a temporary aberration; the homosexual was now a species." A similar observation emerges from the travel literature of gay studies. In a book called *Out in the World*, the writer Neil Miller compared gay life in a dozen countries around the world, and discovered that the variations are extreme. In some countries, not even the homosexuals consider themselves homosexual. Visiting the black townships of South Africa, Miller discovered that people there weren't sure if male homosexuals should count as male or female or as a third sex that might even be capable of bearing children. He discovered a homosexuality that was strictly regimented by a notion of "male" roles and "female" roles, so that everyone was either a "king" or a "queen," more or less like the old-fashioned American lesbian bars. In Thailand, Miller stumbled on a sexual atmosphere dominated by prostitution, straight and gay. In Latin America and elsewhere, he discovered a way of categorizing male homosexuality that considers the "passive" role homosexual but the "active" role not, which used to be a common idea in the United States, too. And from these observations Miller speculates that a modern-style homosexual identity—Foucault's "species"—crops up only at a particular moment in the development of society. This moment arrives when four minimum requirements have been fulfilled: a fair amount of personal freedom and tolerance; a degree of economic development that is strong enough to allow people to get away from home and move about at will; a relatively high status for women;

and what Miller calls "a decline in the power of the family and religious institutions in defining and determining every aspect of an individual's life."

Reading the gay travel literature, you'd have to conclude that before these four rigorous conditions have been met, many people might experience homosexual urges and might even act on them in a regular way, though probably with a lot of angst and inconvenience, exactly as in the different stops on Miller's world tour. But once the conditions have been met, those same angst-ridden persons would probably notice that life can hold out better possibilities for themselves, and ever-growing numbers would leap at the chance to live as homosexuals in the modern style of the West, perhaps keeping up a false front in public but no longer pretending to themselves. In the United States, Miller's four requirements were met during the late nineteenth and early twentieth centuries. After that, people, very small numbers of them at first, did begin to work up distinctly gay and lesbian senses of themselves, one step at a time, even if the straight world never quite figured out what was going on.

But once the new feeling about being gay had been fanned into street demonstrations by the insurrectionary breezes of the late 1960s, the campaign for gay liberation in America did, it seems to me, take the form of a movement for enfranchisement. The people who had now come "out" could never exactly go back "in." Human dignity doesn't bob up and down like grain prices. Naturally the gay movement is unlike any of the movements for enfranchisement that have come before, but then, each of the movements for enfranchisement has been unlike the ones that came before. Everything that has happened in American history would lead us to suppose that, if the gay movement does in fact count as such a movement and not just as a moral campaign, some kind of inevitable force does come into play, and the ever larger wing of the gay movement that has gone from bohemian anti-militarism to wanting a place within the armed forces and the rest of mainstream society has made a logical decision, and the zigzag progress of American liberty will increasingly mean not just the freedom to live the life of Christopher Street but also the life of Main Street, and be gay even so.

It is tempting to propose a still more grandiose claim. The variations on homosexuality that Neil Miller discovered around the world testify to the splendid multiformity of man; yet in each of the stops on his journey, he also stumbled on a few portentous signs of the single newer idea about homosexuality whose origin is the United States as well as Western Europe (where in Holland, Denmark, and Norway, gay rights, having been inspired by the post-Stonewall movement, have prospered beyond anything achieved so far in the United States). "It was significant," he tells us, "that in many of the countries I visited, the leaders in creating a gay movement"—here he mentions the names of gay leaders from Cairo, Hong Kong, and Bangkok—"had all spent time in the West." Random copies of the American gay magazine *The Advocate* turned up in Cape Town. A lesbian leader in Japan, where there are not many lesbian leaders, told him, "You know, they say that whatever happens in the United States happens ten years later in Japan."

Plainly the spread of AIDS has prompted people to put together some of the embryonic gay political organizations that can now be found in one country and another. But cultural factors seem to be the main impetus behind the new organizations, and chief among these factors, say what you will, is the world-wide spread of American pop culture and of the American-influenced culture of Western Europe. Miller, being a reasonable man, is of two minds about the ubiquitous creep of American images and ideas. Yet he noticed that even the lowly and much-reviled Western porno videos spread the kind of message that ought to be called "socially redeeming." From watching Western pornography some people in other parts of the world have learned the strictly modern news that the same person can have sex in both the "active" and "passive" positions, that "kings" can be "queens" and vice versa, which constitutes a turn against social hierarchy in a realm that Tocqueville never got around to mentioning. And since the Americanization of culture around the world appears to be something that no one has yet figured out how to stop, at least not for long or in a total degree, some of the new thinking about homosexuality that already figures in popular American culture does seem bound to spread, regardless of the outrage and the scimitar-brandishing it might inspire.

Given the degree of wealth and secularization that

produces Miller's list of four preconditions for a modern gay identity, what can possibly prevent the new thinking from producing some actual gay movements in countries around the world? And given some further progress toward secularism and democracy, what will prevent these movements from one day bursting into the open, to the amazement of everyone, with genuinely modern demands for the right to dignity and a new kind of personal freedom—exactly as the feminists have already done in large parts of the world?

A grand spectacle does seem to be taking place before our eyes, and this spectacle, when you get it into focus, has every appearance of being "history from below"—not the history that is written on the page, but the history that is written on the street. When the sounds from the noisy spectacle on the street reach our ears, they seem to be saying: "Ordinary individuals and lowly despised corners of society do make their own history—at least they *can*, and someday they will, and history shows their capacity to do so, and in fact some of us ordinary and despised people are doing it right now." We seem to be hearing: "There are no marshals today—not on the question of heterosexuality versus homosexuality. On that most crucial and personal of questions, you, each and every one of you, are responsible for yourselves." We are hearing: "Concerning homosexuality, it is forbidden anymore to forbid."

In earlier times, in the era that was only yesterday, many a solid citizen would have laughed at cries like that. Rights for the small minority of persons whose impulses in love and sex are not absolutely typical: what hilarity! A giant smirk crosses nine-tenths of the globe even now. There is reason to think that the battles over gay liberation will go on wavering, now forward, now back, very likely with violent shocks and setbacks for generations at a time. But there is reason also to think that, along with the other consequences and quarrels of modernity, those battles will spread and not grow narrower, and the final vector will point toward more liberation, not less. There is reason to think that on the matter of homosexuality, some small but important aspect of human personality has begun to change, not just in two or three cities, or in two or three countries, but, weird though it is to suggest such a possibility, *everywhere*.

Zappa and Havel

I

In January 1990, less than a month after Václav Havel had risen to the presidency of Czechoslovakia, but well before he and the other democrats were securely in power; before even the Communist secret police had come under democratic control; before anyone could quite tell who was running Havel's personal security among the guards at Prague Castle; in a period when rumors of Communist counter-revolutionary coups punctuated every telephone conversation and when the brave students who had begun the Velvet Revolution were silently returning to the conformity that is induced by fear; at a moment when the exhausted Praguers were holding back from signing any more radical petitions, *just in case*—at that ominous moment in the first shaky months of the Eastern Bloc Revolution, the distinguished Frank Zappa made his visit to Prague.

Zappa was on his way to attend the Czechoslovak parliament and to confer with President Havel, a long-time fan of *Bongo Fury* and other albums. In his pocket he carried earnest suggestions to rescue Czechoslovakia from decades of economic stagnation by means of tourism, cellular phones, and something called magnetohydrodynamic technology. Five thousand fans (in Zappa's own estimate) waited for him at the airport. A TV news crew from Prague deployed its equipment to record the historic arrival. And by sheerest luck, the crew spotted at the airport still another distinguished American, the United States ambassador, catching a plane out of the country. The American ambassador was none other than Shirley Temple Black, the dimpled, tiny-tot princess of the movies, grown up now. What excitement! Real-life Americans—straight from Hollywood! The TV crew rushed over to the ambassador from the United States and asked her to comment on Mr. Frank Zappa's impending arrival.

From an American point of view, that was a bizarre, at any rate a foreign, moment in the Eastern Bloc Revolution. No right-minded American would dream of asking Shirley Temple about Frank Zappa. Americans know that the United States is a divided country, at war with itself since the mid-1960s or earlier, splintered into culture and counterculture, right and left. Or who can say what the divisions are, except that they persist, like a guerrilla war that has festered in the jungle unto the second or third generation? The charming Temple, beloved for "The Good Ship Lollipop" and other entertainments, is not from the same America as the pirate-bearded performer of those classics from 1967 and '68, "Lumpy Gravy" and "We're Only in It for the Money." Not to mention "Alien

Orifice" and "Dicky's Such an Asshole!" No way on earth was Shirley, the sweetheart of the GOP, going to have anything to say about Frank, the Mother of Invention. The TV crew, however, did not consist of right-minded Americans. The crew was in the grip of a delusion. They seemed to think that Ambassador Black was going to say, "We in the United States are proud of our contributions to music and blah blah blah. . . . On the occasion of the arrival of such a distinguished . . ., allow me to express. . . ."

The telecast of Frank Zappa's sensational airport arrival in the midst of the revolution ran that night on Prague TV, along with a clip of what the ambassador from the United States did manage to say. As was endlessly recounted to me by every Czech I met in those revolutionary, frightening weeks, Mrs. Black looked horrified, even humiliated. Head turned away from camera. Face buried itself in hands. Televised mortification! Mr. Zappa's music loomed like a distant sun that had never once cast a beam on Mrs. Black's lonely shore. Face reemerged from hands. The ambassador from the United States volunteered that she did know something about Mr. Zappa's daughter, Moon Unit. Czechoslovakia was aghast. People had no way to account for the United States ambassador's boorish airport behavior, except to mark her down as a cultural ignoramus who lacked the aplomb to boast to all of Central Europe about one of America's finest sons, the brilliant Zappa, a world figure in the field of popular music.

There was a lot of that in the early months of the

Eastern Bloc Revolution. Visiting Americans had to rub their eyes. American artifacts were not exactly everywhere in sight, the way they are in much of the rest of the world. But the artifacts that did turn up seemed to radiate, and the Easterners stood around basking their faces in the glow. It was astonishing to see. Perhaps we should have been inured. In the past, though, we had always found reasons to discount or distrust the popularity that American culture seems to enjoy around the world. We always knew that large numbers of people flock to American movies or music, but we noticed that large numbers of other people express disdain for those same movies and music; and pro-Americanism and anti-Americanism seem to cancel each other out. We had suspected that foreign enthusiasm, where it exists, is mostly resignation in the face of superior force. In the last week of 1989, while the world's attention was focused on Havel's struggles in Prague and the violent mob assault on the Communist tyranny in Romania and other spectacular events of the Eastern Bloc Revolution, President Bush took the opportunity to launch a U.S. invasion of Panama in order to capture the Panamanian dictator and spirit him away to a Florida jail; and the American reporters who followed the troops into Panama City were struck by how much enthusiasm the Panamanians expressed for the United States (mixed with a few nationalist resentments). But was that so impressive? Paratroopers descend, and what would any sensible person do, except show appreciation for the culture of the conquerors?

For a long time we had observed American culture's vast popularity in France (among some people), along with an even vaster unpopularity (among others). But in France, too, American paratroopers had descended once upon a time, and afterward came who knows what manipulations by the American embassy. We suspected a relation between popularity and capital. Obviously Parisians took to nibbling fast-food hamburgers not because of the superiority of the cuisine, but because American (or, after a while, American-style) investments made hamburger nibbling cheap and efficient. American films penetrated movie houses not just because people enjoyed those movies, but because Hollywood's financing allowed expensively made movies to be distributed with superior efficiency—not to mention that, in negotiations over the decades, U.S. policy had done everything it could to inhibit the French and every other government from sensibly protecting their own national film industries. Not to mention the CIA! In short, we had always had our suspicions about America's cultural popularity. And more than suspicions. Whole libraries, the literary product of the left-wing passions of the 1960s and '70s and '80s, were devoted to the Marxist theme, "America, enemy of peoples." Which went too far, no doubt. Yet surely had a point.

But then, how to account for the passion for every American thing that seemed to burst into flower during the early euphoric months of the Eastern Bloc Revolution? Material explanations for America's popularity could hardly apply. United States soldiers have never conquered a Slavic country, except for a few miles at the end of the Second World War, when General George S. Patton briefly pushed into what would shortly become a corner of the Soviet Bloc. Penetration by American capital could not explain the phenomenon. American products had never dominated the Eastern Bloc consumer markets, if only because, under Communism, consumer markets did not exist. No giant agencies had conspired to saturate society with American tastes and sounds.

On the contrary, giant agencies, namely the Communist system, had conspired to keep the tastes and sounds as far away as possible. "America, enemy of peoples" was the universal theme of every official medium, and the only conduits of alternative information were a couple of static-filled stations on shortwave radio, plus occasional letters from long-gone emigrated cousins, the mini-Rockefellers, who told of factory exploitation in faraway dystopias like Cleveland or Brooklyn. Pro-Americanism, which in Panama might have gotten you a job, once the U.S. troops had staged their invasion, guaranteed arrest in the old Soviet zone. Yet instead of impeding the spread of American influence, the official obstacles and prohibitions in the Eastern Bloc seem only to have induced a warp or distortion to an American influence that remained powerful nonetheless, so that after long decades of Communist rule, people adhered to a notion of America that was even more appealing than the notion that loomed elsewhere in the world—a deluded idea,

loco in its extravagance, of America as a golden moun-
tain beyond the seas.

In Prague during the revolution's second month,
I went to a party in a clean, modest, cinder-block
housing project in a suburban neighborhood. Afterward a doctor and I left together, and as we strolled
to the curb, he gestured to the building where our
party had been held and said, in a tone of disgust,
"This is socialist housing." He meant, "Dear visitor
from America, this, a travesty of a dwelling, is what
the Commies, those bastards, have done to us." What
oceans of delusion about America lay in that single
sneer! Any American could have told him: You want
to see housing projects? I'll give you housing projects.
Ever hear of the Bronx, buddy?

Frank Zappa participated in a version of the same
conversation. From the Prague airport, he checked in
at the Hotel Intercontinental and set out to receive
his keenest fans in the wine cellar of the Union of
Socialist Youth, around the corner from the historic
balcony where General Secretary Klement Gottwald
had long ago announced Communism's original sei-
zure of power. Zappa's keenest fans looked like Goths
and Vandals in leathers and caveman haircuts. They
were hippies from 1968, preserved in amber. They
stood up to express their gratitude and reveal their
wounds. For love of pirated Zappa tapes, these people
had undergone every kind of official torment. "We're
going to beat Frank Zappa out of your heads," the
police used to say. And here at last was the real-
life Zappa standing before his persecuted fans in his

oversize black undertaker's suit, puffing Winstons in the smoky marijuana Communist wine cellar, now answering questions, now grabbing a mike and bursting into song. For them alone! Just for them! The hero himself was shaken by the scene. He felt constrained to remind the ebullient hairy mob that in America, too, in the land of loony fundamentalists and would-be censors, not everything was wonderful. "You've been living with secret police for a long time," he told them, looking grave under the spotlight in the hazy smoke. He searched for the *mot juste*. "It will take Americans a while to realize that we have them, too."

A silly remark! Truly thoughtless—given the different scale and function of secret police in the United States and the Eastern Bloc, where every fourth person seems to have been enrolled as some kind of informer. Nevertheless, every American who traveled to the East in those revolutionary days ended up in conversations like that. Honesty required it. The Easterners measured their lives by what they took to be an American standard, and simple decency on our own part obliged us to instruct them in the reality behind their dream. Dickensian horrors spilled from our lips. We warned them about the popular culture that seemed so alluring to their distant, adoring eyes. "Welcome," we told them in Philip Roth's deadpan phrase, "to the World of Total Entertainment."

We reminded those people that culture in America is anything but unitary, that left and right, North and South, different classes and tribes, all represent serious divisions. We tried to tell them that to admire Martin

Luther King and Ronald Reagan at the same time (as so many Easterners liked to do), or to applaud free trade unionism and also the free market (a veritable fad), wasn't really possible. We mentioned the gringo fondness for invading the little republics of Latin America. And talking on, we won a point or two, and our friends in the East, hanging on to our every word, promised to remember henceforth that all was not one and well in the distant World of Total Entertainment. They knew that capitalism can run amok and that getting home at night in the United States is sometimes no small experience.

We, the visitors, nodded in satisfaction. We felt welcomed into the fraternity of all who suffer. And then, horrified, we watched, one breath later, as the backsliding began, and the old naive habits revived, and the Easterners clustered around any available American artifact to bask in the brilliance one more time. It was as if they had concluded from listening to us that maybe in the present things are less than ideal in the United States—but the future will be different. Material prosperity in the here-and-now was, after all, only part of their American fascination. All right, possibly it's true about housing projects in a place called Bronx. A shame! But better housing was never the main idea. And when the more-than-materiality of their concept sank in on us, when we at last understood that these people had credited to us a liberating mission irrespective of mere facts, that we were expected to lend them a hand because our inner nature was thought to be intrinsically altruistic, our astonishment deepened two, three times over. For these Easterners had not only conceived an extravagant affection for American life in spite of every totalitarian obstacle. All by themselves, they had arrived at a venerable idea from out of the remotest American past, a nearly forgotten relic of New World folk culture. It was the idea of a world revolution for liberal democracy conceived in its simplest, most primitive form, namely, the notion that America and the Americans, from their home across the seas, were not going to enslave the world, after all. No, they were going to liberate it. America, friend of peoples.

A classic discussion of that idea, too little known by modern readers, was written in the 1880s by Henry Adams. It is Chapter VI, "American Ideals," of his *History of the United States of America During the First Administration of Thomas Jefferson, 1801–1805*. Adams described America in the year 1800. The concept of a world democratic revolution spreading outward from the United States was already recognizable. It was partly an idea that America was going to triumph through wealth. The Americans of 1800, as he pictured them, bragged obsessively about the national wealth, even if their own share of it was laughably small. To every inquiring traveler from Europe, they would say, "See these solid mountains of salt and iron, of lead, copper, silver, and gold! See these magnificent cities scattered broadcast to the Pacific!" And partly their idea was a commitment to libertarian activism. "European travelers who passed through America noticed that everywhere, in the White House at Washington and in log-cabins beyond the Alleghenies, except for a few Federalists, every American, from Jefferson and Hamilton down to the poorest squatter, seemed to nourish an idea that he was doing what he could to overthrow the tyranny which the past had fastened on the human mind." Such was the national tone. "Every American democrat believed himself to be working for the overthrow of tyranny, aristocracy, hereditary privilege, and priesthood, wherever they existed."

Of course even then, in the remote Jeffersonian past, the idea of the United States liberating the world was, in the perspective of sophisticated people, a bit much. The inquiring travelers from Europe were highly educated, not at all eager to be bamboozled. They took one look at the America that actually existed and replied, "Gold! cities! cornfields! . . . Nothing of the sort!" They saw a dismal scene. It was, in Adams's description, "nothing but tremendous wastes, where sickly men and women are dying of home-sickness or are scalped by savages! mountain-ranges a thousand miles long, with no means of getting to them, and nothing in them when you get there! swamps and forests choked with their own rotten ruins! nor hope of better for a thousand years!" The Europeans noticed southern slavery. And they said, "Your story is a fraud, and you are a liar and a swindler!" The notion of America overthrowing tyranny everywhere it existed was too preposterous for words. "Nothing was easier than to laugh at the ludicrous expressions of this sim-

ple-minded conviction, or to cry out against its coarseness, or grow angry with its prejudices."

So the skeptical visitors returned to Europe, wrote
their bemused and irritated reports, and revealed the
American experiment as a vaporous deception. But
was that the only view of the American phenomenon?
Adams was clever. He noticed that every one of the
European writers on American themes circa 1800 came
from the upper classes, and that humbler people from
lower classes saw things very differently. The humbler
people—"the poorest peasant in Europe"—believed
those skeptical exposés for not one moment. The poorest peasant gazed westward toward America and saw
"the gold and the jewels, the summer cornfields and
the glowing continent." He saw "the outline of a
mountain-summit across the ocean, rising high above
the mist and mud of American democracy." What
the educated observers from the European elite never
could discern—an American ideal, a liberation, a
dream of opportunity and freedom for even the poorest
and most persecuted person—was, to the peasantry
of Europe, unmistakably visible.

In those first months of the Eastern Bloc Revolution, our American eyes widened because the people
who flocked to an airport to greet a visiting rock star,
the dedicated Zappa freaks, the wacked-out longhairs
in their leather pants—these people were, almost two
centuries later, the peasants of Europe, and they did
seem to regard the arrival of a character like Frank
Zappa as a liberator's triumphal entrance into their
humble midst. They seemed to believe that every

American, from the president and the hippie celebrities down to the poorest squatter, nourished an idea of doing what he could to overthrow the tyranny which the past had fastened on the human mind. The material realities of poverty or hypocrisy in distant America, the mist and mud of American democracy, everything that had been reported by knowledgeable observers with a claim to insight into American life—all that was, for them, no big deal. They listened. They nodded. Then they turned back to gaze gaga-eyed once more at our rock princes and our third-rate politicians and our silly ambassadors and, by God, they saw the gold and the jewels.

II

A few days after Zappa's conquest of Czechoslovakia, I joined a British reporter and his translator and departed Prague for zones where the hipsters were less hip but the mysteries of American influence no less profound. We drove southwest into the Šumava region of western Bohemia, past the city of Pilsen, industrial homeland of Pilsener beer, to a quaint ancient settlement called Sušice (pronounced Sue-SHITS-a). Twelve thousand people lived in that town, according to its mayor, or else twenty thousand, according to the glossy pamphlet that he passed out. It was the safety-match capital of the world. Kitchen drawers all over the world contain wooden matchboxes that were manufactured by the SOLO woodworking enterprise in industrious Sušice.

As everywhere in Europe's eastern zones, the history of that provincial spot was a multigenerational saga of ethnic grisliness. Bohemia was originally Czech, but in the late Middle Ages, Germans colonized the western region around Sušice and became the dominant class. The two groups, Czechs and Germans, battled back and forth ever after, until in 1938, with all of Bohemia firmly in the hands of a Czechoslovak government, Germany's leaders figured that five or six hundred years of dispute were enough and sent the Wehrmacht marching across the border. Germany annexed a grand swath of Bohemian territory as the German Sudetenland, to the cheers and applause of the local Germans, who tended to be ardent Nazis. An elderly Czech resident of Sušice, Kamil Svelch, showed us photos of a Nazi rally that was held at the Hotel Korun in the town square, opposite from the Hotel Fialka, where the SS troops lodged. In one photo, the swastika flag droops in the dismal industrial air. A third ethnic component in those long-ago times, after the Czechs and the Germans, were the Jews, who formed as much as a third or more of the population, according to what I heard, and ran shops and a boot factory.

Most of those people were deported and never returned. Sušice must have looked like the heart-breaking Slovak movie *Shop on Main Street*, with its scenes of Jewish shopkeepers herded into the town square on their way to the railroad. The synagogue was pulled down and the tumbledown Jewish cemetery with its corroded stone Hebrew letters fell into disrepair (though in the 1980s, someone began to take care of it again). The town also had a fourth group, the Gypsies, whose experience must likewise have been something to weep over. A nasty place, Sušice. The history of that town was such that, in Havel's play *Temptation*, the Faust character turns to the Devil and says, apropos of the sulfuric odor but conceivably with Sušice's SOLO woodworking enterprise in mind, "I'd guess you work in a safety-match factory."

The town lay at the base of a valley and burned cheap brown coal. From a distance, it looked like one of its own matches, silvery smoke wafting up from deep within an ashtray. The outer districts were modern, barracks-like, depressing. Yet Sušice's downtown, to call it that, remained a picture of ancient Bohemian charm. Two- and three-story buildings with steep tile roofs the color of match heads surrounded a cobbled square. Gingerbread dormer windows arched like eyebrows overhead, as if deploring the goings-on down below. The air was filthy, but the streets were empty and clean. And by an odd circumstance of war, on May 6, 1945, after seven years of Nazi rallies and firing squads, across those narrow cobbled streets had rolled some expensive-looking cars, according to what people in town still remembered, bearing American soldiers. It was the Fourth Armored Division of the United States Third Army (George S. Patton, commander), come to liberate the safety-match capital of the world. The expensive-looking cars halted. GIs clambered out. Officers of America's 738th Field Artillery Battalion moved into the same Hotel Fialka where the SS used to stay; the enlisted men were billeted elsewhere; and the story of American influence in Europe's faraway eastern regions took an unexpected, little-known twist.

The soldiers set up a hospital, passed out army tins, published a newspaper aggressively called *Attack*, and in these ways managed to spread a shiny surface of American good cheer. One of the surviving photographs shows an exuberant Gene Kelly of a GI wearing an army cap at a crazy tilt and a Yankee grin at an opposite tilt, sitting on a tank with the air of a man who has nary a worry in the world. A battalion band put on dances, which marked a big change from the old Nazi custom of extinguishing that dangerous fuse, popular music from the United States. And what with the expensive cars, the tins, the band, the dances, the good cheer, and the Gene Kellys, the 738th Field Artillery Battalion set off, judging by people's reactions to my questions forty-five years later, a sexual tizzy that had still not entirely subsided. The desk clerk at the Hotel Fialka, when she reflected on those exciting months of 1945, broke into high-pitched giggles; Svelch, into low-pitched giggles; a younger man recalling what had been told to him by his elders, into giggles at a medium pitch. The U.S. Army—tee-hee!

Sušice girls dressed up in peasant costumes to celebrate the American liberation, and the dashing GIs responded with so much enthusiasm as to marry five of them, according to one account, or eight, according to another account; and given the pregnancies in town, ought to have married, according to everyone, a larger number still. As an indication of the American army's standing among Sušice's population, the street that led past the Hotel Fialka was officially renamed the Street of the American Soldiers (less formally, American Street). The town erected a plaque in the square catty-corner from the Fialka saying, in Czech and in English,

> IN MEMORY OF THE LIBERATION OF THEIR
> TOWN BY THE 4TH
> ARMORED DIVISION OF THE 3RD AMERICAN
> ARMY ON MAY 6TH 1945
> —THE TOWN OF SUŠICE

with the words cast in raised bronze to maintain the joyful memory forever.

That was nice, and doubly so to render the words in English. But to anyone who recalls the debates of cold-war America, the inscription on that plaque also raises a delicate question. America's duty, in Adams's phrase, to promote "the overthrow of tyranny, aristocracy, hereditary privilege, and priesthood" around the world—does that exist? If it does, America's duty in regard to Hitler was clear. But what about Stalin? Did duty require America to overthrow that man as well? In May 1945 Europe's entire eastern region was about to fall into the hands of tyranny, privilege, and priesthood in a Communist version (with "priesthood" connoting the role of party ideologists in a Communist regime). Even as the American officers settled into the Hotel Fialka horse-drawn wagons were dragging the huge Red Army forward from the east. Did the United

States have a duty to keep that Red advance to a minimum—for instance, by sending the American troops onward to Prague and beyond, in order to preserve the newly liberated zones for a democratic future?

The decision at the time, back in 1945, was to avoid any kind of hostile encounter with the Soviet Union. President Roosevelt met with Stalin at Yalta in February, and by way of guaranteeing Soviet cooperation against Hitler and perhaps even with the hope of drawing the Soviets into the war against Japan, he conceded the whole of Europe east of the Elbe to the Soviet sphere of influence—though Stalin did agree to hold free elections, once his army was in place. It was an unavoidable arrangement, given that Germany and Japan were enemies enough and Stalin was a mighty ally. Yet even at the time, in the first months of 1945, the alternative policy had no lack of clamorous supporters. Among the British leaders, General (Sir) Bernard Montgomery was all for pushing the Allied armies into Berlin, even though Berlin was supposed to lie within the Soviet sphere. Churchill was similarly disposed—though he had signed the Yalta accords, together with Roosevelt.

Patton himself was furious about any order to hold back. He muttered under his breath about going all the way to Moscow, a mad idea, and besieged General Eisenhower with requests to press onward at least to Prague, which was, from a military standpoint, not mad in the slightest. German forces were rushing to surrender to the Americans in order to spare themselves the consequences of surrendering to the Soviets. On the same day that American troops took over Sušice and Pilsen (or else the day before, in an alternative account), the anti-Nazi Resistance staged an uprising in Prague and could have used American support. The Red Army was three days to the east, and the American units at Pilsen, Sušice, and elsewhere were only a few hours to the west. One or two American jeeps are said to have driven into Prague, just to have a look. A general advance was entirely possible.

Or so it has been argued. Among cold-war conservatives in America the impression lingered ever after that grand opportunities were thrown away. And not just among the Americans. Yet another surprise of the Eastern Bloc Revolution—a surprise to some of us left-wing naïfs, anyway—was to discover how many people in the East agreed with that estimation. The United States should never have signed the Yalta accords; the U.S. armies should have pressed onward to the East in 1945; America has a mission in the world that should have made it grab Stalin by the throat. Those were the attitudes. By failing to push harder and by consigning the entire region to Stalin's control, the United States—this is what people kept saying— betrayed the East, at any rate "abandoned" it, in Adam Michnik's word, together with all hope for democracy and freedom for several decades.

How should we look at America's cold-war influence in the East, then? As a tragic lost opportunity? Conceivably—though during the decades of debate about lost opportunities no one ever seemed to ask what the Eastern Bloc prospects for democratic development might have been, back at the cold war's point of origin. In 1945 towns like Sušice had their little complexities. Among these was the Communist Party. A fly in the ointment! The party dated from 1921 in that town. It boasted of antecedents that reached back into the workers' movement of the late nineteenth century. The thing had roots. Naturally the war against the Nazis was hard on the Communists. The Sušice party chief, František Hájek, died in a German concentration camp in 1944, according to the town literature. But his organization survived. When the town was at last occupied by the 738th Field Artillery and the Nazi shadow was lifted and the Americans established a political environment that was free and open, what sprang up in the town square of Sušice were political movements in which Marxism-Leninism held pride of place.

Probably the enthusiasm for Communism was less ardent in little towns like Sušice than in the big capitals like Prague. The strongest of Sušice's parties proved to be the Social Democrats. But in the excitement of the war and the ideological confusions of the 1940s in the East, Czechoslovak Social Democracy somehow lost its anti-Communist principles in favor of what Havel calls a "strange collusion of democrats and Communists," in which the non-democrats had the whip hand. The whole environment in Czechoslovakia leaned toward totalitarian solutions. Even before the Americans decamped for Western Europe and left the country to the mercy of the Soviets, the Czechoslovaks busied themselves with solving the ethnic tension by packing up the Sudetenland's entire German population, more than three million people, and deporting them *en masse*, without any effort to establish who had been a Nazi criminal and who had not. The old totalitarian custom of judging people by group characteristics, of resolving political problems by means of population transfers, the policy of treating entire peoples as if they had no individual and inalienable rights—all of that, which for years had been the Nazi rule, survived the Nazi defeat in the less horrifying and indeed understandable but still tyrannical form of German deportation.

So the Sudeten Germans exited from Sušice for a new life in West Germany, and into their homes came Slovaks who themselves had been deported from somewhere else. The 738th Field Artillery Battalion and all the American soldiers in Czechoslovakia retired westward at the end of a few months, as per America's agreements with the Soviet Union. And soon enough, in 1946, even without the Americans on hand to bestow the blessings of democracy, Czechoslovakia did hold an election, exactly as was specified by the Yalta accords. Was it free? Since the Communists were already a powerful party, and never did subscribe to the principles of democratic freedom and were, on the contrary, accustomed to using compulsion as a political method, voting conditions were, of course, not those of a genuinely democratic country. Still, no one doubts that the Communists enjoyed authentic support. In Sušice, the people voted (or were reported to have voted) a Communist plurality—with Social Democracy a strong second. Given the "strange collusion," the place voted, in effect, for Communism. Those charming townsfolk lining up for their delicious tins from America and dancing to the infectious rhythms at the American dances, the costumed girls going out with the dapper GIs, the Sušice locals posing for the camera with that exotic species, the dark-skinned African-Americans who formed part of Patton's liberating army—those enthusiastic Bohemian admirers of the 738th turned out to be, at least some of them, due to confusion or coercion or principle, pro-Soviet.

What would have happened if Patton's army, unleashed, had done its militant duty and had subjected the entire Bohemian region, Prague included, to a lasting American occupation? Would Communist loyalties and enthusiasms have withered away, and would towns like Sušice have voted for someone other than the party of Lenin and its deluded Social Democratic allies? It's hard to see how or why that would have occurred. What if a Communist-dominated government in Czechoslovakia had demanded a U.S. withdrawal? Would the Americans have found themselves in the classic quandary of all modern American history, fighting in the name of liberal democracy against an aroused populace that had chosen something else?

The debate that lasted more than half a century over Yalta and the American reluctance to press ever eastward ought to remind us of one other element in the grand folkloric theory about America and its libertarian mission. The notion that America has a democratic vocation outside its own borders, that a global purpose hovers over the national history, that American freedom is for the world, not just for the Americans—this notion emits an intoxicating fume. You start to contemplate the American vocation; grandeur swirls about your head; and you find yourself banging a glass on the bar and calling in the cavalry, perfectly illustrating Adams's complaint about "prejudices" and "coarseness" among Americans and the "ludicrous expressions of this simple-minded conviction." The line between liberating the world and enslaving the world is amazingly thin. Likewise the line between liberating the world and throwing yourself off a cliff. Adams himself understood the dilemma. In any case, he credited such an understanding to Jefferson and the Americans of 1800. The Jeffersonians, who subscribed to every lavish belief about America's duty to liberate the world and especially Europe, were skeptical, he wrote, about doing any of that by force of arms. Economic competition from the United States, not military confrontation, was their idea. And if the Europeans failed to respond to competition and preferred to knot a rope of despotism around their necks, so much the worse for Europe. "When the day of competition should arrive, Europe might choose between American and Chinese institutions, but there would be no middle path; she might become a federated democracy, or a wreck." It was their choice. By

"Chinese" institutions, Adams meant, of course, a system of total state domination.

The American withdrawal from western Bohemia took place in September 1945. Three years later, when General Secretary Gottwald climbed out on the balcony in Prague and announced the "Proletarian Revolution," the "Chinese" alternative was at hand. Every aspect of Czechoslovak life fell under the scheme of universal nationalization by the vanguard party. Even history was "nationalized," chiefly for the purpose of showing that people owed a debt of gratitude to the heroic Soviet Union for liberating them from the Nazi yoke—and did not owe anything to Stalin's cold-war opponent, the United States. The kind of tedious labor that George Orwell's Winston Smith performed at the Ministry of Truth in *1984*, rewriting the past to make it concur with shifting events of the present, began with a vengeance in proletarian Czechoslovakia.

Communism's revision of history went on even in the little sulfurous town that had been inconveniently liberated by the Fourth Armored Division of the United States Third Army. In the years after the Communist takeover, teachers in the Sušice schools, strictly under orders from above, instructed their students that Sušice was liberated not by Americans at all but by the Red Army—wearing American uniforms! American Street lost its name. One day the authorities sent workmen into the square to the building cattycorner from the Hotel Fialka, and the plaque in two languages that commemorated the liberation of Sušice by the United States Third Army was unscrewed from the wall and quietly stored away. America's mark on the safety-match capital of the world, memorialized in raised bronze for all eternity—gone!

III

How did the Eastern Bloc countries—some of them—eventually arrive at the non-"Chinese" alternative, given that hard-line American fantasies, Patton style, never did go into operation, and the Western armies failed to capture Berlin and Prague, and democracy was not imposed by the sword? It's easy enough to identify the stages of development. In a fit of prophetic intuition back in 1948, Orwell described them in *1984*.

Orwell's hero, poor old Winston from the Ministry of Truth, sick and tired of his job rewriting history, rebels against Big Brother by committing himself to two attractive and indomitable persons. One of these is Orwell's Trotsky character, Emmanuel Goldstein, the radical with wire glasses and a goatee. Goldstein has written a subversive tract against Big Brother called *The Theory and Practice of Oligarchical Collectivism*. He stands for authentic socialism—against its totalitarian distortion. He says that Big Brother's ruling party "rejects and vilifies every principle for which the Socialist movement originally stood, and it chooses to do this in the name of Socialism." The principle he articulates is, in effect, left-wing archaicism. He wants to return to the ancient socialist virtues of the nineteenth century, which Big Brother has so gruesomely betrayed. Goldstein's revolutionary conspiracy, "the

Brotherhood," aims at "the gradual spread of enlight-
enment—ultimately a proletarian rebellion." Winston
becomes an ardent Goldsteinite. At the same time, he
takes up with a girlfriend, Julia, who is likewise no
friend of Big Brother, without being much of a polit-
ico, either. Winston invites Julia to Mr. Charrington's
secret upstairs room and reads to her from Goldstein's
Oligarchical Collectivism. But Julia can barely bring
herself to listen. Goldstein's ideas appeal to her not
at all. Her interests are strictly personal. She lives
for sex—that grand contraband in the world of Big
Brother. An honest fidelity to her own desires is her
passion.

It's an odd thing to notice, but these two stages
of Winston's progress through *1984*—the Goldstein
stage of left-wing purity, the Julia stage of personal
integrity and private life—tell the history of nearly
the entire radical left in modern times. In the 1940s,
when he was at work on the book, Orwell hung out
with the intellectuals of the libertarian left, which in
Britain and America was going through exactly that
two-stage development—in London among some of
the people around the anarchist journal *Freedom* and
other publications, in New York among the people
around Dwight Macdonald's *Politics*, in San Francisco
among the members of Kenneth Rexroth's anarchist
literary group, the Libertarian Circle. The people in
those groups were left-wingers who had started out
with the idea of a proletarian revolution in a very
pure, anarchist fashion, and had ended up promoting
an idea of personal liberation, sometimes in a sexual

version, sometimes in a free-verse version, sometimes in ways too vague to define. Twenty years later the same two-step evolution—from a dream of orthodox social revolution to a movement for personal liberation—took place on a far huger scale in the New Left student movements in Western Europe and the United States and to some degree elsewhere. The progression went from socialist revolution to feminism and gay liberation and the several other components of post–New Left radicalism: left-wing archaicism to personal liberation, Goldstein to Julia.

But the biggest example of the two-stage evolution was the one that took place among the opposition movements in the Eastern Bloc. Goldstein-style movements arose in the Soviet Union (in the 1920s, led by Trotsky) and in the European satellite countries (in the 1950s, led by disgruntled Communists) and drew their ideas from the Communist tradition itself, or from neighboring bookshelves. The official Communists called the Goldstein-style dissenters "revisionists" (when they didn't call them "fascists"). But the revisionists were mostly honest Leninists, unblinded by the totalitarian razzle-dazzle, who understood that Communist despotism had turned the socialist idea upside down. They championed the Young Marx against the Old Marx; Hegel against Engels; Marx against Lenin; Lenin against Stalin; left-wing humanism against scientific leftism; the artists and intellectuals against the bureaucrats and censors; the avant-garde against the party-mandated arts. They weren't less faithful to the Marxist idea, they were more.

Were they unrealistic? The great hope was to convert to their cause the good-souled leaders of the official Communist Party, which in retrospect seems hard to imagine, when you think about the official Communists. Yet from time to time the official Communists did convert and revisionism came to power. In Poland and Hungary the revisionists got hold of sections of the Communist Party in 1956, when Khrushchev's Moscow reforms briefly loosened the Soviet tether on the satellite parties. The revisionist idea tended to be fairly moderate: not to abolish Communism or one-party rule (at least not at first), but to give decision-making more of a grass-roots democratic character, to allow enterprise managers more freedom to maneuver, to permit a diversity of views and freedom for the intellectuals. There was a modest little notion of establishing national independence from the Soviet Union. Unfortunately, the Soviets took a dim view of modest little notions, and down came the Stalinist heel, violently in the case of Hungary.

No one could fail to notice, however, that revisionism was a living possibility for the Communist world. In Czechoslovakia, a small revisionist tendency within the Communist Party clung to life in the years after 1956 and withstood every pressure from the orthodox Communists, until finally, in the first weeks of 1968, Alexander Dubček and his comrades took hold of the state, and revisionism was again in power. Ever so carefully Dubček began to enact the revisionist reforms, and the excitement grew, and the "Prague Spring" and its idea of "socialism with a human face" began to look genuinely promising. Prague under the revisionists became a far more revolutionary place than Paris or the precincts of student rebellion in the United States during those same insurrectionary months—given that Dubček and his comrades were running a government and not merely rioting in the streets. Then the Soviets took another dim view, and in August the armies of the Warsaw Pact rolled into Czechoslovakia, and the experiment was at an end.

Still, revisionism's influence was immense. The revisionists pulled the serious believers in socialist ideals out of the official Communist ranks, they exposed official Communism as a sham justification for power, they revealed the Soviet Union as an occupying power instead of the liberator that it claimed to be. All of which proved devastating to the official Communists. Revisionism was the leak that couldn't be plugged. In that one respect the revisionists did have their triumph over official Communism, though the victory was a little sad, from their own point of view. For the notion of being more Communist than the Communists, more idealistic than the party that claimed to be idealistic, the idea of opposing left-wing dictatorships with a truer, more socialist left and thereby returning to the nineteenth-century ideals of Karl Marx—that idea, the Goldstein aspiration, slowly evaporated into something ever less plausible, pleasant but gassy, like a plan for revolutionizing the world by building communes in the countryside. So the Goldstein stage came to an end, and beginning in the 1970s a different sort of opposition movement began to prosper in the Eastern Bloc, not a movement for socialist values but a movement for personal integrity: a Julia stage.

The person who stood at the center of that development in Czechoslovakia was Václav Havel, an unusual man. Other intellectuals in Czechoslovakia went through a few years of Communist commitment in their youth, sometimes with a lot of fervor, the way that Milan Kundera has described from his own experience. Not Havel. He grew up in a wealthy bourgeois home in Prague that gave him what he calls "a heightened sensitivity and aversion to various manifestations of social inequality." He considered himself a socialist, only he was one of the few who insisted on drawing the proper line between socialism and Communism. Socialism for him, as he has written in his *Summer Meditations*, was "a temperament, a nonconformist state of the spirit, an anti-establishment orientation, an aversion to philistines, and an interest in the wretched and humiliated." It was an ethical commitment to greater social justice and equality. It meant (in his phrase) "man liberated from the clutches of an alienating social machinery." He pictured freedom of opportunity and workers' self-management as proper socialist achievements. But rigid economic planning and ownership by the state of the entire economy, not to mention police-state tyranny and dictatorship by the vanguard party—no, that was never his concept.

So he had the wrong family background and the wrong ideas, and he found himself traveling a route that never once crossed into Communist terrain. Other young intellectuals moved straight from the university into the ranks of the state-sanctioned Writers' Union, which was crucial for getting published. Havel went to work in a lab. He performed his military service without being able to get good jobs there, either. He built boat bridges, toiled as a machinist. After the army, he applied to the Drama School at the university—and couldn't get admitted, not at first, anyway. Communism is not meritocracy. Somehow he did establish himself as a writer, in spite of every obstacle, and as early as age twenty attended a Writers' Congress. But that was in 1956, a year of Eastern Bloc rebellion. The revisionists had come to power in Hungary, and a revolution broke out, which caused a lot of excitement at the exact moment when the Writers' Congress met, and so Havel's "entry into public literary life," as he says, began with "a whiff of rebellion."

The journal that he affiliated with in the 1960s, in the years when he kept pursuing his unsanctioned but unstoppable drama career at Prague's Theater on the Balustrade and other "little theaters," was *Tvár* (*Face*), which was utterly of the opposition, more libertarian than the revisionists (or, as the revisionists were called in Czechoslovakia, the "antidogmatic" Communists). One day in 1968, when the revisionists had at last come to power in Czechoslovakia, Havel met President Dubček at a reception and tried to talk him into abolishing one-party rule altogether and legalizing the old hapless party of the democratic left, the Social Democrats—which was something that Dubček and the reformers never got around to doing. Revisionism had its limits. For that matter, Havel wished that *Tvár*, too, would go a little further, give up its own dogmatisms, stop enforcing its own political line. But where is the iconoclastic magazine that has never had a few icons and purge trials of its own? Anyway, in came the Warsaw Pact armies, the moment of freedom was over, and Havel finally found the opportunity, now that political activity was out of the question, to work up his own ideas.

His thoughts were about philosophy and personal morality. He pictured something that he called the moral horizon, which might mean other people aside from oneself, or might mean something grander— the Absolute, spelled with a capital A, German style. With that horizon fixed in his glance, he wanted to define his own life by a responsibility either toward others or toward the Absolute. In his thinking, the individual person acts in accord with the moral horizon—or betrays himself. Perhaps these ideas, as some people have said, did bring Havel into the sphere of religion—though he called himself agnostic and spoke about "Being" instead of God. Heinrich Böll, remarking on Havel's prison letters (where he expounds these ideas), commented that "Christ is speaking in these letters." My own impression is that Havel became merely one more slightly befuddled left-wing reader of Martin Heidegger. Those philosophical studies of his turned him into a poorer but more level-headed Eastern cousin, so to speak, of Herbert Marcuse and the Western unorthodox Marxists of the

1950s and '60s, who were likewise the left-wing readers of Heidegger. Havel's emphasis on how people betray their best nature and end up "alienated" from themselves was more or less the same emphasis that you see in the Western unorthodox Marxists. And like those other writers, Havel fixed the final blame on the social system, not on the individual and certainly not on Original Sin.

Naturally the unorthodox Marxists of the West had monopoly capitalism in mind when they spoke about the social system; Havel had in mind Communism. The Westerners cited exploitation and cultural manipulation; Havel, Communist coercion. The Westerners were dreaming of some kind of Marxist alternative; that was not Havel's impulse. Yet his theme was still, like theirs, to show how people get caught in a vast social trap whose ultimate effect is to disfigure the human personality. In one of his essays he wrote: "For fear of losing his job, the schoolteacher teaches things he does not believe; fearing for his future, the pupil repeats them after him; for fear of not being allowed to continue his studies, the young man joins the Youth League and participates in whatever of its activities are necessary; fear that under the monstrous system of political credits, his son or daughter will not acquire the necessary total of points for enrollment at a school leads the father to take on all manner of responsibilities and 'voluntarily' to do everything required." So the schoolteacher, the pupil, the young man, the father, and everybody else in a Communist society end up living a false existence. They turn their backs on their own moral horizons. And since these powerless people can no longer define themselves through moral behavior toward the world, they look inward for meaning, either in intimate relations or in new possessions. They cannot follow their own ideas of right and wrong, but they can buy a refrigerator. Material goods become their gods. They shrink into half-humans. In a word, they are alienated.

Exactly how people could ever climb out of such an ugly hole was never easy to see in the writings of any of the Heideggerian radicals, East or West. Marcuse, when he considered the depths of capitalist alienation, could only imagine one possibility, which was for privileged young people to follow their own deep Freudian instincts instead of the social conventions—and in that way create zones free of psychological repression. A few zones like that might stimulate the larger population to rebel against the general repression. That was Marcuse's hope. It was a theory of countercultural revolution. Havel's idea could hardly be the same, given the differences between prosperous Western capitalism and dusty polluted Communism; yet something in his thinking was not entirely different. Communist society, as he understood, was held together by the party ideology. No one entirely believed the ideology anymore, not really. But there was a lot of intimidation, which produced a me-first atmosphere, which led everyone to go along, which made the ideology functional in spite of everything. So he asked himself: What if a handful of people opted out of the me-first quest for small-scale advantage?

What if, instead, the handful of people followed their own instincts—the instinct for truthfulness, above all—regardless of consequences? What if these people, by "living in truth," managed to establish "parallel structures" free of the general alienation, "where a different life can be lived"? Mightn't the handful of dissidents succeed in revealing the Communist ideology as an empty shell, and mightn't the zones of freedom inspire other people to go do likewise? Mightn't a revolution break out after all—though Havel emphasized the "hopelessness of trying to make long-range predictions"?

He was obliged to work out these ideas under fairly dismal circumstances. Even to obtain the basic readings for a modern philosophical education was a giant labor, given that state repression kept relocating his own personal zone of freedom to the prisons of Bohemia. During his forties and early fifties he spent more than five years behind bars. Yet his theory had the great virtue of pointing to one aspect of society under Communism that was not at all invisible. The rebellious youth scenes that Marcuse admired so extravagantly were more than a Western phenomenon. Havel himself, back in 1956, had figured in one of those scenes, if only as a face among the audience. The crucial details appear in his memoir, *Disturbing the Peace*. The first steps in the development of the youth movement were taken in the "little theaters" of Prague. These places had once been lively centers but mostly disappeared in 1948, when the Communists staged their coup. In 1956, though, at the first sign of reform,

the theaters revived. The works of absurdist play-
wrights, eventually including Havel himself, went on-
stage. And along with those plays came performances
by the very first rock and roll band to become well
known in Czechoslovakia, the Akord Klub.

The band played in the Reduta theater near Wenceslas Square. Havel recalls, "The room would only
hold 60 people, but all of Prague, if I can put it that
way, was jammed in. It was a sensation. I was lucky
enough to discover it early on, and I was there in the
crowds that jammed the room. I could sense at once
that something important was going on here. I didn't
understand music very well, but it didn't take much
expertise to understand that what they were playing
and singing here was fundamentally different from
'Kristynka' or 'Prague Is a Golden Ship,' both official
hits of the time." There was "an entirely different
kind of fantasy, a different sense of humor, a different
feeling for life, different ideas, different language."
Something inspiring. "The atmosphere in Reduta was
marvelous, and what was born in those sessions was
that very special, conspiratorial sense of togetherness
that to me is what makes theater. That was where it
all began."

I wonder what that first well-known rock band in
Czechoslovakia sounded like. Anything like American
rock? The relation between rock in its American and
European versions is a murky business. American rock
is mostly a dance music, and European rock, some of
it, a cabaret music. The European musicians show
(from my point of view) too much interest in poetry

and theater, not enough in African-derived rhythmic sophistication. Too much profundity, not enough groove. Melancholy cynicism, the European disease, oozes from the amplifiers. Was the Akord Klub like that? Havel praises the band's lyrics, which remind him of art songs by Czech poets and writers from between the wars. A bad sign, from an American rock point of view. On the other hand, the historian of Eastern Bloc rock and roll, Timothy Ryback, in his book *Rock Around the Bloc*, reports that Akord's bass player, Jiří Suchy, borrowed songs from Elvis Presley, Fats Domino, and Bill Haley. So the Akord Klub may have been a bit of a combination, art-song pretentious and hard-kicking at once—which sounds like Frank Zappa, come to think of it.

The atmosphere that exudes from Havel's description of those long-ago concerts seems, in any case, entirely familiar. The atmosphere at the Reduta was not especially intellectual, he tells us. Ideology had no place there. The musicians and their fans were not debating the virtues of revisionist Communism versus official Communism. "The performances"—at another theater, the Semafor, which became a lively center in 1959—"were not about anything. They were just a series of songs, one after another, and the songs themselves were about nothing in particular, but it was the delight in performance, the rhythm, the pure fun, that seemed to make all those learned ideological debates seem fundamentally inappropriate, without much in common with real life. It was a manifestation of uncensored life, life that spits on all ideology and all that lofty world of babble; a life that intrinsically resisted all forms of violence, all interpretations, all directives. Suddenly, against the world of appearance and interpretation, here stood truth—the truth of young people who couldn't care less about any of that, who wanted only to live in their own way, to dance the way they wanted to dance, simply to be in harmony with their own nature."

In short, a rock scene. Or putting it another way, the scene was a gathering of characters like Orwell's Julia, who didn't exactly spit on Goldstein's learned ideological *Oligarchical Collectivism* but didn't pay attention to it either. The little theaters were a coterie affair for the avant-garde, not for the masses. The Semafor had only 350 seats. Nonetheless, according to Ryback's history, in the theater's first five years as a countercultural center, nearly a million people, equal to the entire population of Prague, squeezed into those 350 seats. A nice-sized coterie! Something about the combination of American-inspired cultural ideas and the Central European avant-garde had hit the right note, and the population responded. By the time that Allen Ginsberg made his famous trip to Czechoslovakia in 1965 (the same year that Havel established himself at *Tvár* magazine), the popular response was sufficient to present the Czechoslovak authorities with the kind of problem that was already bothering their non-Communist counterparts in America. Ginsberg arrived in Prague (direct from Havana, having been honorably deported by Communist Cuba for denouncing the persecution of homosexuals) and attended the pagan rituals of a student May Day festival. A half-dozen rock bands—out of an estimated thousand such bands in Czechoslovakia at the time, so vast was the rock explosion—performed, along with one Dixieland band on a truck. The visiting poet kept scribbling lines like "the Communists have nothing to offer but fat cheeks and eyeglasses and lying policemen" (along with equal jabs at the capitalists, in "Krail Majales" and other poems). And this of all personalities, the bearded essence of hip American rebellion, got himself crowned "King of May" by a hundred thousand drunken revelers in the Park of Culture and Rest. Which was an omen, or ought to have been, to anyone who paused to consider Communism's future.

Havel himself, by 1968, figured in Czechoslovakia's American connection. In May and June, with Dubček still in power and revisionism's Prague Spring in full bloom, Havel spent six weeks in New York to participate in Joseph Papp's New York Shakespeare Festival and to put on his own play *The Memorandum* and win his Obie prize from the *Village Voice*. Havel hung around the freak centers in the East Village (where, at the Fillmore East, Zappa and the Mothers of Invention were performing, by the way). Uptown at Columbia University, the mass rallies and building occupations and the intermittent fighting with the police were still going on. Havel came to see the strike and participated a bit and gave a talk to a group of students. And having soaked up that springtime 1968 New York radicalism, he went home to Czechoslovakia with a treasured album by the Velvet Underground and a collection of psychedelic posters in his luggage and arrived in time to see the armies of the Warsaw Pact roll across his own country—and to notice something extraordinary. The revisionist Communists in Czechoslovakia, the Marxists with human faces—those people failed to put up any resistance at all. The Soviet Union summoned the revisionists to Moscow to be reprimanded, and they went and bowed their heads. But at least one portion of the ordinary population was not so contrite.

The rock scenes at the Reduta and Semafor had grown by then into a hippie culture that sprawled daily across the National Museum steps in impudent displays of antiestablishmentarian indolence. Semidelinquent, semi-hippie gangs lounged around the little towns. Havel went out to the north Bohemian town of Liberec. A hundred no-goodnik longhairs in that town under the inspiration of someone named "Tramp" visited the mayor, no friend of the Warsaw Pact, to put together a hippie-mayoral alliance. The mayor sent "Tramp" and the longhairs into the streets to take down the street signs, just to make driving less of a pleasure for any foreigners who might happen by in a tank. The image that Havel retained was of young rebels walking the streets in their blue jeans, strumming guitars and warbling a song called "Massachusetts," a Bee Gees hit from 1967.

The tanks ushered in a renewed ice age in Czechoslovakia, an epoch of totalitarian controls so overwhelming as to be peaceful, which is the coldest of all tyrannies. But when the shock eventually wore off and the post-'68 Czechoslovak dissident movement arose, beginning in 1976, rock and roll finally moved to the center of Czechoslovak politics. The entire development was an odd Eastern Bloc confirmation of some of the wilder youth-culture theories that became popular circa 1969 in the American New Left (to be factionally precise, in SDS–Revolutionary Youth Movement, in Abbie Hoffman and Jerry Rubin's Youth International Party, and in some of the underground papers with their guitar-and-guerrilla themes), except in an anti-Communist version (which, by the late sixties, would have been inconceivable to the American New Left). In the post-invasion age of "normalization," rock music, at least the music that was any good, was banned in Czechoslovakia. Most of the groups broke up or took to playing in other styles.

Still, a number of rockers did cling to the old idea, among them a group from Prague called the Plastic People of the Universe, who spelled their name in English. The Plastic People featured a singer from Canada and a repertoire that, at least in the band's early days (before they switched to original compositions), drew from hip New York bands like the Fugs and the Velvet Underground—thanks to the album that Havel had brought back from New York. (That one album "played a significant role" in Czechoslovakia's history, according to what Havel told the Velvet's Lou Reed, after the revolution.) The Plastic People performed along with groups like the Old Teenagers, specialists in Chuck Berry, at rock festivals in small villages because they had trouble getting permission to play in Prague. And around these bands grew another version of the same scene that had caused such a stir in the little theaters of the 1950s. The Plastic People's manager, who doubled as a radical theoretician, called it the "second culture," which was a good name, full of unspoken challenges to the official culture.

The "second culture" was not a political movement. Its goal was to keep you focused on your own passions. But then, as Orwell knew, fidelity to self cannot be tolerated for more than a moment in a totalitarian system. The Plastic People were soon enough under arrest. The indictment cited lyrics of "extreme vulgarity with an anti-socialist and antisocial impact, most of them extolling nihilism, decadence and clericalism." Clericalism! The Communist Party newspaper railed against the band's "moral filth and efforts to infect our youth with that which every decent man condemns." It was Havel and a couple of others who formed the defense committee in 1976, then transformed the committee into a larger group around a petition called Charter 77. Hundreds of intellectuals—some 1,300 eventually—agreed to sign. Havel and the philosopher Jan Patočka served as spokesmen for the group.

Charter 77's campaign departed in every way from the revisionism of earlier times. Like the Plastic People and the "second culture" as a whole, the new opposition did not propose a program of political change, did not call for a truer socialism, did not invoke the left-wing ideals of the nineteenth century, did not propose to be what the Marxist vocabulary calls a pre-party formation. The new movement was for personal integrity. With Havel's campaigns for the Plastic People and for Charter 77, Goldsteinism, you could say, had finally passed from the scene. Julia-ism took its place—though as something more than a spirit of youth or an impulse for excessively cheerful May Days in the Park of Culture and Rest. For the new campaign's achievement was to add to the notion of personal integrity one extra brick on top of the barricade, which was the insistence that people have a *right* to their own integrity.

And so the apolitical inspiration acquired a modest political dimension, even while claiming to have done nothing of the sort. In regard to foreign affairs and the cold war, the new movement took no position at all. Still, the cold war played its role. The human rights policy of President Carter, the American and British shortwave radio broadcasts, the meddlings by Western embassies (American, Swedish, and West German, especially), the petitions and pesterings by rights groups in the West, the letters to the editor in the *New York Review of Books*, and the committees at the writers' organization PEN had their influence, not just on Czechoslovakia. Western agitations made the Eastern governments hesitate an extra second before ordering arrests. And these several political and ideological efforts, together with the music, literature, and all kinds of other ideas that filtered in from America and the West, worked a noticeable effect on the dissidents themselves.

The dissidents from Havel's generation, the '68ers,

were, in the beginning, by no means sympathetic to the United States on political questions. Throughout the 1970s and even afterward in some instances, the most common idea in the dissident ranks was some kind of "Third Way" politics, neither pro-Soviet nor pro-American. In the early 1980s President Reagan terrified half the world with his campaign to scatter Pershing II and cruise missiles across Western Europe, and Havel, as a dedicated antiestablishmentarian and a proper man of the left, identified with the anti-Reagan peace protesters in the West, the German Greens especially, whose shaggy looks he admired on the TV news. He didn't consume himself with worry that the Greens and the protesters were Communist dupes, as the hard-line cold warriors of the West liked to say. The word "socialism" eventually dropped from Havel's vocabulary, out of frustration at the different definitions that people ascribe to it. Even so, he liked to horrify his disapproving friends, as his adviser Rita Klímová once told me (looking up from her Prague coffee table with a copy of the New York journal *Commentary* aggressively on display), by saying "My heart has always been on the left"—placing his hand on the appropriate spot to lend a punny touch of irony. But by the 1980s, what did that mean, a left-wing heart?

Slowly, slowly, the meaning evolved. From his lonely home in Prague and in the prisons of the Communist state, Havel gazed at the cold war and the superpowers, and at a certain point in the struggle against Reagan and the American missiles, the Western peace activists, his own comrades with their admirably long hair, began to trouble him. He came across excerpts from a book about nuclear strategy and the Western peace movement by André Glucksmann, the French '68er, who had gone through a considerable evolution. Glucksmann was no longer obsessed with Western imperialism. He had finally taken a hard look at the Soviet Union. In Glucksmann's view, the Western peaceniks failed to understand anything at all about Moscow, failed to understand how terrible was totalitarian oppression, failed to understand that Soviet ambitions and not the United States posed the danger to Europe. Glucksmann did think the peaceniks were dupes, the German Greens especially.

Havel invited Glucksmann to Prague. The philosopher arrived, held a seminar for the members of Charter 77, stayed up late chatting with Havel about the good old days of '68, and expressed his opinion that intellectuals ought to be Cassandras and do their best to trouble the tranquil souls of their fellow citizens. All of which evidently resonated in Havel's imagination. For what did those Western peaceniks, his own comrades, know about living under a Soviet-style totalitarian state? About spending year after year in a Communist prison? Havel's left-wing heart began to feel that the world, as he would later tell the U.S. Congress (in his moment of triumph), was "bipolar": divided between "two enormous forces, one a defender of freedom, the other a source of nightmares." And the Third Way was behind him.

The Goldstein movement, back in the first stage of

the Eastern Bloc opposition, had continued to identify with the bloc whose capital was Moscow—even if the Goldsteinites were always plotting to turn Moscow right side up with democratic reforms. But Julia, when she got around to adopting a political stance, turned out to be pro-American. It was not that Jefferson and the Jeffersonians got it wrong. No one can doubt that economic competition from the United States played an enormous role in strengthening the democratic opposition in the East. But the competition from America and the Western democracies was cultural and (aided by the occasional French philosopher) intellectual, too.

IV

In hindsight, we know that the ideas of the dissident intellectuals resonated all along among the ordinary unhappy citizens of the Communist republics. But hardly anyone was too sure of that before the revolution had occurred. Totalitarian societies are, of all societies, the hardest to decipher. The same struggles go on there as everywhere—political and ideological disputes, class struggles, ethnic and religious controversies, struggles that are generational or regional. But in totalitarian societies these struggles become miniaturized, as if shrunk into a thimble by a mad wizard. The more stable and mature the government, the less visible the repression. Crowds march in the streets chanting praise of the party, government slogans decorate the walls, and nothing at all indicates, if you glance around in a normal way, that anyone might find merit in the two or three dissidents whose names may have become known. Stability is the visible spectacle, and to see anything else you have to put your eye up close, looking for infinitesimal wavelets.

The history of little Sušice in the years after General Secretary Gottwald's 1948 coup shows the miniaturizing effect. In that town, there were always recalcitrant individuals who never did approve of the Communist decision to expunge from history the town's experience of having been liberated by the U.S. Army. Protests went on from the very start—on a miniature scale. People squirreled away the artifactual evidence of what had once occurred. They preserved the American flag that used to fly from the Hotel Fialka and other flags, too, along with a poster of Franklin D. Roosevelt and a lot of photographs. They savored the leftover American army rations as delicacies. The son of Kamil Svelch, the man who showed me his photograph collection, dined on U.S. Army rations as late as 1961, which is an appalling thought.

In the schools most of the teachers followed the official curriculum and taught the students about the Red Army and its sneaky way of conquering Sušice disguised in American uniforms. But there were other teachers, the older ones, who couldn't bring themselves to stand in front of a classroom and straight-out lie. So the truth emerged at school, now and then. Parents, too, eyed their children carefully, and when they figured the children were old enough to bite their tongues, they passed along the shocking information about which army had driven into the Sušice square on May 6, 1945. Such was the resistance. The town was engaged in what Kundera calls a battle between memory and forgetting. Yet the battle was so discreet, so intimate and cautious, that no one outside of those individual homes or school rooms had reason to suspect that the happy safety-match capital of the world was silently nursing a grievance.

For a brief moment in 1968, at the time of the Dubček reforms, the authentic feelings of Sušice moved into the open. The municipal government brought the old bronze plaque out of storage and reinstalled it on the square around the corner from the Hotel Fialka. Once more the people could read the inscription in Czech and stare at the English translation that said:

In Memory of the Liberation of Their
Town by the 4th
Armored Division of the 3rd American
Army on May 6th 1945
—The Town of Sušice

Such was the radicalism of 1968 in one little town. Then came the invasion that all too honestly wore the uniforms of the Warsaw Pact, and the plaque was again unscrewed from the wall and put back into storage. That was in 1969 (or possibly as late as 1972, according to Sušice's mayor). The miniature struggle resumed. Since memory had meanwhile won a victory and forgetting had suffered a defeat, the municipal authorities evidently felt shy about leaving the town utterly bereft of all references to the United States and its army. So the authorities put together an official "citizens' movement" that demanded a new and different plaque, which duly went up on the wall and said something to the effect of (as the mayor told me):

IN THIS PLACE USED TO BE A PLAQUE
COMMEMORATING THE 4TH ARMORED
DIVISION
OF THE UNITED STATES ARMY. BUT IT WAS
TAKEN DOWN AS A
PROTEST AGAINST
AMERICAN ATTACKS ON VIETNAM.

Only that plaque, too, got to look a trifle odd, especially after the United States pulled out of Vietnam. At the end of the 1970s, the ingenious authorities, concerned about their credibility, put up still another plaque on exactly the same spot. The plaque commemorated somebody named

MAX PIRNER

who was a professor of fine arts. Only the Pirner plaque, too, proved to be less than popular among the ungrateful population. It was because this newest of plaques gazed out on the town square like an eyepatch for no other purpose than to cover up the place from which the historic marker from long ago had been wrongfully plucked. And a new effort began at the end of the 1970s on behalf of the original plaque.

Three brothers from a Ukrainian family, the Černegas, who had ended up living in Sušice, led the campaign. Old man Černega had been a soldier in the Soviet Red Army, but had never liked Bolsheviks, and his sons felt the same. The Černega brothers, ordinary workers all three, were outraged by the lie about the American army. They came to a popular workers' bar and got people to sign a petition demanding that the original plaque go up in its proper place on the square. People with privileges were reluctant to sign, given the ease with which privileges could disappear. But humbler workers had no such worry. One of these was František Holy, a Sušice factory garbageman with hippie hair and a chubby build who was born in 1950 and therefore had no memory of Americans in Sušice. He did know that teachers in school were lying to his own children about Soviets in American uniforms. That was enough to arouse his indignation. Holy affixed his signature to the Černegas' petition and reasoned that "they," the authorities, couldn't do much to a man like him, since his garbageman's job already put him close to the bottom of the occupational ladder. Some four hundred people finally came to reason along similar lines and signed their names to the Černega brothers' document.

Then troubles did begin, even if the signatories, many of them, had nothing much to lose. The troubles were less than dramatic. In the stable developed

countries of the Eastern Bloc, firing squads and concentration camps were a thing of the past. Nothing
about the new-style repression was likely to attract
the attention of the foreign reporters who might
fly into Prague once a year or the faraway Western
committees on human rights. Holy's predicament
illustrated the method. The garbageman had
arranged to build an extra room on his house. The
workers arrived, the building materials were depos-
ited on the ground, construction was set to go. But
when the news got around that Holy had signed the
barroom petition, he was called in for a discussion
with the deputy mayor.

"Why did you sign?" the deputy mayor asked.
"You weren't even born then."

Holy answered (as he told me), "I signed because
Americans liberated the town. If you can put red
stars everywhere, why can't you put up a plaque for
the Americans?"

A moderate argument. There was no talk of overthrowing Communism or changing the political system in Czechoslovakia. It was simply a question of
affirming the historical truth. Holy made his explanation and went home—and next day, the construction
workers failed to show up at his home, the construction materials disappeared from his yard, and that
was the end of it until six years later, when bygones
were at last bygones and Holy was able to put up
his new room. At his factory, he told me, the director
meanwhile came under instructions to wreak on-the-
job vengeance against whoever was vulnerable among

the signatories. One worker suffered a pay cut, which was a favor on the director's part, since the man wasn't fired outright. Life for the Černega brothers became so bad that all three ended up applying for visas and left Czechoslovakia, not that the authorities admitted to any harassment (though it's significant that a few weeks after Communism was finally over-thrown in 1989, the state prosecutor for Sušice blew out his brains, presumably in fear of what might some day be learned about the local repression).

The original plaque about the United States Army remained hidden away in municipal storage, news was never made, ripples from little Sušice never trou-bled the smooth public image of life in the Czechoslo-vak Socialist Republic. But what events had occurred in that town! That barroom petition represented, if you interpret it broadly enough, the outbreak of class struggle in western Bohemia. It was a workers' protest for historical truth on behalf of the entire commu-nity. Nor did things quiet down after the instigators fled the country and the petition was shelved. The United States embassy in Prague, getting wind of these several events, took up the cause. There was a fine nineteenth-century tradition of American embassies making themselves obnoxious to European tyrants, for instance, by plotting to overthrow mon-archies. And in what remained of that ancient spunki-ness, the embassy staff in Prague adopted the custom of driving out every May to the Šumava regions that had been liberated by the United States Third Army to hold commemorations in the public squares, no matter what the Czechoslovak government felt about these ceremonies. On May 6 every year, the embassy cars rolled into the square at Sušice.

Mostly it was the secret police, the StB, who attended those embassy rallies. Police photographers filled the square and agents harassed anybody else who had the temerity to attend, which did keep the crowds away. Nonetheless some older people came every year. Pensioners who had no boss to threaten them with demotion or a lowered salary, the aging townsfolk who had stood in that square on May 6, 1945, and had witnessed the arrival of the never-forgotten expensive-looking American cars—they were the crowd. The older Svelch stood among those people, year after year. So the StB photographed him—so what? What could "they" do to a man who was already retired? Some younger people began to attend, too—not the university students, whose privileges could be easily revoked, but the young workers, which might have seemed a portent, if anyone had been analyzing the political meaning of that crowd. Only nothing sensational seemed to be going on, and to analyze the meaning was not so easy.

On November 16, 1989, in Prague, the high school and university students went into the streets to begin the democratic revolution at last, and in the next few days the "second culture" and Prague's theater world and even the Czech Philharmonic filled Wenceslas Square to add their support, and Havel and the other leaders waved to the crowd from a balcony and urged the revolution on. But none of those people really knew how things stood in the regions outside the capital. The students and theater people organized teams of agitators and speakers to go out from Prague to announce the revolution and invite everyone to join, and the revolutionary teams got in their cars and drove into the countryside nearly trembling with fear. On the fifth day, November 21, one of those teams— it was a group of Prague theater actors—drove down the valley into smoky Sušice, expecting what—hostility? apathy?

Yet in Sušice, as it happened, any number of people were already prepared to respond to an uprising in Prague. Charter 77 had some signatories in Sušice, who had organized a local chapter of Havel's new group, Civic Forum. The younger Svelch had enrolled in its ranks. Holy, the garbageman, had enthusiastically participated. It was not as if the democratic revolution in Sušice had to scrape together an activist group from scratch. People in a town like that knew perfectly well how to confront authority. Philosophically, the place was already vibrating to the higher ideas of the dissidents from the capital. The theories of Václav Havel that were guiding the Prague revolutionaries—the instinct to avoid rigid ideological systems, to maintain a unity of personal character and political action, to value individual integrity, to emphasize the principles of "living in truth"—came easily to people who had been campaigning for the simplest honesty about local history. The concepts of alienation and truth, which for so many years had seemed like intellectual phrase-mongering, were a gar-

bageman's wisdom. The "existential revolution"—
Havel's phrase—had been going on in Sušice for forty
years.

A solid two thousand townsfolk turned out in the
square to hear the Prague actors announce the wonderful news from the capital. Next day the crowd was
bigger. The demonstrations in Sušice became a scaled-
down version of the larger events going on in Wenceslas Square, swelling day by day until the crowd at
Sušice reached seven thousand persons. A sizable percentage of the entire population was suddenly standing
in the town square. A few weeks later, after Havel
and his Civic Forum in Prague had been able to put
together the beginnings of a democratic government
(with the participation of Dubček, just to show that
Goldstein had finally come out in favor of Julia), the
dissidents in Sušice, exulting in their suddenly public
popularity, called still another rally. It took place at
the regular spot in the square, between the old Town
Hall and the Hotel Fialka. Once again a motorcade
from the United States embassy drove out to the town,
only this time to discover quite a different spectacle
from the sad crowd of nasty StB photographers and
stubborn pensioners and young workers who every
year in the past had greeted the American officials.
This time the square was packed. Two American colo-
nels and the aides of Ambassador Black (unfortunately
not the ambassador herself—those were busy days for
American embassies) climbed out of the cars. And to
the astonishment of the embassy staff, the crowd was

waving—but where did they get these things?—a sea of American flags.

It would be easy, faced with a scene like that, to exaggerate the meaning that America had assumed for the Eastern countries in the course of the anti-Communist revolution. To the Easterners, America had come to represent anti-Sovietism, liberty, and liberalism; and as long as the revolution was still in a liberal phase, American symbols were a logical thing to adopt. In Prague the revolutionary students had decorated the site known as the "John Lennon Wall" with slogans from the American Pledge of Allegiance (". . . and Justice for All . . ."), and when the students went marching through the streets, the anthem they sang was "We Shall Overcome." The old hymn of the American civil rights movement had by then become the worldwide anthem of democratic resistance. Yet liberalism was, of course, only one aspect among many in the Eastern Bloc Revolution. The moment that Adam Michnik predicted almost at once, the triumph of nationalisms of every sort, of ethnic bigotries and novel fascisms and ancient traditions invented on the spot—that moment was visible from the start, and to the degree that it came to dominate the scene, libertarian America was bound to seem that much less attractive. Sooner or later even the Eastern Bloc writers and artists who had exclaimed the most enthusiastically over American virtues were bound to sink into the same envy and resentment that had overcome their counterparts in Western Europe in the 1950s, and sooner or later were bound to look down their cultivated, impoverished noses at wealthy America's lack of culture.

Sooner or later ordinary working people in the formerly Communist countries, ruing the day that a word like "socialism" had disappeared from the dissident vocabulary, were bound to discover the anti-labor biases of free market ideology, and were bound to blame their troubles (correctly!) on right-wing economic doctrines foisted on them by the economics department of the University of Chicago. Eventually the people of the East were fated to get a clearer idea of American bleakness and social decay and the me-first ethic in its capitalist manifestation. And what would they make of golden America when they learned, as was certain to happen, that America's devotion to freeing the world of tyranny, priesthood, and all the rest is, on any given day, blather? That the land of the free is not necessarily the home of the brave? Or the intelligent? The American moment was never fated to be a permanent affair.

Then again, maybe the people in the East, less naive than was sometimes supposed, always knew that. At Sušice on that day of tribute to the United States, the sea of Stars and Stripes was not necessarily intended to extoll every last breeze from across the ocean. The flags waved for truth, for the immutability of history whose symbol is the immutability of bronze. The tribute was to the past. For there on the wall catty-corner from the Fialka was, once again, in its proper place, lettered in Czech and English, a declaration of simple reality, namely:

IN MEMORY OF THE LIBERATION OF THEIR
TOWN BY THE 4TH
ARMORED DIVISION OF THE 3RD AMERICAN
ARMY ON MAY 6TH 1945
—THE TOWN OF SUŠICE

Nor was the pro-American zeal quite what it seemed. The embassy staffers and the townsfolk turned their heads and noticed that not every one of those fine-looking American flags was identical. Some of them had forty-eight stars. These were the banners left behind by the retreating army of George S. Patton. The forty-eight-star flag that had once hung over the American officers' quarters at the Hotel Fialka was once again drooping in the industrial air.

Other people waved flags with fifty stars. During the frantic first weeks of the 1989 revolution, citizens of Sušice took the sudden opportunity to drive to the Federal Republic of Germany on shopping expeditions, and some of those people chose to spend their not-very-valuable Czechoslovak crowns on properly up-to-date American flags. Then, finding themselves abroad and discovering that every kind of foolishness is for sale to the willing tourist, they bought a few other flags, too. As a result, waving among the honored relics of Patton's army and the proper banners of present-day America were, here and there, the Stars and Stripes with the face of Marilyn Monroe superimposed. And here was a James Dean! These were flags that will someday be banned in our own home of democratic liberty, if the advocates of an anti-flag-desecration amendment to the U.S. Constitution ever get their way. Let me hazard a serious interpretation of what those desecrated banners signified in western Bohemia at the height of the Eastern Bloc Revolution. They were jokes! The star-spangled Marilyn Monroes and James Deans were flags of humor and affection. They were flags of sex appeal, of antipolitics. They were flags from the homeland of Frank Zappa and of Shirley Temple—but not necessarily from the hardscrabble streets of American suffering and failure.

The visiting officials from the U.S. embassy waved, and the Monroes and Deans waved back, and those bobbing flags might even have said, to anyone willing to listen: We Eastern Bloc revolutionaries know all about the difference between reality and aspiration. We are celebrating freedom. We are celebrating the overthrow of tyranny, privilege, and ideological domination. And we have no intention of submitting to solemn new orthodoxies of the present, not even yours, kind friends from America. We salute the victor in the cold war, whose capital may or may not be Washington. But it is certainly Hollywood! And if there are traumas and troubles on the way to building a new society, these can come later—and will.

A Backward Glance at the
End of History

I

Was there a larger meaning to the liberal and nationalist revolutions that began to break out in the fall of
1989? Did some crucial truth about the nature of man
and the shape of history, previously hidden under the
cloud of events, stand suddenly revealed, bright and
obvious, to an astonished world? To be any kind of
political thinker at all in the age of Václav Havel
and Boris Yeltsin was to work up theories on this
question—and to scotch those notions two seconds
later for newer, better ideas. Crowds surged through
the Central and Eastern European streets, and theories
surged through the political journals. Yet for all the
lush variety in the many new analyses, there were, if
you look closely, only two main ideas. There was the
idea that things change, sometimes in spectacular ways,
but without ever arriving at any kind of order or final
shape, and history is like a kaleidoscope. And there
was the idea that things change, and eventually the
chaos adds up to progress, and in a roundabout way
history does get somewhere. Like a corkscrew.

The corkscrew theory was the more famous, and the less well regarded. It was upheld by just a handful of writers, not always with a lot of literary skill or intellectual authority. Yet among the handful was Francis Fukuyama, whose professional résumé beamed a bright spotlight on his own ideas. Fukuyama was that novel blossom of the Reagan era, a Washington intellectual. He worked as a foreign policy analyst at the U.S. government's RAND Corporation (the "BLAND Corporation" in Stanley Kubrick's *Dr. Strangelove*), took a State Department post, and during the Reagan and Bush years rose to the rank of deputy director of the State Department Policy Planning Staff. Nothing that he had written had ever attracted much attention, outside of what are known as "policy circles." But in the summer 1989 issue of the neoconservative journal *The National Interest*—at a moment when the Soviet empire was just beginning to totter, still a few months before the Berlin Wall came down—he published an article called "The End of History?"

It was the corkscrew theory. Serious presentations of political philosophy (Fukuyama's idea was definitely serious) almost never become overnight sensations, yet his "End of History" became the rule-making exception, on a world scale. The fame was perhaps not everything an author could wish. The first commentaries were chilly, the next worse, and laughter began to accumulate, until at last, like a bicycle left outside in a blizzard, hardly anything remained of poor Fukuyama's original notion except a comical shape. History finished! No more events! Human perfection finally achieved, with boredom as result! Such was the unfriendly summary version. In 1992 he expanded the article into a book, *The End of History and the Last Man*, and the book, too, attracted something other than applause. The soulful heavy-lidded young man's face staring outward from the author photo on the jacket flap was that of a worldwide butt of humor—though why his theory, if it was so ridiculous, would stir so much interest in so many countries was a question that might have given pause to his innumerable merry critics.

The kaleidoscope idea was more popular, and less clever. None of its upholders came up with anything to rival a phrase like "End of History." Still, some very intelligent arguments were made, including one by André Glucksmann, the old Paris "Mao." He proposed it at the Frankfurt Book Fair in October 1989, a few months after Fukuyama's article had come out, though still a couple of weeks before the Berlin Wall came down. The West German publishers had decided to award the Frankfurt Peace Prize to Václav Havel, but because the Communist Party still ruled Czecho-slovakia, the prizewinner, prevented from attending his own ceremony, sent the text of a speech instead, which was read by the actor Maximilian Schell. Glucksmann delivered the official homage. His speech carried the title "To Exit from Communism Is to Re-enter History." It was the rebuttal to Fukuyama. Then Glucksmann, too, expanded his argument into a full-scale book, which came out in Paris in 1991 under the title *The 11th Commandment* (in French, *Le XI*ᵉ *commandement*).

It's very striking to examine those two books side by side, Fukuyama's and Glucksmann's. The arguments they make are perfectly parallel. The Reaganite State Department theorist and the '68 Paris revolutionary have each concluded that Communism's collapse, together with that of sundry right-wing dictatorships around the world, requires an ambitious reexamination of the philosophical foundations of the whole of Western civilization. Each author has decided that we need to think about history in a new way, and each has justified his proposed new way by glancing back to ancient Athens, then forward to the revolutions of 1989 and the Persian Gulf War and other modern matters: Plato to NATO. Yet the final conclusions could not be more opposed. Logically speaking, if Fukuyama's corkscrew theory has any merit, Glucksmann's kaleidoscope theory has none, and vice versa—which helps us not a bit in deciding which, if either, of these grand ambitious efforts to imagine the post–cold-war world is the one with merit.

II

Glucksmann's theory is simple enough, but he expounds it with sulfurous intensity; and the intensity is something you can understand only by recalling how people of his generation took up politics in the first place, and what happened to them next—in France and elsewhere. His family background was hair-raising. His father was a Romanian Jew, his mother a Czech Jew. Separately the parents embraced Zionism, met each other in Palestine, converted to Communism—and were sent by the Communist movement into Nazi Germany to work in the underground. André himself was born in 1937 in France, which meant that, during the years of his infancy, people all around him were either disappearing into Auschwitz or else were fighting in the Communist wing of the Resistance, and life offered and/or choices between courage and death. There was the example of his sister, twelve years older than himself, who remained in Germany during the war distributing tracts on behalf of the Resistance, and was lucky, and survived.

At age thirteen in 1950, a time of peace, André joined the Communist movement in Paris. He attended an elite school, the Lycée Henri IV, and remained part of the Communist group there until 1956, when he and everyone else from his circle, the student radicals, were expelled from the party for failing to endorse the Soviet invasion of Hungary. Communism in an orthodox version could never hope to retain the allegiance of someone as frisky and intelligent as Glucksmann. In Paris, Marxist philosophy and social criticism were alive and well, but only outside the party, among the left-wing thinkers who could not bring themselves to take out a party membership, or who criticized the party in some way, or who harbored reservations about the Soviet Union. Those writers, the unorthodox Marxists, had conceived of a grand project, which was to reread Marx through the nine-teenth-century lens of his own philosophical predeces-sor, Hegel, and through a twentieth-century lens that came from Heidegger, and in that way to discover new energies in the old doctrine, maybe even to rescue the Communists from their own intellectual failures. Glucksmann studied the arguments. He enrolled at the École normale supérieure of Saint Cloud, took a seminar on Hegel with Althusser, became an assistant of Raymond Aron at the Sorbonne, published an arti-cle in Sartre's magazine. And when he began to work up ideas of his own, he focused his attention on Hegel's influence on Western thought and on the greatest of Hegel's Parisian disciples, Alexandre Kojève—about whom something should be said.

Kojève was a slightly terrifying figure. He was a Russian aristocrat from before the Revolution, a nephew of Wassily Kandinsky, the painter. When the Bolsheviks came to power, Kojève was obliged to flee, first to Germany (where he studied philosophy), then to Paris (where he taught it). Yet in spite of his own experience in Russia, his attitude toward the Bolshevik Revolution remained approving. He regarded himself as a Communist—in his own words, a "strict Stalin-ist," which was a phrase that always puzzled his more levelheaded friends. In some deep way he was not unlike his uncle the painter (who had likewise sup-ported the Bolsheviks back in Russia, and had to flee to Germany, then to France). The blotchy dark yellows and steely blues in Kandinsky's paintings, the intricate designs that look like electronic diagrams, seem to have oozed onto the canvas direct from the unconscious. They are pure irrationality in color and shape. And that sort of extreme radicalism—the celebration of the irrational, the violent turn against sentimentality of any kind, the dramatic strokes—was Kojève's spirit, too.

During the 1930s Kojève conducted a seminar on Hegel's *The Phenomenology of Spirit* in the main building of the Sorbonne, and a Who's Who of brilliant students trooped in to attend. Raymond Queneau, Jacques Lacan, Georges Bataille, André Breton, Maurice Merleau-Ponty, not to mention Raymond Aron, Glucksmann's future teacher—those were the faces in the class. Kojève delivered his interpretations, and the Hegel who emerged was violent, half-mad, hard and heartless, cynical, provocative, revolutionary, wise, and lucid; and behind Hegel lay a panorama of human history consisting of lordly masters and cowering slaves, obsessed with combat and death, fighting over insignificant issues of prestige. Grim! In later years Kojève turned away from teaching in favor of a position as *éminence grise* in the French Ministry of Economy and Finance. He became an architect of the GATT treaty, which may sound like an odd enterprise for a Marxist—except that socialism's purpose in Kojève's view was to bring the irrationalities of the market into the realm of rational social decisions, meaning that well-designed trade treaties might almost count as socialism itself. In any case, the turn away from teaching hardly brought his philosophical influence to an end.

One day in 1962 Kojéve showed up at a Paris lecture hall and discovered that fully three hundred students were waiting to hear him speak. He had become, at least he could have become, a guru to the student world nearly on the scale of Marcuse or Sartre. Guruship seems not to have interested him, though. The crowd at his lecture made him feel, in his own self-deprecating phrase, like a "twist instructor." In 1967, with the European student movement getting under way, he met in Berlin with Rudi Dutschke and other leaders of the German student left. Only instead of counseling his young admirers to plunge into ever wilder and more dangerous projects, as Sartre, the man of mischief, would surely have done, Kojève, the sphinx, merely urged the German students to study Greek.

Aron was never swept away by Kojève's ideas but came to be his friend anyway and looked on him as something of a genius—"more intelligent than Sartre," which was saying a lot. You can imagine the impression he must have left on people who did get swept away. For Kojève, in his lectures on Hegel, seemed to have discovered some inner murderous essence of human character, and having identified the inner essence, he seemed to have located the hidden mechanism of world history; and, no, the hidden mechanism did not make a pretty picture. But neither was Europe a pretty picture, not in the mid-twentieth century, nor at any time. And so, in Paris during the 1950s and '60s, if you were any kind of philosophical thinker at all, you had to be a Kojèvian, or an anti-Kojèvian; but you could not ignore the man.

In that atmosphere Glucksmann sat down to write his first book, under Aron's supervision. The book was called *The Discourse of War* (in French, *Le Discours de la guerre*). It came out in 1967. Ostensibly it was an analysis of military theory from Clausewitz to Mao, with a long discussion of American nuclear strategy in the thinking of Secretary of Defense Robert McNamara and the sages of the RAND Corporation. But underneath the military discussion was a strictly philosophical argument. It was an analysis of Kojève and of Kojève's Hegel. Glucksmann was an anti. He looked at Kojève's ideas and instead of seeing a properly subversive, hard-nosed, left-wing view of the world he thought he saw a celebration of naked power.

In 1967 the Vietnam War was at high tide and the United States, in the grip of its own military ideas, was raining bombs on rice paddies; and Glucksmann became convinced that not just America but Western civilization, taken as a whole, was fixated on death. And at the heart of that fixation lay the long philosophical tradition of the West, whose greatest modern thinker had been Hegel, as revealed in the interpretations of Kojève. You could say that between Glucksmann and Kojève was a difference in generations. Kojève expressed the idea that society is monstrous, and we should accept the fact and see the greatness in it (or, in his later years, at least resign ourselves to it). He was the voice of the totalitarian generation. Glucksmann expressed the horrified feeling that society, at least in its modern Western form, is exactly as Kojève described, but nothing is great about it. He was the voice of the children of the totalitarian generation.

Glucksmann's *Discourse of War* could be compared to the classic Marxist analysis that came out of the student movement in the United States in the late 1960s, *Empire and Revolution* by David Horowitz, which likewise extended the condemnation of America's role in Vietnam to Western institutions as a whole—except that where Horowitz's American volume offered a somewhat plodding political analysis in a Trotsky-influenced vein, Glucksmann's *Discourse* offered a razzle-dazzle philosophical criticism of the whole of Western civilization. But both books, Glucksmann's and Horowitz's, claimed to have discovered the new revolutionary alternative. In Glucksmann's version, the alternative was to turn away from high-tech militarism and the quest for centralized power, in short the Western cult of death, and to take up, instead, the patient, militant, revolutionary policy of a low-tech guerrilla resistance movement—a movement not so different, all in all, from the low-tech Communist Resistance in which his own parents and his sister had participated during the Second World War. In Glucksmann's opinion, a movement of that sort was going on in Vietnam in the present, again under the leadership of the Communists. And in the writings of Mao Zedong (*On Protracted War, On Practice, On Contradiction*), Glucksmann felt that he had discovered the master texts of guerrilla resistance, the philosophy of anti-Hegel and anti-Kojève, and the theoretical basis of the world revolution.

The year of Glucksmann's book, 1967, was a wonderfully productive one for revolutionary manifestos among the younger French writers. Régis Debray, sitting in his prison cell in Bolivia that year, published *Revolution in the Revolution?*, which was nothing less than the principal theoretical expression of the Marxist guerrilla movement in Latin America. The Situationist writers, Raoul Vaneigem and Guy Debord, came out with, respectively, their *Treatise on How to Live for the Usage of the Young Generation* and *The Society of the Spectacle*, which laid out the prospect for an anarchist revolution in Europe. Glucksmann's book was not quite comparable. It was brash, impossibly woolly in some passages (a characteristic flaw), but, finally, scholarly, a volume directed at philosophers.

He made plain that he himself was no kind of prophet, had no weapon, and was announcing no sort of Maoist affiliation. Still, reading Glucksmann on Kojève's Hegel and the theory of war, you could reasonably wonder, why stop where he had stopped? If his condemnation of American nuclear strategy and of Western philosophy and civilization was on the mark, if his high estimation of the human qualities of Mao's guerrilla alternative was even halfway accurate, why *not* turn his book into a genuine manifesto, as revolutionary as those other books, and proclaim the greatness of Mao? Why not do the logical thing and form some kind of guerrilla movement to struggle against the death obsessions of Western thought and technology? Why not revive the Nazi-era Resistance in Europe—just as Debray was trying to do in Latin America? Anyone who had followed Glucksmann's argument about Kojève and Western civilization could hardly think those were unreasonable possibilities.

Then came the student uprising of May–June 1968, and Glucksmann, as might have been expected, threw himself into the ferment. By then he was teaching at the Sorbonne, but he took the occasion to tell his students to go out into the street and join the revolution. He wrote articles for the weekly newspaper of the student insurrection, *Action*. The barricades came down in the summer, and most of the students and the workers who had joined the movement went back to the pleasures and doldrums of ordinary life. But Glucksmann stood among the large fervent minority who felt that May and June had demonstrated the practical usefulness of revolutionary action, and that what had taken place in the student quarter of Paris could take place in the working-class regions everywhere in Europe and even in the oppressed countries of the Soviet Bloc, if only the effort were made. And so he embraced the particular spirit of fanaticism that, in France, went under the name *gauchisme* (meaning leftism of an ultra sort), in a "spontaneist" version (meaning direct-action protests and provocations, not institution building).

Now he did write explicitly revolutionary tracts. He helped organize a group with the derisory name the Base Committee for the Abolition of Wage Labor and the Destruction of the University, which was

pretty much the French counterpart of Abbie Hoffman's "Plans for the Destruction of the Universities"
in the United States (as can be observed with a glance
at Chapter 7 of Abbie's classic of American-style spontaneist *gauchisme* from 1968, *Revolution for the Hell of
It*). And like Abbie in the American colleges,
Glucksmann went around the halls of the left-wing
university at Vincennes, leading his mob of followers
and waving his copy of *Quotations from Chairman
Mao* and disrupting classes, including the classes that
were taught by Marxist professors—those classes especially, given that Glucksmann looked on Marxism's
conquest of the academy as a government conspiracy
to defuse the revolution (which in France and especially at Vincennes was actually the case).

In January 1969, the Vincennes students occupied
the administration building, and Glucksmann took
his place among them, and he and Michel Foucault,
the supermilitant profs, climbed to the top of the
stairs, Foucault wielding a fire extinguisher, to resist
the police. Glucksmann and the *gauchistes* fought off
the Communists, who were always trying to reestablish
some kind of order at Vincennes (if only because
gauchisme had every intention of overthrowing the
Communist Party and even the Soviet Union, in the
name of a higher Communism). And afire with the
revolutionary idea, in the spring of 1970 Glucksmann
enlisted in the strangest and most extreme of the tiny
splinter groups of the student left. It was the group
that had begun at the École normale supérieure and
had split away from the official Communists and had

called itself, first, the Union of Communist Youth (M-L) and, later, the Proletarian Left—and was fondly or not so fondly known to all as the "Maos."

The Proletarian Left had a certain attractiveness—combined with some other qualities, obviously. The Maos pointed their accusatory fingers at the treatment of immigrants and of prisoners in France, and at unsafe conditions in the factories and mines (these were their main political concerns, along with zealous opposition to Zionism and American imperialism), and their accusations, at least the ones that referred to French society, were not mistaken. The Maos wanted to break down the barrier between the student left and the world of the oppressed workers, and they took their faithful cadre from out of the universities and sent them into the factories and the immigrant neighborhoods. They were unfazed by the likelihood of getting arrested or beaten by the police. They had a swaggering air, half-brilliant and half-crazy, full of dash and combativeness, a style of leather jackets and alarming slogans, which is to say, they were rebellious, thuggish, hostile, alluring. A familiar enough style in twentieth-century Europe: a posture of extremism and violence, slightly dandified.

Several of the older, left-wing intellectuals, the ones who had always looked for something more revolutionary than the Communist Party, positively doted on the young militants. Glucksmann worked on the journal of the Proletarian Left—it was called *J'Accuse* (of course)—and among the contributors and editors at his side were not only Foucault but also Sartre himself, Simone de Beauvoir, Jean-Luc Godard (pseudonymously), Gilles Deleuze, and some others, too, the luminaries of Paris. The Maos put out a newspaper called *La Cause du peuple*, and when the government arrested the editor-in-chief, it was Sartre who agreed to take the editor's place, at least on a titular basis. The police arrested vendors of the paper. Sartre and de Beauvoir went out on the Boulevard St.-Germain and took to hawking *La Cause du peuple* themselves. Eventually the Maos put out a second paper, *Libération*, intended for a wide daily readership; and Sartre again was on the masthead.

Yet there was never any doubt where the Proletarian Left intended to take those many charmed and astonished followers. The direction was already visible, faintly, in Glucksmann's early book about Kojève and Mao. Then it became less faint. In the analysis that Glucksmann and other party journalists began to present to the public, the France of circa 1970—bourgeois, constitutional, unegalitarian, stuffy, rigid, moderately democratic France—was fascism incarnate, no different from the France that was occupied by the Nazis in the Second World War. And drunk with this dotty idea and with expectations of revolution and with the moral arrogance that comes from believing your opponents to be Nazis, the Maos prepared for war. The party leaders quietly organized a clandestine wing of the Proletarian Left called the New People's Resistance for the purpose of reviving the old Resistance from the Nazi era. And in May 1970 the "clandos" went underground. Their intention was no different from that of the Weather Underground and the other guerrilla groups in the United States. But mostly the French "clandos" resembled their guerrilla comrades in West Germany and Italy. In those countries, the ones on France's borders, the guerrilla tendencies turned out to be amazingly tough and hardy. The governments cracked down, but the guerrillas succeeded in recruiting new young fighters year after year, and they kept finding new sources of political and material support, and they managed to survive straight into the 1990s. Was there any reason why the fraternal movement in France should have been any feebler, shorter-lived, or less bloody? No reason at all.

The conditions for a genuinely gory struggle were excellent in France. The Proletarian Left was splendidly talented. Glucksmann and one or two other young writers in the movement gave a genuine sophistication to the argument for guerrilla revolution. (In the United States, by way of comparison, the guerrilla-war pamphlets and tracts that came out of the Weather Underground Organization and the Bay Area Research Collective and the Black Liberation Army in that period could be considered laughably crude, except that guerrilla tracts are never laughable.) As for the older intellectuals who gathered around the Proletarian Left at *J'Accuse*, *La Cause du peuple*, and (later on) *Libération*, these people, some of them, were giddy with the anticipated joys of mayhem. Foucault, the maestro of excess, took to speaking with relish about how, during the French Revolution, "people's justice"

paraded the heads of enemies on pikes. It was fashionable to speak about the fashionableness of terror.

Maoism's popularity on the streets was unmistakable. In February 1972, in the course of one of the
Proletarian Left's protests, a scuffle broke out at the
plant gates of the big Renault factory at Billancourt
in the Paris suburbs, and a young man associated with
La Cause du peuple, a worker named Pierre Overney,
was shot and killed by a company guard. The Maos
responded by sending the New People's Resistance to
seize a Renault executive and smuggle him into a
safe house, more or less in the style of the guerrilla
kidnappings in Germany and Italy. Then came the
public funeral for Overney. Two hundred thousand
people marched in the cortege through the streets of
Paris—an enormous crowd, big enough that Althusser, in his addled memoirs, recalls it as two million.
And anyone could see that, if the Maos had ever gone
ahead and launched their war, the sea of sympathizers
and the cultural and intellectual strength of the movement might easily—surely would—have sunk France
into the same ugly predicament that proved so durable
and bloody in Germany and Italy.

Still, something about the Maos in France was not
entirely like the German and Italian guerrillas. The
French Maos were not utterly opposed to thinking a
new thought. Adulation in the streets had the paradoxical effect of sobering them up. They gazed at the
endless blocks of marching mourners for Pierre Overney, and sank into their own reflections. Glucksmann
found himself asking why, if he and his hyper-revolu-

tionary comrades were so well liked, they insisted on behaving with such bitterness toward society. The kidnapping of the Renault executive seemed bold and inspiring at first, but the weeks went by, and the man remained safely imprisoned in the secret apartment under the masked guard of the New People's Resistance, and a bad odor, morally speaking, began to seep from that secret apartment. There wasn't much to do with the man from Renault except parade his head on a pike. But for what reason?

So the Maos lost heart and let the man go (to Sartre's displeasure!). Then it was September 1972 and time for the summer Olympic Games in Munich. Those were the games in which the most famous guerrilla movement of all to emerge from the radicalism of the sixties, the Palestine Liberation Organization, launched its assault on Israel's athletic team, with the aid of the West German Red Cells. The fraternal revolutionary groups in other countries, some of them, applauded the PLO attack, without making prissy little noises about the choice of tactics. The German terrorists, in close alliance with Palestinians, persisted in the years to come in making random attacks on Israelis (and, in fact, on non-Israeli Jews). By their own principles, the French Maos should have looked on the PLO assault with a similar feeling of warm fraternity. Israel's role as linchpin of world imperialism was an unquestioned postulate everywhere in the guerrilla revolutionary movement, and the Maos were nothing if not orthodox in these matters. In the past they had painted up Baron Rothschild's home in Paris to show their sincerity, and they had tossed Molotov cocktails at the police on behalf of the oppressed Palestinians. Their student "colonizers" in the factories and workplaces had set up Palestine Support Committees, which recruited a good number of Arab immigrant workers. No one could question the Proletarian Left's anti-Zionism. Yet when the PLO staged its action in Munich, the response from within the organization was curiously divided. The Arab workers who had been recruited through the Palestine Support Committees tended to go on admiring the PLO and its daring exploits in Munich, and were not about to turn against terrorism just because the publicity was less than favorable.

Among the Maoist leaders, on the other hand, a plain majority happened to be, like Glucksmann, Jewish. That was truly an oddity. These people were suffering from epic confusions about Jewishness and its place in the world. There was the remarkable case of the Proletarian Left's topmost leader, the Mao of the Maos, Pierre Victor, whose real name, all too Jewish, was Beny Lévy. Young Lévy was an Egyptian who had fled to France to escape the Arab nationalist revolution, had established a reputation for brilliance at the École normale, and had led his fellow students into Maoism and anti-Zionism without ever having stopped to consider the relation between reality as conceived by his doctrines and reality as reflected in his own refugee existence. (Later, when the *gauchiste* moment was over, he would take a job as Sartre's personal secretary and then go on to embrace a new life devoted to . . . Talmud study!) In the political imagination of the revolutionary left everywhere around the world in the late 1960s and early '70s, a sympathetic knowledge of the Jewish question was the great absence; and nowhere was the absence more present than among the brilliant-and-stupid Jewish ultra-leftists of France. But that could not last forever. For here was the PLO in Munich, and the Israeli corpses were stretched out on the German soil, and the French revolutionaries, Jewish and otherwise, had to make a judgment.

Among the Maoist leaders, the judgment was to be horrified. Eyes suddenly opened. The Maos were shocked—by themselves, not just by the PLO. And now, with amazing speed, they began to hold up for critical inspection every one of the violent ideas that they themselves had so carefully stockpiled as party doctrine. They thought about terrorism as a whole, about what it means to make deliberate plans to kidnap or murder random persons for political gain. They gave some consideration to the theory of collective guilt, which was a topic that had managed to escape their attention until that grisly moment. Perhaps they recognized that *gauchisme*, in their own conception of it, was never really intended to go around painting the sidewalks with blood (except that things do get out of hand). Over the course of their revolutionary adventures, they had seized the Odéon Theater and they had broken the windows at a gourmet shop at La Madeleine, and all of that was grand to do, because of the theatricality; but theater is defined by its limits.

So the Munich massacre sent the Maos into a spasm of reflection, and reflection led to the most extraordinary action that any vigorous and reasonably popular political group can take, which is to disband. In France, a different group, Direct Action, anarchist in its leanings (though led by a former member of the Proletarian Left), went ahead with guerrilla attacks over the next few years. But Direct Action was small, without support from the intellectuals, without a popular following on the street, and it got nowhere. Guerrilla violence in France was going to be Mao or never. And at exactly that moment of psychological vulnerability—by then it was late 1973, early 1974—the Maos, having dismantled their own organization and having sunk into the fumes of political despair (post-'68 psychological depression was another worldwide trait, by the way, shared by the student revolutionaries of the United States, Mexico, and half the other countries on earth), looked up from their volumes of Mao's quotations and military essays and the impenetrable tomes of French Marxism that had served them so poorly. And they noticed in the press the earliest translations into French of Aleksandr I. Solzhenitsyn's detailed portrait of the Soviet concentration camp system, *The Gulag Archipelago, 1918–1956: An Experiment in Literary Investigation.*

In the entire history of literature there has probably never been another book that altered public attitudes and political events so swiftly and radically as the French translation of Solzhenitsyn's *Archipelago*. In

1975 alone, Volume 1 sold 600,000 copies in France, and Volume 2 some 175,000 more, and if the effect of these sales seemed huge at first, time has only made the huge seem huger—though exactly why may need an explanation. For surely, by the 1970s, everyone on the left knew about the camps in the Soviet Union, didn't they? But, no, everyone did not, and the lack of knowledge came in two versions. The French Communist Party, pathetically Stalinist though it was, still commanded the loyalty of nearly a quarter of the electorate, which meant that any number of ordinary working people, the faithful readers of the party press, would still have said, in Sartre's immortal words from the 1950s, "the worker has two countries, his own, and the Republic of Soviet Russia." The position of most of the people who had participated in the '68 student uprisings was, of course, very different, both in France and in most of the Western countries (the Third World was another story). The student insurrectionaries were not the partisans of the Communist Party, and they were sincere in insisting that, in regard to the Soviet Union, they did know the reality, and needed no lessons on the topic.

Yet what exactly did they know? To be on the radical left in the first years after the student uprisings meant that you harbored the expectation, at least the hope, that the society of the present was going to be overcome, that a newer, higher society was going to arrive, that capitalist relations of production were going to be superseded. In the Soviet Union capitalist relations had already been superseded, in an unattractive way, due to the terrible Soviet bureaucracy. Politically the Soviet Union might be worse than the West (though some people were reluctant even to grant that much). But economically wasn't the Soviet Union an advance? At least in principle? And didn't Marxism argue that, in the last analysis, economics counts for more than politics? And so, great portions of the radical left in the Western countries—not everybody, but undoubtedly a majority—found themselves ambivalent about Soviet society. The ambivalence was expressed by a theory of two Communisms. Life in the Soviet Union might be lamentable in almost every respect; but Communism in the Soviet Union was a kind of pregnancy, and out of the pregnancy would be born a second, better Communism, perhaps the direct democracy that almost everyone on the radical left expected to see.

There were different ways of picturing the pregnancy and the second Communism. In the Third Worldist version, Communist revolution in the Soviet Union was thought to have already given birth to a superior Communism in China, Vietnam, Cuba, and several other countries, not to mention a non-Communist state socialism in places like Algeria. So there was reason to be grateful to the Soviet Union, even if Soviet society itself was nothing to admire. In the Trotskyist version, Communist institutions and ideas were recognized as deficient in every one of the Communist countries, not just in the Soviet Union. But by collectivizing economic life, the deficient Communisms had, at least, established the social base for a superior society to come, and sooner or later the social base was going to sweep away the superstructural deficiencies, and the second, higher Communism would come into being. There was a not-quite Trotskyist version which expected revolutionary movements to break out in the Soviet Bloc—perhaps in a democratic style along the lines of Dubček's Prague Spring; perhaps in a syndicalist or anarchist style along the lines of the Hungarian Revolution of 1956; perhaps in an expanded version of the 1968 Paris uprising (which had been Glucksmann's hope, for a while). But one way or another, the deplorable Communism of Soviet reality was pregnant with possibility, and the higher Communism was going to be born.

The factions of the radical left defined themselves according to which of those analyses they preferred, and the differences, in the eyes of the competing groups, loomed large. Yet the logical implications that followed from each of those variations were finally the same. Capitalism, not Communism, was the greatest danger facing the world. America, not the Soviet Union. Or, if the Soviets did pose a more or less equivalent threat, they also offered a solution. For the Soviets, in their inadequate and objectionable way, were giving birth to the better future. Exploitation and imperialism were the essence of capitalism, but slave labor and prison camps were not the essence of Communism, and sooner or later, peacefully or violently, the labor camps and the prison system were going to be eliminated.

In that manner, a great number of people on the

radical left felt they knew everything they needed to know about Communist realities, and felt extremely sure of themselves on that point, and flew into a rage at anyone who accused them of Soviet sympathies; yet they saw no reason to pay any attention at all to the camps and the prisons. Theirs was the knowledge of averted eyes. They believed themselves to be more sophisticated than the simpletons of the pro-Moscow Communist rank and file all over the world, who cheerfully subscribed to every foolish lie and delusion about the workers' homeland; and they could not see that their own non-simpleton naïveté was almost equally impressive. And now, in Paris, for those brave and hyper-educated Maos suddenly to pick up Solzhenitsyn's enormous tomes about the Gulag prison system and to read about the camps of Kolyma and all the rest, to discover that camps in the Soviet Union were not a tumor or growth on the Communist system but were integral to it, to learn at last that Marxist-Leninist societies could survive only through a consistent threat of terror, to understand finally that Communism and totalitarianism were inseparable—that was a new experience. The virtuosos of social indignation discovered how preposterously deaf had been their own indignation. And now, suddenly, they turned Solzhenitsyn's pages, and in a flash recognized the moral disaster that stood at the heart of their own movement. And they felt shaken.

Among the Maos who looked up from Solzhenitsyn's pages as if waking from the reverie of a lifetime, the most prominent was Bernard-Henri Lévy—never much of a Mao, actually, and certainly not a hero of 1968, yet a man with a decided talent for television appearances and book promotion, also a knack for coining a phrase like "the New Philosophy" to describe his new thinking and that of his comrades. In the mid-seventies Lévy's was the principal name that wafted westward to the United States. But Glucksmann, a decade older than Lévy and a decade better-educated, was more serious and more eloquent. He published two books in rapid order—in 1975 *The Cook and the Man-Eater* (in French, *La cuisinière et le mangeur d'hommes*) and in 1977 *The Master Thinkers* (which has been his only book to come out in English translation). In the English-speaking world, his political turn-about never did make much of an impact, except indirectly. He gained the reputation of a left-wing zealot who, in the grand old tradition, had become a right-wing zealot and therefore was not worth reading. Yet that reputation was never really deserved. In his books of the mid-seventies Glucksmann raised two questions about the basic principles of the radical left, and, in hunting for answers, he followed his natural instinct, which was to turn even further left, not to the right.

He asked: How should we understand the Soviet Union, given everything that Solzhenitsyn has revealed? And he looked for analyses from the most theoretical-minded of the several small groups of the radical left that had always declined to accept the theory of two Communisms. That was the circle of post-Trotskyists in France. The tradition of left-wing anti-Stalinism that, in the United States, was associated with the radical offshoots of Max Shachtman's brand of American Trotskyism (the Detroit group around C. L. R. James and *Facing Reality*, the New York group around *New Politics* magazine, and above all the New Leftists of Philadelphia Solidarity) was represented, in France, by the group around Cornelius Castoriadis and Claude Lefort. These were the lonely anti-Sartreans of the Paris left. They had published *Socialisme ou barbarie* magazine and a few successor journals ever since 1949 and, from time to time, had even succeeded in finding readers. The Situationists of the 1960s were indebted to *Socialisme ou barbarie*, and so, too, were the student anarchists, Cohn-Bendit included (not always consistently). Because of their very clear understanding of Communism, combined with their desire for a libertarian revolution, the *Socialisme ou barbarie* group had always been the purest of the pure on the radical left. They were the avant-garde's avant-garde. And yet, brilliant though they were, their influence had never managed to penetrate very far beyond the little world of the libertarian ultra-leftists.

Why was that? One reason was a quality of weird archaicism in their analyses. They had begun as Trotskyists and orthodox Marxists (as they understood orthodoxy), and they had never entirely gotten over the need to proclaim themselves truer and more orthodox than everyone else. They formally rejected Marxism in 1963, and even then they stuck by the orthodox instincts. Yet they were serious about trying to understand the Soviet Union. And so they took the old language about factories and exploitation and did their best to apply it to the twentieth-century world of totalitarian prison camps and forced labor, which obliged them to twist and stretch the ancient socialist vocabulary into tortuous new meanings. Soviet Communism, due to the relation between workers and managers, was capitalism, except worse—in Castoriadis's formula, a "total and totalitarian bureaucratic capitalism." What a phrase! The satirical passages in *1984* where Orwell makes fun of Goldstein and his underground anti–Big Brother *Theory and Practice of Oligarchical Collectivism* were aimed at writers like Castoriadis and the *Socialisme ou barbarie* group, and they deserved the attack, strictly from a prose stylist's point of view.

Even so, there was a virtue in what the *Socialisme ou barbarie* writers managed to achieve, which any left-winger who took the trouble to decipher their texts was free to discover. Their argument was a refutation of the theory of the two Communisms. By denying that Soviet Communism was in any respect an advance over capitalism, by defining Communism as, in fact, a backward step, Castoriadis and his comrades allowed themselves to look Soviet reality in the face, to see the camps and not blink their eyes, and to feel for Communism's victims the indignant solidarity that is supposed to be leftism's reason for being. That was their achievement, and a very great achievement it was, in its time and place. Their approach now became Glucksmann's, too, wooden language and all, mixed with a few additional observations about mass incarceration that he derived from Foucault. The book that

Glucksmann wrote about Solzhenitsyn, *The Cook and the Man-Eater*, expressed everything that he had so suddenly learned. It was a classic statement of left-wing anti-Communism, post-Trotskyist style—ferocious, rigorous, morally deft. In order to demonstrate the continuity of impulse between his 1968-era leftism and his new anti-Communist clarity, he made a point of beginning his book with a quotation from George Jackson, the prison martyr of the California Black Panthers. He wanted everyone to see the clench of his left-wing fist. Yet for all the revolutionary gestures and the ostentatious appeals to left-wing orthodoxy, Glucksmann's *The Cook and the Man-Eater*, by clearing away certain confusions about Soviet society, allowed him, in *The Master Thinkers*, to ask a further question, which touched on the orthodoxy itself.

He wanted to know: How did totalitarianism come about in the first place? What were its roots? Again he turned to the extreme left for an answer—this time, to his own *Discourse of War* and his criticism of Kojéve and Hegel. Only now he updated his own argument by rendering it harsher and more confident. His old delusion about Mao was gone, of course. Now he had no difficulty in recognizing that Maoism was itself a branch of the Western cult of death. Hegel had always been his *bête noire* among philosophers, but now he looked at Fichte, Marx, and Nietzsche, too—the great German philosophers of the late eighteenth and nineteenth centuries—and saw them in the same terrifying light. They were the philosophers of total domination, of universal mastery, the state, and death. They were the creators of totalitarianism. They had invented the idea in the eighteenth and nineteenth centuries, and the twentieth century had merely put their notions into effect.

Fascism, Nazism, Communism, and, for that matter, the American bombing raids over Japanese cities (and other crimes of the Western countries) were their legacy. As analyses of totalitarianism go, Glucksmann's argument was fairly extravagant—which is not necessarily a flaw, for hasn't totalitarianism been extravagant? But the argument was, in any case, true to his own experience. A certain kind of personality arose in the course of the rebellions of 1968, at any rate in the Western countries—the impudent heckler, the obnoxious respecter of no one at all, the person who makes fun of every sacred object in sight, who goes too far. Among the popular student leaders, Cohn-Bendit displayed that personality in France, Abbie Hoffman in America. Among the serious novelists who came out of the student movement, the English language author of *The Satanic Verses* made that kind of personality a worldwide scandal. And Glucksmann was the philosophical version. He was outrageous. He treated Fichte, Hegel, Marx, and Nietzsche like lunatics. "The Four Aces," he called them. He was gleeful. Contempt gave spring to his step.

But the peculiar quality in his obnoxiousness and railery, the trait that made him different from Cohn-Bendit or Hoffman or for that matter from Salman Rushdie, was an irresistible impulse to rail at himself, too. In *The Gulag Archipelago* Solzhenitsyn explains how, in his younger days as a Soviet army officer, he was a loyal Communist and a follower of Stalin— and only gradually did he come to realize the insanity of his own beliefs and the process of insanity that had overtaken Russia and the Soviet Union as a whole. That was exactly how Glucksmann viewed himself. He looked back, and he realized that he, too, in his Maoist days, had been out of his mind, had been fully prepared to sink society into a pit of blood, to the cheers of the crowd and of France's greatest intellects. And now nothing could prevent the old journalist from the Maoist *J'Accuse* from accusing himself. He wrote about "the Russia in our heads," meaning his own head. He was like a street rioter who suddenly realizes that, if anybody's house deserves to be burned down, it is his own house.

You could worry about Glucksmann. In the middle 1980s, when the anti-nuclear movement was growing all over Europe and the United States, he wrote another book about nuclear strategy, this time defending the American policy against the Soviets (which brought down on his head a round of left-wing denunciations, including one from me), and his defense bubbled with enthusiasm for the virtues of nuclear weaponry (even if he did, at least, draw a line at President Reagan's Star Wars). He wrote a polemic against the French Socialist Party and called it *Stupidity* (in French, *La Bêtise*) because of the party's lingering sentimentality for Marxist tradition. The notion that his own political foolishness in the past ought to have tempered his style, that modesty might have suited him better, never seemed to enter his mind.

Still, in those responses of his to Solzhenitsyn and to the collapse of the Proletarian Left, Glucksmann had made a genuine contribution to political understanding. The truism that every generation has to rediscover anti-Communism for itself applied as much to the '68ers as to anyone who had come earlier; and among the people who made the rediscovery for the generation that had fought on the student barricades all over the world, Glucksmann, it seems to me, was the leading figure, at least in the West. His mishmash of anti-Kojèvianism, Solzhenitsyn, post-Trotskyism, Foucault, and self-accusation somehow cohered into a loudspeaker, and the true nature of Communism went beaming outward to the French intellectual left, and from France outward to the world (even if the English-speaking radical public was notoriously slow in hearing the news). And now that two decades have gone by, it's impossible to deny the results.

When we think of Communism, we are likely to imagine an imperial system with Moscow at its historic center and a few provincial centers like Havana and Beijing. But straight into the 1970s, Communism was also something of an intellectual system. The pinnacle of that system consisted of one or two thinkers who were, in a formal sense, Communists themselves. But mostly it consisted of left-wingers who were not themselves Communists but kept finding arguments for conferring a moral superiority on the Communist world, Soviet or non-Soviet. The capital of *that* sector of the worldwide Communist system, the intellectual capital, was neither Moscow nor any other city under Communist rule. It was the city of Kojève, Sartre, and Althusser. In Latin America, for instance, the Communist and near-Communist political theory that proved so influential during the whole era from the 1960s through the 1980s came from Paris, more than from any other place, except possibly Havana.

The same had always been true in large parts of Africa and East Asia, especially wherever the French empire had once ruled. And if the "Solzhenitsyn effect" of the mid-1970s in Paris proved to be enormous, that was because the entire younger generation among the French writers and thinkers who might otherwise have carried on in the old way, the rebels from 1968, converted *en masse* from one or another variety of Communism or pro-Communism to outright hostility. Neither Glucksmann nor any of his fellow thinkers from the French generation of '68 ever managed to produce a genuine classic of anti-Communism—something that could be compared, say, with the writings of Orwell or even with those of Lefort and Castoriadis. In Glucksmann's books the pomposity, woolliness, high-handedness, ungraciousness (especially toward other writers whose ideas he had borrowed), and generally the air of excess were all too easy to discover. This is a man with flaws! Yet the damage to Communism had been done. If people like André Glucksmann were not going to become the new generation of pro-Communist philosophers in Paris, Communism was going to find itself with no defenders at all. Actually, it was not only the younger generation who suddenly worked their way to a new attitude. Among the writers who were a few years older, Foucault, happy to discover how useful were his own writings for making sense of Communist totalitarianism, made a point of applauding in print Glucksmann's book about totalitarianism and its philosophical origins, *The Master Thinkers*. Sartre, older yet, found no difficulty in appearing publicly with Glucksmann, together with Aron, Glucksmann's old professor (whose unfashionable anti-Communism now turned out to have been right all along), on behalf of the Vietnamese boat people. In the capital of the left-wing intellectual world, the philosophical collapse was total. You could almost say that, in regard to Communism's ultimate worldwide collapse, Paris in the mid-1970s was the first to fall. The Berlin Wall came later.

The argument about history that Glucksmann made in 1989 at the Frankfurt Peace Prize ceremony for Havel, then expanded in *The 11th Commandment*, came out of those experiences with Maoism and *The Gulag Archipelago*. By 1989 Glucksmann no longer took any interest in the left-wing categories of analysis. But his feeling of having made an error in his own life, his horror at having discovered his own capability for supposing himself to be a man of splendid intentions while in reality trying to lead a totalitarian revolution in France, his lack of faith in anything like progress or the reliability of reason, his antipathy to

Kojève and Hegel and the philosophical principles of mastery—all of that was alive and crackly with emotion. And from those many vivid feelings of chagrin and disillusionment he now extracted quite a bit.

He took the story of his own early Maoist fanaticism and his later awakening to skepticism and doubt and projected the entire experience onto the history of Western civilization and philosophy, beginning with the Ancient Greeks. Man has always consoled himself with a harmonious belief in solid certainties. Then came the Greeks, who began to question and doubt. That was a forward step. Questioning led to reason. But because the forward step broke up the old consolations of faith and dogma, reason proved to be a terrifying thing. And so the Greeks rebelled against their own best achievement and tried to reestablish the old reassuring faith in solid certainty. There is no chaos, said Plato, because everything is One. There are no inner contradictions; everything resolves. There is no basis for doubt, except temporarily. And from Plato onward, the war between skepticism and certainty has been unceasing. It is the war that lies at the heart of Western civilization. As theories go, this notion of Glucksmann's is perhaps less than original. The heart of the argument was laid out long ago in Karl Popper's classic of anti-totalitarianism, *The Open Society and Its Enemies* (1943). But, then, Glucksmann's talent has always leaned more toward drama than toward innovation, and the picture he painted in *The 11th Commandment* succeeds in being dramatic in the extreme.

As he sees it, the history of the twentieth century has been nothing other than the ancient war between skepticism and certainty, only now in an apocalyptic modern version, spread to the four corners of the globe. The old Western certainties of the nineteenth century—the conviction of European superiority and of Europe's mission to civilize the world—blew up during the First World War, and the blowup was apocalyptic because it was inexplicable. Even so, Europe's power and influence went on expanding, and cultures around the world that had always been certain of their own non-European convictions were suddenly consumed with doubt, which was terrifying. The non-European cultures could no longer believe in their own traditional doctrines, and they could not believe in Europe, either. And in response, one revolutionary movement after another rose up to do the impossible and to reestablish the reign of certainty. The revolutionary movements got their start in Europe itself during the First World War. But they spread everywhere. They took the form originally of Soviet Marxism. But they were protean.

Glucksmann's term for those revolutionary movements is very curious. He calls them "fundamentalist" because, in his view, the fundamentalist religious groups provided the original model—even for the Marxist movements that have always viewed themselves as atheist. The basic concept comes out of the Book of the Apocalypse. It is the idea that evil is right now at its greatest height, and right now the whores of Babylon are fanning a fire that will consume every evil thing in vast metaphysical calamities, and soon enough the Kingdom of God will be established. Glucksmann doesn't mean to say that every one of the revolutionary or totalitarian movements of the twentieth century has shown an interest in biblical references or in the exact terminology of the Book of the Apocalypse. But from one twentieth-century movement to another, several of the central ideas have remained curiously linked to the biblical text, with only slight variations.

Each of the revolutionary movements has posited the notion of a single evil—a mono-evil—that is destroying the purity and unity of virtue. The mono-evil might consist of a sinister force that is penetrating our previously glorious society from within. It might be "the Jews" (in the imagination of the Nazis) or "the Zionists" (in the imagination of the Arab nationalists, the Islamic fundamentalists, and the Eastern Bloc Communists during their anti-Zionist phase). Alternatively, the mono-evil might be "cultural imperialism" (in the imagination of the anti-imperialists and the anti-Americans). The mono-evil encircles and humiliates us from outside, perhaps in the form of "capitalist encirclement" (in the case of the Soviet Union), or in the form of "imperialism" (in the case of the Third World revolutionaries), or in the form of Soviet and American "pincers" (in the image proposed by Heidegger to describe the danger posed to Nazi Germany).

Each of the twentieth-century revolutionary movements has pointed to a messiah class that will rescue mankind. The messiah class embodies the virtues that are currently being destroyed by the mono-evil, but that will ultimately triumph. The messiah class might be the Russian masses and the world proletariat (in the case of the Stalinists). Or it might be the German *volk* and the "metaphysical people" (in the case of Nazis like Heidegger). It might be the peasantry of Asia, Africa, and Latin America (in the case of the Third World revolutionaries), or the people of the Koran (in the case of the Islamic fundamentalists). But in each case the messiah class promises to create a new society dramatically different from the world of the present.

The new society might be a "Kingdom of God" pictured from the past, such as the Golden Age of Islam (for the Islamic fundamentalists), or the Spain of Christ the King (for the Spanish and Latin American ultra-rightists). Alternatively, the Kingdom might be pictured in the future, such as the reign of the proletariat (for the Marxists). The Kingdom might go under different names: Third Reich, Third International, Third World. But no matter its name or its home in the past or the future, once the revolutionary forces and the messiah class have succeeded in bringing the Kingdom into being, all of human life will undergo a change. The fractures of modern society will at last heal over. The organic solidarity of the masses and the elite will be achieved. Culture will form a single granite wall of defense against the dislocations of modern life. And behind the impenetrable wall, in the organically unified society of the Kingdom, a reign of purity will at last get under way.

Each of the revolutionary movements has described the purity in its own way. It might be the purity of labor untouched by the speculative parasitism of bourgeois exploiters (for the Communists). It might be the genetic purity of the master race (for the Nazis). It might be the purity of the sacred word (for the Islamic fundamentalists) or the purity of the national culture (for revolutionary nationalists). And thus purified, unified, and defended, the Kingdom is bound to sweep away the confusions that come from doubt. It is going to liberate us from the terrors of the free circulation of things and ideas. It is going to reestablish the One—though not right now. For there is always a grim part of the message, which announces an apocalyptic struggle to the death. There is going to be a war that will be physical and metaphysical at the same time—the war that Glucksmann regards as nothing more than a spiraling global extension of the horrific war that broke out in Europe in 1914. It is the frankly irrational war, the war that in the past was led by supermen (Hitler, Stalin, Pol Pot, Fidel, Saddam) who proved irresistibly charismatic precisely because they were visibly mad and therefore had a touch of the divine. In the "fundamentalist" vision, the war is going to destroy conventional morality, and it is going to carry us across the gulf that separates the presently existing world of absolute evil from the Kingdom of absolute good.

The collapse of the Berlin Wall in 1989 was a grand

moment, but if Glucksmann's picture of revolutionary fundamentalism has any merit, why should we suppose that even the grandest of moments will bring about an end to crazed and bloody rebellions against the threat that is posed by skepticism and doubt? The philosophers of the nineteenth century, the prophets of total mastery, kept looking for the world's great struggles to arrive at a happy resolution. They were always trying to say, each philosopher in his own fashion, that evil doesn't actually exist—that evil is somehow an aspect of good, and everything finally adds up to One, and the endless struggles against evil will someday achieve the desired result, and order and certainty will at last be achieved. Even Nietzsche, with his idea that evil possesses a certain beauty, found a way of saying that evil is ultimately good, if only aesthetically. But that is not Glucksmann's opinion.

No, the One is fantasy, and evil is evil, and not even beauty emerges from it. To the optimistic souls who, at the end of the cold war, hoped that the atrocities of the twentieth century would at last yield to a world of peace, he says: "Not a chance!" There will be no kind of unity or universal agreement about what constitutes the good society. For the struggle between certainty and doubt that has taken such apocalyptic forms in the twentieth century lies at the heart of Western civilization, and with the spread of Western civilization around the world, the struggle is never going to be resolved. It is eternal. It is the unstoppable uproar that arises from the terrifying news, which is Western civilization's gift to the world, that nothing is certain and people are vulnerable and free and are at the mercy of their own decisions. In Glucksmann's interpretation, huge historical events may well take place, and from time to time everything around the world may well get rearranged, and new colors and patterns will emerge. But the new colors and patterns will never never result in a lasting order or arrive at a final destination.

What can we learn, then, from the immense events that began sweeping halfway across the world in 1989—these revolutionary events to which Glucksmann himself, from his writing desk in Paris with the volumes of Solzhenitsyn piled before him, had made a distinctive contribution? The lessons that he proposes are humble in the extreme—even if his way of describing these lessons is characteristically grandiose. He wants us to construct a new humanism, wholly unlike the old nineteenth-century humanism that wished to submit all peoples to the same idea of the good and the true. The new humanism should begin by recognizing what is inhuman in man. The eleventh commandment that Glucksmann wants to append to the biblical ten is this: to know thyself as capable of being a monster— even if that means saying (and here the imp of excess wraps its fingers around Glucksmann's neck one more time), "Hitler c'est moi."

Glucksmann is not in the reassurance business. He wants us to feel horrified not only by the things we have seen in this worst of centuries but above all by what we have observed in ourselves. He wants his readers to return to the dark idea of sinful humanity that lies at the origin of certain liberal ideas about limited government. He proposes that mankind try to construct a new kind of solidarity: not a solidarity based on positive principles, but a solidarity (here he credits the Czech dissident philosopher Jan Patočka) of the "shaken." He wants a solidarity designed to protect people from evil, but not to lead them to the good. A solidarity without illusions; a solidarity of mutual deterrence; a cold brotherhood of man to follow the cold war.

Glucksmann's picture of the twentieth century as a series of revolutionary fundamentalist movements spiraling outward from the calamity of the First World War is his own fanciful notion. But nothing is especially new about the lessons that he wishes to draw. The chilly humility that he advocates, his refusal to see any sort of forward-marching direction in history or any kind of meaningful unity in world events, his antipathy for Hegel and Marx—these are main pillars of modern liberal thinking, one brand of it, everywhere in the world. I could go around my bookshelf plucking volumes from one writer and another to find variations on the same ideas. Here is Isaiah Berlin in England. Berlin asks, "Can anybody in the twentieth century—certainly one of the worst centuries of human history—really believe in uninterrupted human progress? Or general progress as such?" Here is the critic Nicola Chiaromonte from Italy. Chiaromonte warns against the idea "that the course of things must have a single meaning or that events can be contained in a single system."

Here is Richard Rorty in the United States. On the topic of lessons to be learned from the overthrow of Communism, Rorty advises us to pull back from any kind of grand-scale theorizing at all: "I hope we have reached a time when we can finally get rid of the conviction common to Plato and Marx, the conviction that there just *must* be large theoretical ways of finding out how to end injustice. I hope we can learn to get along without the conviction that there is something deep—such as the human soul, or human nature, or the will of God, or the shape of history—which provides a subject matter for grand, politically useful theory." Rorty warns against anything that might serve as a "successor to Marxism"—"a large theoretical framework that will enable us to put our society in an excitingly new context." He wants a more "banal" language of political theory.

These writers wish to see a bit of intellectual teetotaling. No more inebriating theories—not even one, thank you! Drunken highs were the philosophy of the nineteenth century, and drunkenness-turned-ugly was the totalitarianism of the mid-twentieth, and the intention of the late-twentieth-century anti-Hegel-and-Marx wary liberals is to remain clear-eyed, soft-voiced, precise, modest, sharp, sober. The idea is to keep ourselves cool and contained—though nothing is cool or contained about the experiences that lie behind the modest admonitions. For these are the thinkers who have never gotten over the shock of watching how Marxism, mankind's liberator, turned out to be a plague. The passion in their call for dispas-

sion comes—as I imagine it—from the kind of bio-
graphical fact that is fairly widespread in a century in
which an Isaiah Berlin is a refugee from Bolshevism,
and a Chiaromonte was a participant on the losing
side of the Spanish Civil War, and a Rorty (whose
father was an old comrade-in-arms of Sidney Hook)
grew up in the perfectly peaceful but entirely bitter
ideological wars of the New York left-wing intellectuals.

Glucksmann's version of the wary liberal position
has an odd quality, due to the grandiose way he likes
to posture and the lack of interest he shows in the
pesky little details of liberal political theory. Yet nothing about him is odd from the perspective of his own
generation. He is the model of the besotted revolutionary who sobers up with a look of horror on his face.
He is the looniness of 1968 repentant. The autobio-
graphical in philosophy is always powerful, and the
kaleidoscope theory about the end of the cold war has
power in Glucksmann's version because you can turn
his pages and hear the echoes of an earlier revolutionary
moment, not so long ago, when a brilliant young
philosopher could go tramping through the halls of
a first-rate university in a democratic country leading
a mob called the Base Committee for the Abolition
of Wage Labor and the Destruction of the University
and waving *Quotations from Chairman Mao*.

III

Francis Fukuyama's theory is the opposite in every respect—yet (a very odd point) contains nothing that Glucksmann had not already thought to denounce, down to the tiniest particulars. Glucksmann had begun his career back in the 1960s by expressing horror at the foreign policy analysts of America's RAND Corporation and by attributing to those power-mad strategists a Kojève-and-Hegel style of thinking, which might have seemed fairly implausible to anyone familiar with the habits of American political thought. Yet in 1989 here came Fukuyama, the man from RAND (not to mention the State Department), suddenly proclaiming a doctrine based on, of all people, Hegel, in the specific interpretation made by Alexandre Kojève. As if straight from Glucksmann's fervid Maoist imaginings!

Exactly how the doctrines of Kojève's violent left-wing Hegelianism ended up circulating among the conservative theorists of the Reagan and Bush administrations is a curious story. Kojève achieved his original influence back in the 1930s by teaching his seminar and cultivating friendships with his students and other thinkers, which was adequate for spreading his ideas within the hermetic world of Paris, but not beyond. In the United States he had no influence at all, and was not likely to develop any. Americans who wanted to look into Hegel could read Hook's *From Hegel to Marx* (1937), or Marcuse's *Reason and Revolution: Hegel and the Rise of Social Theory* (1941), which were, from a literary point of view, superior to anything Kojève had done (though not as precise and detailed).

Still, rumors of Kojève's brilliance did eventually cross the Atlantic. One of Kojève's friends from his days in Germany was the conservative philosopher Leo Strauss, who, like Marcuse, fled to the United States in the 1930s. Strauss taught in New York, then in Chicago, and established what is sometimes called, though not by its adherents, an academic cult: the "Straussians," conservative elitists one and all. (Strauss himself was happy to embrace the word "sect.") To be a Straussian was to be instructed in the wisdom of superior intellects from Ancient Greece to the modern age. And among those intellects was, as it turned out, the Marxist philosopher who happened to have been Strauss's personal friend: Alexandre Kojève. In that curious manner, Kojève's reputation, which in France flourished among the left-wing intellectuals, in America came to flourish, in a more modest way, among the conservative thinkers who studied under Strauss at the University of Chicago.

One of those thinkers was Allan Bloom, who became famous during the Reagan years as the author of an idiosyncratic manifesto in favor of intellectual elitism, *The Closing of the American Mind*. Bloom was full of enthusiasm for Kojève. A footnote on page 222 in Bloom's book refers rather dogmatically to "Alexandre Kojève, the most intelligent Marxist of the twentieth century," though without any remarks to explain the superlative. It was Bloom who, back in 1968 (the year that Kojève died), finally succeeded in presenting Kojève to American readers. Bloom brought out an English-language edition of Kojève's lectures, *Introduction to the Reading of Hegel: Lectures on the Phenomenology of Spirit*, which carried the elaborate byline, "By Alexandre Kojève, Assembled by Raymond Queneau, Edited by Allan Bloom, Translated by James H. Nichols, Jr." The book was Bloom's contribution, strictly pedagogical in purpose, to the student insurgencies of the '68 era. Bloom seems to have reasoned that, if the students were going to insist on being left-wing, let them be left-wing intelligently.

Thanks to him, American university students in the golden age of academic Marxism during the 1970s and '80s sat down to study their Hegel by reading the analyses of Alexandre Kojève. Which was not necessarily a joy. *Introduction to the Reading of Hegel* is a guide to Hegel without being any less convoluted than Hegel. Little diagrams with circles and arrows, exactly like the diagrams in Uncle Kandinsky's essays on art, indicate the differences between Plato, Aristotle, Spinoza, and Hegel. Italics and capital letters give a pop-eyed Germanic tone to the prose. Due to one strange Kojèvian trait and another, the academic left in the American universities never did come to agree with Bloom about Kojève being "the most intelligent Marxist of the twentieth century." Bloom must have been heartbroken. And yet, because chance plays as great a role in the history of ideas as in any other kind of history, *Introduction to the Reading of Hegel* by Alexandre Kojève did attract one energetic young disciple—who was none other than Professor Bloom's undergraduate protégé at Cornell in the early seventies, Francis Fukuyama.

Student leftism—SDS, anti-war organizing, draft resistance, Black Power—was strong at Cornell, and Fukuyama, although never any kind of militant, did not entirely escape its influence. The students held anti-war demonstrations, and his was a face in the crowd. When he finished at Cornell he went on to study literary deconstruction, which (in those years especially) gave off a pungent odor of the left, "in the tradition of a certain Marxism," as Jacques Derrida puts it. Fukuyama spent half a year in Paris, and every week he went to the École normale supérieure on the rue d'Ulm and audited a seminar with Derrida himself. Then it was off to New Haven, where he continued his studies with Derrida's disciple, Paul de Man.

Fukuyama seemed to be destined for a comfortable place within the academic left. Yet all the while he felt the lingering conservative influence of Bloom (and, through Bloom, Strauss), and the further he progressed in his studies with Derrida and de Man, the more the influence lingered, until left-wing deconstruction and Yale were at last behind him, and he was a neoconservative student of political theory at Harvard. From there, through the network of Strauss's disciples, Fukuyama moved on to the RAND Corporation, to the State Department under Reagan and Bush, to his position as deputy director of the department's Policy Planning Staff, then back to RAND. And he returned to his old student interest in Kojève and Hegel—now in a spirit that owed everything to Bloom and Strauss and nothing to Derrida and the deconstructionist breezes of the academic left.

Exactly what does Kojève teach? The violent vision of mankind, the appreciation of the irrational in human events, these Kojèvian ideas against which Glucksmann has so fervently rebelled—what do they add up to? For that matter, what does Hegel teach? The argument that Glucksmann makes about Hegel and Kojève as the philosophers of totalitarianism is perfectly coherent and plausible, in its own terms. But to Fukuyama the lesson was something else. Hegel lived in Germany from 1770 to 1831, which meant that, when the French Revolution broke out, he was young and in school and eager to put together his own ideas. The hopes that were raised by the revolution—the expectation that feudal superstition and oppression could be overthrown everywhere, that ordinary people could become educated and rational and control their own destiny, that man could be free— were Hegel's, too. The French conquered Germany, and Hegel welcomed the invasion because he saw in it the spread of revolutionary principles and the overthrow of German feudalism and cultural backwardness. The philosophy that he developed was intended to express those ideas—to show that human history had begun in darkness and was fitfully advancing to the light, that freedom (as he defined it) was going to be the end result.

Kojève's gloss on these ideas emphasizes a single section, "Lordship and Bondage," from Chapter IV ("The True Nature of Self-Certainty") of Hegel's *Phe-*

nomenology. But instead of describing the gloss, I will describe the one aspect that so strongly guided Fukuyama when he sat down to write *The End of History and the Last Man.* Kojève's gloss proposes, in good Hegelian style, a theory of history and human nature—which is to say, proposes everything that the wary liberals have warned us against. According to this theory, human nature has three dynamic components.

These are (1) Desire, which leads man to be active in the world instead of just sitting under his palm tree. (2) Reason, which leads man to figure out ever more clever ways to fulfill his Desire. And (3) a quality that cannot be named in ordinary English but was known in Ancient Greek as "Thymos," meaning, roughly, "spiritedness" (which is an idea that Fukuyama took more from Strauss than from Kojève). Thymos craves prestige, which is to say, recognition from other people. Animals experience desire, but only man (according to this theory, anyway) craves recognition from his fellows. Just as man must be willing to risk death to satisfy his animal needs, he must be willing to risk death for prestige, too. Taken together, these three components of human nature—Desire, Reason, Thymos—account for all the main developments of history.

Kojève explains this by invoking a myth about the origins of society, as found in Hegel's discussion of "Lordship and Bondage." In the mists of prehistoric time, according to the myth, Thymotic impulses led the earliest people to lift themselves above the animals by engaging in a primal battle to the death with one another for pure prestige—an irrational battle, rooted in instinct, aimed at nothing more than winning recognition from one another. The winners became masters, and the losers, because they feared death more than slavery, sank to their knees and became slaves. Such were the beginnings of society (and this emphasis on the murderous violence and irrational impulses at society's core is exactly what has so horrified Glucksmann). The society that resulted was fatefully unstable, however. The masters wanted recognition and prestige, and achieved it; but the version they achieved came merely from slaves and was therefore never satisfactory. The slaves enjoyed no satisfaction at all. Yet in going about their masters' bidding, the slaves applied Reason to make their own work easier and more efficient. The slaves developed technologies. They worked improvements on the material world. In these ways the slaves, too, in spite of everything, began to achieve a more than animal existence. Thus both masters and slaves ended up partly animal, partly human, though in different ways.

The situation of the masters was a dead end, since all they could do was issue orders and continue to risk death to maintain their own status. Not so with the slaves. In the course of transforming nature and inventing technologies, the slaves began to conceive the idea that they, too, ought to enjoy freedom and in that way become fully human. So the slaves began to construct a series of doctrines to explain the difference between their real-life condition and the freedom that they desired. The first of these doctrines, back in

Roman times, was Stoicism, which told people to ignore the real world of slavery and unhappiness. One of the next doctrines was Christianity, which acknowledges that real-life slavery actually exists, but insists that freedom also exists—in the world to come. Next came a series of efforts to take Christianity's promise of freedom and make it a reality in the unheavenly world of the here and now.

According to Kojève's Hegel, man becomes fully human only when the qualities that Christianity imputes to heaven have been brought to earth and individuals enjoy the recognition of other individuals in an atmosphere of freedom and rational knowledge. To be fully human means living in a society of reason and mutual esteem, without masters or slaves—a society of creativity, individual freedom, and (most of all) informed self-awareness. Kojève, summarizing Hegel, describes such a society as a "universal and homogeneous state." The state would be universal because it would make no distinction between degrees of humanness among its citizens. Everyone would enjoy equal rights. It would be homogeneous because no one would have a motive to start a revolution or do anything else to make the system fall apart. And because man would at last have achieved his full potential in such a society, the history of progress toward freedom and toward human understanding would have reached a climactic high point: the End of History.

Exactly what would this stable and satisfying system look like, if ever it came to exist? Its political institutions, for instance—what shape would they have? Here the entire philosophical system plunges into deepest murk, which can be explained with a glance at the French Revolution and (by way of comparison) at the French Revolution's counterpart in America. The revolutions in France and America were both intended to achieve freedom and justice for all of mankind. But while the American Revolution defined itself in terms of specific political ideas (democratic representation, constitutional law, and so forth), the French Revolution kept turning from one political idea to another, now republican, now dictatorial, now monarchist, without settling on any single one. And so Hegel, too, with France and Europe as his model, kept looking this way and that for the perfect political system.

He knew that freedom presupposes rights for all, guaranteed by law. But he could never decide what kind of institutions that would require. Democracy as such never appealed to him. Democracy, to Hegel, meant something like Ancient Athens, which was a good place for civilization to begin but could never accommodate a modern society (mostly because democracy in its Athenian version had no room for individualism). He preferred some sort of rigorous law-abiding authoritarianism. In 1806, when he was finishing his *Phenomenology of Spirit*, he happened to see Napoleon himself, the hero in person, ride by, fresh from having defeated German feudalism, and Hegel concluded that here, in the revolutionary military dictatorship of Napoleon Bonaparte, was the perfect state. Then Napoleon was defeated and the philosopher imagined that a law-abiding authoritarian state ruled by a constitutional monarch was the best of all systems. Or maybe questions of political structure were secondary, and man's realm of freedom could best be found in the zone of pure thought. That was the philosopher's deepest idea.

Hegel's disciples have not been much more helpful on the proper way to achieve human freedom. Kojève, as a weird sort of Marxist, pointed to a paragraph in Marx's *Capital*, Volume III, where Marx explains that during all of history, man labored in the Realm of Necessity. But once industry's progress has reduced the workday and societies have learned to master economics and people no longer have to stand around getting battered by economic changes the way they get battered by hurricanes, man will enter the Realm of Freedom—and, in Kojève's eyes, *that* is the meaning of a universal and homogeneous state. But Marx's explanation is no more useful than Hegel's, apart from reminding us that freedom has an economic component. For what kind of institutions would the Realm of Freedom require? As a "strict Stalinist," Kojève believed that Stalin's Soviet Union was the model, and the rest of the world was destined to follow the Soviet example, and freedom, when it arrived, would speak Russian.

Then again, there was a playfulness in Kojève, a flexibility that could be either amusingly nutty or slightly sinister, which allowed him to reinterpret his Stalinism in all kinds of paradoxical and ironic ways. Maybe the universal and homogeneous state at the end of history wasn't going to be Communism in the Soviet style at all. Maybe the Western states would succeed in mastering market economics, presumably through such mechanisms as the GATT treaty on which Kojève himself labored so diligently, and prosperity would result; and, therefore, the rational non-Communist countries of the West, taken as a group, would become the world's truest example of a universal and homogeneous state. Or maybe the end of history had already been achieved. Maybe it could be found in the most powerful of the Western states, and the true universal and homogeneous state was, of all places, the United States of America, otherwise known (to conventional Marxists) as the seat of world imperialism.

A very strange passage in Kojève's book on Hegel lays out the analysis. "From a certain point of view, the United States has already attained the final stage of Marx's 'communism,'" Kojève writes, with the explanation that, in America, due to the national wealth and the democratic system, class divisions have ceased being much of a problem and people no longer have to work too hard. A nice idea! Was he serious about that? You never know with Kojève. That tone of his is supremely whimsical. Maybe the United States was not the end of history at all. Maybe the truest end is snobbery as practiced in . . . Japan! You could imagine Kojève waving his finger in front of a classroom of astonished French students, as if to tell them: Never mind about the real-life meanings of these Hegelian ruminations, these are strictly philosophical concepts, intended to bear on nitty-gritty practicalities only in the vaguest of ways.

Still, the American possibility was one of Kojève's ideas. It's easy to imagine that Hegel, on four days out of five, would have been horrified. Hegel wrote about the United States a number of times, and most of what he wrote was dismissive in the extreme. America in his eyes was a place of biological stuntedness, religious insanity, and uncontrolled lust for wealth. And yet, in a couple of enigmatic passages, Hegel, too, played with the American possibility. America, he wrote (in his lectures on the philosophy of history), was "the country of the future. . . . It is up to America to abandon the ground on which world history has hitherto been erected." In another passage (in his study of aesthetics): "If one wants to have an idea of what may be the epic poems of the future, one has only to think of the possible victory of American rationalism, living and universal, over the European peoples . . . If one wishes to escape the European prison, it can only be in the direction of America." Probably most of the people who have sat down to read Hegel over the years have shrugged off those passages as so much idle speculation.

Yet with Hegel, due to his profundity or due to his famous impenetrability (or due to both), it has always been possible to fill out his strange formulas with ingenious explanations of your own. You could argue that Hegel on the surface level said many a strange thing and was never able to explain his political ideas adequately; but what he really meant in his theory of freedom and history was to praise liberal democracy, which is the only system in which individual freedom and mutual self-recognition can have any reality. Hegel might have used some not-very-liberal words from time to time; but anything other than liberal democratic meanings would be at odds with his larger theory. And if that interpretation has any validity, the pinnacle of Hegel's idea about history and freedom would have to reside in liberal democracy's original home, the United States of America, freedom's golden cupola. Those enigmatic phrases about "the country of the future" and "the possible victory of American rationalism" must, in that case, lie not on the margins of Hegelian philosophy but at its center—regardless of what Hegel managed to say in any number of other ill-considered passages. He wrote: "The nation whose concept of the spirit is highest is in tune with the times and rules over the others." Germany, he surely had in mind (because of its superiority in philosophy). But, in the liberal democratic interpretation, he should have meant the United States.

Political readings of Hegel's philosophy conventionally divide into "Right Hegelian" (some of whom ended up fascists) and "Left Hegelian" (some of whom, like Kojève, ended up Marxists). But this third interpretation—I'll call it the Yankee Hegelian—is nearly as venerable and has always had its own highly distinguished champions, even if it has never, until now, received a full-scale exposition. It is sometimes forgotten that the earliest academic philosophy in the United States was Hegelian, based on a school of St. Louis philosophers who put out the *Journal of Speculative Philosophy* beginning in 1867. And the influence on American thinking is not hard to discover.

There is the example of Walt Whitman, who wrote a poem called "Roaming in Thought (After reading Hegel)," which is not much of a poem (mostly it hits the ingenuous note of Hegelian optimism) but does provide a key to understanding the poet's larger doctrine. Whitman may have been the first to insist that Hegel, in his vision of freedom as the destiny of man, must have had America in mind—the America that, in Whitman's phrases, had developed the "only stable forms of politics upon the earth" and was destined to spread its system into a "world democracy." The "formulas of Hegel," Whitman wrote, "are an essential and crowning justification of New World democracy." Whitman could scarcely believe that Hegel composed those grand formulas—"the most thoroughly American points of view I know"—in any place except some cozy American home: "It is strange to me that they were born in Germany."

In his early years, John Dewey, under the double influence of Whitman and the *Journal of Speculative Philosophy*, entertained the same general notion about Hegel and America's evangelical role in world affairs. It's true that Dewey didn't stay with those ideas. He came to prefer something more scientific. Instead of Whitman's idea of "religious democracy" Dewey took to speaking about "moral democracy." The Hegelian vocabulary dropped away entirely. But you could argue that something of the old Yankee Hegelian idea survived in those later ideas, and that Dewey's notions of freedom and of self-realization and of America's role in spreading world democracy came from that original inspiration. In the middle years of the twentieth century the same idea popped up in Marxist versions, too.

So far as I know, Hook never took up the question of Hegel and America, though it would have been natural for him to do so, given the trajectory of his thinking, from Hegelian Marxism to social democratic pragmatism. But you do find the idea in Marcuse, if only in passing. He stumbled onto it in 1941, when he brought out *Reason and Revolution*. Marcuse pointed out on the very first page that Hegel had "a keen insight into the locale of progressive ideas and movements," and the locale in question was the United States. It was because of a "rational spirit" in America, which was destined to play "a decisive role in the struggle for an adequate order of life." And this same idea now became Fukuyama's, too. Only since Fukuyama arrived at these ideas via his readings in Kojève, he seems to have had no awareness of how much intellectual history in America lay behind him.

The originality in Fukuyama's version of Yankee Hegelianism consists mostly in taking Kojève's version of Hegelian metaphysics and trying to give it a scientific basis. In Fukuyama's view, the progress made by Hegel's mythological slaves in altering nature and developing technology and dreaming about freedom went on for thousands of years in a wholly unreliable manner. The slaves would progress, but now and then barbarian hordes would sweep across civilization, and all the progress that had been made would go up in flame, and mankind would go hurtling backward into an animal life of savagery and ignorance. Nothing could be done about that. Around A.D. 1600, however, human Reason underwent a decisive change. Scientists perfected the scientific method, which gave to progress a surer footing. Barbarian hordes might still descend upon civilization, or, in our modern case, the bomb might go off, and the world might turn to rubble. But so long as even a handful of people with a knowledge of scientific method survived, the setback could never be permanent. The handful of people would set society back on the road of scientific progress, and one invention would succeed upon the other. And the society that produced science would sooner or later find itself dominating other societies all over the world.

Why is that? It is because a mastery of scientific method leads to ever more powerful technologies, which lead in turn to a superiority that is either military or economic or both. There is nothing that less powerful societies can do to resist, except to imitate the methods of the stronger society; but resistance by imitation is no resistance at all. Sooner or later every society on earth is doomed to adopt the methods of science, or else find itself dominated by societies that do adopt the methods. That is why history is universal, just as Hegel said—no matter how much we might wish to believe, with Isaiah Berlin, that every culture has its own characteristics, not all of which are mutually compatible. Some societies will lead, others will follow; but all will go in the universal direction. The process that pushes history forward along that path is what Fukuyama calls "the Mechanism," which is more or less what Marxists mean by "historical materialism," except that Fukuyama puts his emphasis on science ahead of economics.

What makes him think, though, that mankind's universal path of science and technology will eventually lead (and here Fukuyama's Yankee Hegelianism is in the grand Whitman tradition, though without Whitman's flag-waving) to the spread of liberal democracy, too? Anyone who looks around the world today will have no trouble finding societies that love science and hate democracy. Why shouldn't those societies, the scientific anti-democratic ones, prove very successful at staying exactly as they are, loving science and hating democracy forever? Communism was that kind of society. The Communists made a mistake, though, which was to combine their cult of science with a hostility to economic competition. Communist economic ideas stifled the creative impulse, and, as a result, neither the economy nor technology could flourish and Communist societies were unable to survive. But not every society that loves science and hates democracy hates creative competition. Gruesome right-wing dictatorships can be wonderfully creative and efficient at bringing together economic competition with a scientific business spirit, as in the cases of Generalissimo Franco, General Pinochet, and the generals in South Korea, not to mention the Chinese

Communists, whose Communism long ago ceased being Communism.

Iron-heel dictatorships might prove to be even better than democracies at generating economic progress, given that a clever dictator can rid himself of labor unions and journalists and anything else that is likely to stand in the way of wealth and military power. Fukuyama figures that if the human soul consisted only of Desire and Reason, people would be satisfied with capitalist dictatorships, and the right-wing free market rulers might thrive forever. The dictators would issue harsh but rational directives, and the obedient populations would toil at their jobs, and, even without trade unions and social legislation to bring about a better life, some portion of the profits would eventually trickle downward into the slums and villages. The kind of happiness that is strictly private and domestic would ensue, and people would feel no reason to rise in rebellion against the dictatorial government. But people are not content with being well-fed animals. The soul consists of Thymos, too. Thymos demands recognition, which for the mass of the population can only be achieved in a society of liberal democracy, where everyone is mutually and simultaneously recognized by everyone else.

Perhaps when people are still languishing in the miseries of a pre-industrial economy, they might not be able to fight very hard for recognition—though sometimes they fight anyway. Fukuyama observes that the American farmers of 1776 were as rustic and pre-industrial as anyone, yet raised a rebellion for democracy. You could point to a democratic country like Costa Rica in Central America, which has never been *rica*, except in people willing to insist on human rights. In any case, the progress of science and technology eventually allows people to escape from the worst sorts of poverty; and once they do, they will begin to experience Thymotic urges, and the fight for democracy will have begun. In Fukuyama's view, industrial wealth may not be a necessary condition for liberal democracy, but it does seem to be a sufficient one. At some point in the rising tide of wealth (at the lofty level of $2,000 per capita annual income, according to research by Samuel P. Huntington, whom Fukuyama invokes), the push for democracy becomes irresistible, and the non-democratic systems begin to totter. In the modern world, virtually all of the highly industrialized countries, and very few of the extremely poor countries, are stable democracies.

Mightn't there be some societies in which, due to science and technology, people become richer and, even so, due to peculiarities of culture or religion, decline to fight for liberal democracy? Islamic fundamentalists despise liberal democracy. Mightn't Islamic society find an alternative way of organizing itself, based on values that are Islamic but not liberal? It is sometimes argued that, for cultural and religious reasons, Islamic societies are incapable of embracing liberal democracy, no matter how rich they become. But that is not Fukuyama's argument. In his estimation, the fundamentalist movement in the Islamic world has something in common with the fascist movement in Europe earlier in this century, which ought to mean that, like European fascism, Islamic fundamentalism cannot be expected to last forever. As for Islam itself, why should we suppose that cultural and even religious traits will never change? Not so long ago it was said that Catholicism, too, was incapable of generating a democratic society.

Countries like Spain and Portugal were deemed to lie outside the zone of even dreaming about democracy, due to Catholicism's authoritarian heritage. Even to suggest that Catholicism in Southern Europe had anything to learn from the democratic practices of its northern neighbors was considered to be arrogant or ethnocentrist, on the part of the northerners. And yet the Catholic societies of the south did begin to acquire the democratic traits of societies to their north. Beginning in the mid-1960s, Catholicism itself, from the pope on down, began to change, and in the 1970s democracy not only overthrew the Iberian dictatorships but managed to flourish (with a few ups and downs, of course). Why shouldn't something similar take place, eventually, in the pseudo-democracies and authentic dictatorships of Latin America? Fukuyama, in an over-optimistic mood (as I judge it), is a little quick to declare that the Latin pseudo-democracies have already become real ones. But his point about Catholic societies and their newfound ability to democratize holds true nonetheless. And if the Catholic countries, against every prediction over hundreds of years, can make such a transformation, why not the Islamic societies?

He concludes that such will be Islam's future, though maybe not in the next twelve hours. If a workable alternative to liberal democracy does arise, he thinks it will probably have to be something newer than Islamic fundamentalism, perhaps some kind of Confucian authoritarianism from East Asia. The thrust of his political analysis makes the Confucian alternative seem quite likely in the short run; but his philosophical analysis makes it seem unlikely in the long run. For as we have seen in one East Asian country after another, Confucians, too, want the human recognition that only liberal democracy can provide—even if liberal democracy in East Asia is likely to end up looking slightly different from liberal democracy in Western Europe or North America. But, then, national or cultural variations were always part of Fukuyama's idea, either in a small way (in *The End of History and the Last Man*) or in a large way (in his next book, *Trust*). "The French can continue to savor their wines and the Germans their sausages," he writes; and in his second book he makes clear that societies and businesses will also come in wine versions and sausage versions. But the wines and the sausages will exist within political and economic systems that are fundamentally the same.

From Fukuyama's perspective there are, then, some specific lessons to be drawn from the revolutions that began breaking out in 1989. The overthrow of dictatorships in one country after another was something more than a cyclical event that would in turn give way to other cyclical events on an equal scale. The liberal revolutions that began in 1989 were the lived demonstration that Hegel's notion of history (as interpreted by Kojève with a few Yankee emendations by Fukuyama himself) is correct. The progression from animal-like oppression to human freedom is not a fable. And if for a moment we agree with Hegel that history represents the slow blossoming of the innate possibilities in man that can someday allow for a truly human life of freedom—if we accept this notion, and do not keep insisting that history is merely a meaningless succession of events—then it does make sense to observe that history is visibly trundling toward its appointed liberal end. For in Hegel's opinion (as per Fukuyama's Yankee Kojèvian interpretation), when a truly human life is finally at hand, when people at last feel themselves to be free, when masters and slaves have achieved for themselves the human qualities that formerly belonged solely to the other, and the masters and slaves have therefore ceased being either masters or slaves but are merely *citizens,* the one equal to the other—then history is, by definition, at an end, even if large and bloody events keep on occurring.

Now, Fukuyama has never quite said that such a moment has arrived. Hegelianism is hyperbole; and even if it weren't, Fukuyama was careful to qualify his own argument. His original article, "The End of History?," was protected by that supremely useful and admirable question mark, and the book that followed, which expanded on the argument, expanded also on the question mark. The idea of history having an end, in its qualified version, means, first of all, that world events are moving in an identifiable direction. During most of the twentieth century, that was not so easy to see. The slow development of democracy went into reverse in many countries. Totalitarianism rose and seemed to prosper, which suggested that social systems apart from liberal democracy can produce dynamic and stable societies.

But the defeat of fascism in the Second World War and of Communism in the cold war made the forward-moving progress of liberal democracy once again easy to see—even if, as is obviously the case, not every forward motion is fated to keep on a progressive path. The democracies that arose on rickety legs between the fall of the Berlin Wall in 1989 and the fall of apartheid in 1994 might, any one of them, or quite a few, be expected to go down rather quickly, with a big crash, too. By the time that Fukuyama's book came out, in 1992, some of the countries that he celebrates in his own pages as newly democratic had already gone down, like alcoholics falling off the wagon, which was too bad. The horrors of the Balkans and the Caucasus and Central Africa in the mid-nineties had not yet occurred. But for the purposes of his larger idea, what matters is the overall direction of things from the vantage point of centuries and not of months or years. And that direction is hard to mistake.

It is the same direction in world events that Whitman had invoked in his poetry and prose. It is freedom's slow development ever since the invention of monotheism and especially since the Protestant Reformation (or, as Fukuyama would have it, the rise of modern science). At the time that Whitman began writing, the United States was the world's only more or less genuine liberal democracy, apart from some Swiss cantons and a few tiny republican entities occupying European mountaintops—and Whitman's America was democratic and stable only in its northern free-labor half. Even there, as Whitman was the first to proclaim, democracy was a stinkhole of corruption. Yet at a lurching rate of two steps forward and one step back, other countries, in solo efforts or two at a time, sometimes in batches, did move in the liberal democratic direction.

Why should we suppose that this long development of liberal democracy is going to stop *now*, having just demonstrated, by achieving a victory over Communism and over several right-wing dictatorships, its enormous strength? The reason why liberal democracy has gradually overcome the old imperialist empires of Europe, the feudal dynasties, the fascists, the Nazis, and finally the Communists involves something more than chance. From Fukuyama's perspective, that reason is inscribed in the three-part nature of the human soul. It might be ages before the rest of the world joins the large successful portion that is already safely established in the zone of democracy, science, and technology. Gruesomeness on a gigantic scale will keep on occurring. Fukuyama's book speculates about nuclear war between India and Pakistan as an example of the terrible things that may very well take place. But because the larger political trend has now become visible, we can now begin to glimpse what mankind's final political shape, history's end, will eventually be. It will be a world in which all other kinds of political systems have given way to the liberal democratic alternative, or have lapsed into insignificance. It will be democracy for all, in all countries, except countries that cannot possibly prosper and grow. Glucksmann and the other wary liberals who have warned against making universal claims—they are wrong! All nations are wending down the same road.

Fukuyama's evocation of the little complexities along this single universal road is sometimes less than stirring:

> Mankind will come to seem like a long wagon train strung out along a road. Some wagons will be pulling into town sharply and crisply, while others will be bivouacked back in the desert, or else stuck in ruts in the final pass over the mountains. Several wagons, attacked by Indians, will have been set aflame and abandoned along the way. There will be a few wagoneers who, stunned by the battle, will have lost their sense of direction and are temporarily heading in the wrong direction, while one or two wagons will get tired of the journey and decide to set up permanent camps at particular points back along the road. Others will have found alternative routes to the main road, though they will discover that to get through the final mountain range they all must use the same pass. But the great majority of wagons will be making the slow

journey into town, and most will eventually arrive there.

Whitman was fond of the Westering image, too. Pioneers trekking westward make a glamorous part of his democratic panorama. But with Whitman a cosmic glow hovers over those dusty caravans. Fukuyama's wagons hint of the silver screen. They are an image from the age of Reagan, as if to say: "The rise of the West, the rise of the Western—what the hell." And we stumble at once on Fukuyama's greatest weakness. He shows himself to be, at least in this first important book of his, a man whose talents are remarkably asymmetrical. No one else in his and my generation in America has taken on a theme as grand as the one you find in *The End of History and the Last Man*. But Fukuyama's literary abilities fall noticeably shorter, and forward he hobbles, admirable and frustrating at once, sinking and rising with every new step, like a man rushing ahead on legs of different sizes.

That wagon train of Fukuyama's does have the virtue, though, of posing a simple question. Why do we imagine that, somewhere along the trail, the wagons will come to a final stop and not go rolling on forever? If we agree for the sake of argument that the entire world is sooner or later traversing a single path of development, with some countries forging ahead and others lagging behind, what makes us suppose that an Oregon lies at the end of the trail, beyond which sparkle the watery wastes of Pacific eternity and noth-

ing else? The idea of history having an end implies
such a thing—not just a direction to world events
but a final destination, too. But why posit a destination? Why not say that, just as feudalism, theocracy,
fascism, and Communism eventually led to liberal
democracy, liberal democracy will lead in turn to some
not-yet-imaginable post-liberal or post-capitalist society? A glance out your own door is enough to reveal
that liberal democracy has left Whitman's stinkhole
of corruption nicely intact. Don't the problems of
modern life guarantee that society in the liberal democratic system will not, in fact, be universal and homogeneous, and violent conflicts will sooner or later break
out, and from the ruins of one society will emerge
something new and different—just as Marx suggested?

Fukuyama's instinctive response to this line of questioning—one of his responses, anyway—is the conservative impulse to look on the social failures of liberal
democracy as mostly a mote in the eye of the left-
wing beholder. "Today in democratic America," he
writes, "there is a host of people who devote their
lives to the total and complete elimination of any
vestiges of inequality, making sure that no little girl
should have to pay more to have her locks cut than
a little boy, that no Boy Scout troop be closed to
homosexual scoutmasters, that no building be built
without a concrete wheelchair ramp going up to the
front door." That is a pretty dismissive way of describing society's campaign for more equality. But with all
due respect to the skeptical conservative instinct, let
us postulate that social problems of the sort that are

invisible only to conservatives actually exist, and that several grounds other than prissy middle-class hyper-egalitarianism might lead to outbreaks of social indignation and all kinds of social crises in the future. What then?

On the basis of Fukuyama's picture of the three-part soul and mankind's evolution through the centuries, you could argue that some very radical social and economic changes lie ahead for even the most liberal and democratic of liberal democracies. The same Thymotic impulses that lead people toward political democracy in a search for recognition and prestige might also lead them to demand greater social equality. Kojève, for his part, never doubted that a "universal and homogeneous state" would have to be, in his words, a "classless society," which could be interpreted in the Marxist way (as a society in which everyone has the same relation to property) or in the vaguer way that Americans mean when they speak of middle-class society, the "American way of life," and "equality of opportunity." Yet merely to achieve something as modest as equality of opportunity would require cataclysms of social struggle.

The democracy that Whitman had in mind extended into regions that were literary, sexual, and religious. It's easy to imagine that in these regions, too, Thymotic struggles for more democracy might cause all kinds of tumultuous upheavals in the future, as Whitman dearly hoped. Similarly with the problems and conflicts of work. In an essay on Strauss, Kojève wrote about the "joy that comes from labor itself"—

and even Strauss, the un-Marxist, conceded an importance to what he liked to call "virtuous or noble activity," which is more or less the same as labor. In Kojève's interpretation, people might be willing to die for the "joy that comes from labor"—which means that, by his measure, the joy of labor should count as another trait that raises man above the animals. But in that case, a truly universal and homogeneous state at the end of history would have to do rather better in guaranteeing satisfactory work than any society has managed to do today. All those 1910-era anarchosyndicalist plans for workers' self-management and democratic industrial systems and reviving the artisan values of pre-industrial production would have to come back into fashion, and desperate conflicts would surely have to break out for even the smallest progress to be made. So here again, even if we accept Fukuyama's general proposition, the liberal democracy that already exists can only be regarded as a setting in which further struggles and conflicts of every sort are bound to take place.

But do any of these likely future battles over democracy and recognition and the joys of labor invalidate Fukuyama's point about liberal democracy as the End of History? It is possible to imagine solutions to all kinds of problems without picturing the end of liberal democracy. In the United States, there have been more than two hundred years of continuous reform, and only one of those reforms, the abolition of slavery, required a violent break with the norms of liberal democracy—as could be expected, given that slavery was itself a violent break with liberalism and democracy. The New Deal of Franklin Roosevelt was always more representative of how liberal societies manage to evolve. Why not have more New Deals in the future—New Deals to abolish social inequality and to transform the way that work is organized, feminist New Deals, New Deals to revolutionize America's relations with the world? Anti-racist New Deals? Anarcho–New Deals that spring from the grass roots and bypass government altogether in the interest of libertarian reform?

This sort of talk makes Fukuyama nervous. *The End of History and the Last Man* alludes grimly to a possible "future left-wing threat to liberal democracy" via an ambiguous harping on rights, by which Fukuyama seems to mean political correctness rendered into a genuine tyranny. Still, in principle he has to concede that New Deals unto eternity do not necessarily pose a threat to liberal democracy: "The desire for a greater degree of social democracy need not come at the expense of formal democracy, and therefore does not in itself refute the possibility of an end of history." If there is an argument that accepts his premises and nonetheless refutes his notion of liberal democracy as history's final goal, the argument would have to show that social and economic reforms are absolutely necessary to avoid disaster and rescue society—but can be achieved only by scrapping the liberal democratic framework, or, alternatively, cannot be achieved at all.

In response to Fukuyama, two of the world's more

prominent left-wing thinkers stood up right away to present arguments along those lines. In Britain there was Perry Anderson, whose *New Left Review* used to be the very journal that published Glucksmann in English translation back in the good old Maoist days. In his book *A Zone of Engagement*, Anderson wrote a long, thoughtful essay on Fukuyama emphasizing the discontents of women and the economic and political crises that are bound to emerge from capitalism's ecological consequences. In France there was the same Castoriadis whose writings had long ago helped wean Glucksmann from the likes of Perry Anderson. Castoriadis took part in a symposium on Fukuyama and pointed to the double dilemma of ecological disaster and Third World poverty. These thinkers would prefer, it's fair to say, a revolutionary movement to overthrow the liberal democratic system altogether, in order to replace it with some kind of updated Marxist or post-Marxist socialism (in Anderson's case) or a society of libertarian "autonomy" (in Castoriadis's case). And, of course, if a revolutionary movement devoted to some such goal did have any kind of chance of remaking society, the end of history would not, in fact, be at hand—at least not until the new society had come about, or maybe not even then. Fukuyama acknowledges the possibility in the last line of his book. He speculates about the wagon trains arriving at the liberal democratic destination, and even so deciding to set out on a "new and more distant journey."

But a decision like that hardly seems likely, when

you look around at the world of the 1990s. And so, from the perspective of either an Anderson or a Castoriadis, a new and different possibility arises. It is the possibility that Fukuyama is basically correct and society has now assumed a shape that will turn out to be permanent. Only liberalism's triumph is mankind's disaster. The stability of liberal democracy guarantees that the intolerable social and economic problems of our present grisly moment will fester forever, or grow worse, and will never be adequately addressed. We are entering an "electronic new Middle Ages," in Castoriadis's withering phrase. The hour is barbarous, and the end of history is the end of hope, and capitalism in its democratic form turns out to be a perfect crime, never to be solved.

IV

Should we see the end of history as something to welcome, then—or something to dread? Fukuyama's presentation is new, but the question is old. The idea that history is leading toward some kind of end has been bandied about in a variety of secular forms for two centuries and more, and people have never been able to decide if they are happy about it or not. In the view of the old nineteenth-century progressives, progress was going to take place, willy-nilly, and the results were going to be excellent, willy-nilly. At one of the high points of *Les Misérables*, Victor Hugo climbs atop one of his own revolutionary barricades and looks out over the Paris of 1832 and proclaims in his boomy demagogic voice, "Citizens, the nineteenth century is great, but the twentieth century will be happy. We will almost be able to say: There will be no more events"—which shows, by the way, that some people did imagine that soon enough events would grind to a halt, and the realm of universal contentedness would be upon us.

Later in the nineteenth century doubts set in. And by the mid-twentieth century, after events had showed no sign of slowing down and happiness had turned out to be an advertising slogan, the idea of an impending end to history went through a flip-flop. Instead of cheery progressivism there was gloomy progressivism. Historical progress was going to take place, willy-nilly, and the results were going to be, willy-nilly, horrifying, and all hope was lost, except perhaps for the remote unpredictable possibility of a miracle. For technology is doomed to be our master, and nothing can impede its victory. Such was the mid-twentieth-century inversion of the old nineteenth-century idea. In those same moments of the early 1990s when Glucksmann was writing his *The 11th Commandment* and Fukuyama his *The End of History and the Last Man*, a German historian named Lutz Niethammer wrote a book with the strange title *Posthistoire* (a French-sounding but German word, coined by a Nazi) and the subtitle *Has History Come to an End?*, for the purpose of demonstrating that, in the mid-twentieth century, intellectuals descended on that pessimistic idea from every conceivable ideological perch.

There were the mid-twentieth-century intellectuals

of the extreme right in Germany who had once hoped that Nazism might rescue mankind from the horrors of modernity but who came to feel that Nazism's defeat was mankind's, and technology was king, and history was at an impasse, and "only a god" (as Heidegger said) could save the world. There were the intellectuals of the extreme left throughout Europe who, for their part, had once hoped for some kind of Marxist or Bolshevik revolution but who came to feel that Marxism and Bolshevism were doomed, and monopoly capital was king and history was at an end, and only a spectacular unpredicted revolution, perhaps in the Third World, could rescue mankind.

There were a variety of 1960s philosophers in France who came out of the extreme left and always knew that student uprisings were impotent and concluded that culture, or language structures, or anything but man was now in command. The "death of the subject," "the death of man," the "end of philosophy"—those were variations on that single obsessive notion of the end. Any number of popular-culture critics in the United States stood up in a similar spirit and announced that television or some other demon had now gotten beyond human control, and the megamachine was king, and onward through the gloomy analysis. Marcuse expressed all of this more vividly than anyone else. His *Reason and Revolution* from the early days of the Second World War reflected a keenly optimistic view of America and its possibilities, which is why he stumbled onto the notion of America as Hegel's "country of the future."

But the postwar years were not so pleasing. The McCarthy persecutions, the cheapness of American commercial culture, the ideological dogmatism that would ultimately lead to Vietnam, and ten thousand others failings and calamities in American life said to Marcuse that, far from being the rationalist liberator of the world, the country of the future had become the capital of oppression. The book that he published in 1964, his *One-Dimensional Man*, offered the classic analysis. Marcuse saw America as a superior kind of totalitarianism, invulnerable to overthrow. "Democracy would appear to be the most efficient system of domination," he wrote, and when he looked for a social force likely to break the grip of that very efficient system, he could think of nothing at all, except maybe an outbreak of Eros, and the world he described was bleak.

There was, however, still another way of looking at these things, which was to conclude that history was progressing in a good direction (as in the nineteenth-century idea), and it was progressing likewise in a dismal direction (as in the mid-twentieth-century idea); and the impending end of history was going to be good and bad at once. Kojève, who was a pioneer in so many other aspects of twentieth-century thought, managed to be a pioneer of that double-pronged idea as well. The strange wavering in his speculations about the end of history, the way he could never settle on Russia, America, or Japan as history's final destination, was fairly screwy, if you judge it logically. But if you take it as a kind of poetry, the wavering in his idea expresses an impossible mix of hope and dismay, which may have been unusual in his own time but has turned out to be a characteristic note in ours: morbid and cheery at once, depressed and giddy, definite and disoriented.

It is an art-world note, mostly—not something that you find too often in political writing. Jean Baudrillard, the French critic, expresses it. In 1986 Baudrillard published a daffy little tract called *America*, which piled up every conceivable gloomy cliché about postmodern life, especially the clichés about American blandness. He sneered at the vapidity of Ronald Reagan's toothpaste smile, at the lack of high culture in America, at the idiotic innocence of the American people, at what he considered to be the primitivism of American life. Baudrillard recognized that, due to the sinister dynamism of the American vapidity, Western Europe was becoming ever more Americanized. He already understood—in 1986, three years before the crowds began their surge through the Central and Eastern European capitals—that America had become the world's last remaining utopian fantasy, and masses of Communist citizens were quietly dreaming of America and of nothing else. Thus the world's future was already visible, and it was America, and it was a calamity. There might even be a sort of universal "Auschwitz"—an "Auschwitz" of culture and thought as well as, possibly, of physical existence, due to the bomb. In which case, the end of history was definitely at hand. Yet Baudrillard's attitude toward all these terrible impending events was strangely laid-back. He noticed the easy egalitarianism of American social relations, and managed not to be upset. The playfulness of American culture seemed to be reflected in the playfulness of his own book. Provocative inanities went chockablock with clever and serious observations. His view of the impending Americanized end of history was so despairing as to be morbid; but the morbidity was ironic, and the irony veered on cheerfulness. He was pessimistic, but not unhappy. Regarding the end of history, Baudrillard stood, in short, on both sides of the question, which is what gave his little book a flavor of the present day.

Fukuyama's argument came out after Baudrillard's, and he is earnest and sincere instead of clever and ironic: a political writer, not a po-mo hipster. Yet Fukuyama expresses the same hyphenated attitude, in reverse. He is optimistic, but not happy. It is because of his three-part picture of the human soul. After Reason, Desire, and Thymos lead at last to the universal and homogeneous state that is liberal democracy and the end of history, Fukuyama sees a new danger arising. It is the gruesome possibility that Thymos will find itself slightly crushed by the weight of egalitarianism and peace. He worries that society at the end of history will consist of nerd-like "men with no chests," the "last men" (the phrases are Nietzsche's, and the idea is Strauss's), who lack nobility or dignity or a sense of heroic willingness to sacrifice for a higher cause. The old aristocratic qualities of dignity and ambition—the qualities that come from an exaggerated Thymos, or Megalothymos—will be gone. In a few passages, Fukuyama speculates that aristocratic impulses like these, which fit less than well in a framework of liberal democracy, might drag society back into "history"—and the whole story of man would have to begin again. But most likely not, and the end of history will turn out to be dismal after all, even if the dismalness is liberal, democratic, and free.

Such is his argument. Not everyone will find it appealing. Five thousand years of plebian ancestors whisper in my own ear that a shortage of feudal traits and of the virtues celebrated by Friedrich Nietzsche is nothing to get upset about. Still, Fukuyama does mean to make a serious criticism of modern life, and if you look into the writings of his old professor, Bloom, you can see in somewhat clearer detail what he has in mind. He means to utter the moan of despair that rumbles up from every page of Bloom's *The Closing of the American Mind.* The Nietzschean phrasing expresses a worry about the moral silliness of modern democratic life. It is the fear that people in modern society want to be comfortable and do not care about anything else, including the state of their souls. And it is the worry that intellectuals have always had about modern life: that, because of mass communications, intellectuals no longer play the prominent role they used to play in earlier times.

Nothing is inherently right wing about those fears. You could take nearly every point offered by Bloom and Fukuyama and render it into a left-Hegelian or Marxist language, and you would end up with Marcuse. For what is Fukuyama's Yankee Hegelianism, if not a grand-scale expansion of what Marcuse had already proposed on the first page of his *Reason and Revolution*, where he described America as the home of the rational spirit? What is Bloom's idea about the closing of the American mind, if not a variation on Chapter 2 of Marcuse's *One-Dimensional Man*, "The Closing of the Political Universe," and Chapter 4, "The Closing of the Universe of Discourse"? Bloom's idea that open-minded supertolerance has produced a novel sort of American idiocy is merely a variation on Marcuse's idea about "repressive tolerance" (according to which, tolerance leads people to the idiotic belief that nothing much matters). The "One-Dimensional Man" and the "Last Man" turn out to be the same unhappy person. Marcuse, too, entertained the notion that nothing in the American-style democratic system would allow it to be overthrown, which means that history is at some sort of end. The one hopeful alternative that Marcuse could think of—the possible outbreak of Eros, leading to a revolution—points in a direction that is more or less parallel to Fukuyama's speculation about an outbreak of Megalothymos, even if Marcuse's Eros seems like a jolly instinct and Fukuyama's Megalothymos highly unjolly.

And so the building blocks of Fukuyama's argument are anything but new. He merely rehabilitated some well-worn philosophical ideas about progress and inevitability, and he found a new way to make the old argument that liberal democracy is progress's inevitable goal all over the world, and he combined these very old notions with an up-to-date contention that democratic progress will turn out to be admirable and dismaying at the same time. He said all that in his original article and he repeated it in his book, and his timing was perfection. For he uttered the enigmatic phrase that summarized these many large ideas—"the End of History"—at exactly the moment when the last great global rival of Western liberal democracy was going down to spectacular defeat.

And at the sound of Fukuyama's phrase, a nervous titter instantly went around the world.

Concerning man and history, there are two main views. There is the idea of Original Sin, according to which man is born with a fatal flaw, which cannot be overcome, except briefly by unreliable feats of virtue, and there will never be a lasting improvement. History moves, but doesn't advance. Like a kaleidoscope. And there is the idea of the Golden Age, which might come at the beginning of history, or might come at the end, but in either case provides a mark against which history can be shown to progress. History goes round and round, and eventually gets somewhere. Like a corkscrew.

Fukuyama's theory says that, for better and for worse, all of history is moving toward liberal democracy. Glucksmann's theory, with its ideas about fundamentalism and certainty and doubt, says: Never! Comparing one author's presentation to the other, I think that Glucksmann's has a number of advantages, which are only partly a matter of superior writing talent. For Glucksmann knows how to paint in a somber hue, and he has had the experiences to make him do so. He is excessive; but not naive.

Fukuyama may be naive; but, then again, neither is he traumatized. The twentieth century has conditioned us to cringe if anyone argues that history can undergo even the mildest of changes—unless the change is said to be for the worse, in which case we almost sigh with relief. As a result it can be very hard to believe that in the revolutions of 1989–94 we have just witnessed the hugest confirmation of the strength and superiority of democratic ideas that the world has ever seen. But Fukuyama doesn't cringe. His combination of Plato, Hegel, Kojève, Strauss, Bloom, and the State Department may look a little odd, arranged across the page; but that peculiar combination has allowed him to underline the immensity of the worldwide event with a thicker and blacker pencil than anyone else.

The messages from these two authors, Glucksmann and Fukuyama, are at odds with one another, but since I am a critic and not a philosopher, I see no reason not to say that both messages seem true enough. In his less than satisfactory manner, Fukuyama has told us that the old discredited ideas about the progress of mankind ought to have their credit restored, though not necessarily in the nineteenth-century style. He has told us that progress need not be confined to the tiny elite portion of humanity whose origins lie in Northern Europe and Protestant culture. He has said that powerful and perhaps irresistible elements are fueling democracy's spread around the world, all of which is nice to hear; and that democracy's final triumph may turn out to be mediocrity's, too, which we already knew (though some of us think of the mediocrity in a different way from Fukuyama).

But Glucksmann has reminded us that, when it comes to grand projects that derive from Hegel or Marx, the world has some experience to go by. He has told us to shudder at certain possibilities that Fukuyama has never really ruled out: that before any kind of freedom or democracy spreads around the world, calamities no smaller than those of the twentieth century will keep on breaking out. Glucksmann has told us that freedom's spread *causes* those calamities. And Glucksmann has told us how the world presently feels, not at some mythological end of history but at the real-life end of the quarter century that began with the dreams of left-wing revolution in the years around 1968 and ended with the outbreak of liberal democratic revolutions in the years between 1989 and 1994. The world feels this: humble, skeptical, anxious, afraid, shaken.

Note on Sources

In the course of the book I refer to most of the writings from which I have drawn important information or ideas. But I have profited from other books as well, a very few of which should be mentioned here. In the still relatively unexamined field of comparative studies of the rebellions of 1968, I have relied on A. Belden Fields, *Trotskyism and Maoism: Theory and Practice in France and the United States* (Brooklyn, 1988); Dany Cohn-Bendit, *Nous l'avons tant aimée, la révolution* (Paris, 1986); Robin Morgan, *The Demon Lover: On the Sexuality of Terrorism* (New York, 1989); George Katsiaficas, *The Imagination of the New Left: A Global Analysis of 1968* (Boston, 1987); and Robert V. Daniels, *Year of the Heroic Guerrilla: World Revolution and Counterrevolution in 1968* (New York, 1989). A book by Alain Finkielkraut, *The Imaginary Jew* (Lincoln, Nebraska, 1994), has been of value to me, together with one by Luc Ferry and Alain Renaut, *68–86: Itinéraires de l'individu* (Paris, 1987).

On the American left I have relied on, among many other books, Max Horn, *The Intercollegiate Socialist*

Society, 1905–1921: Origins of the Modern American Student Movement (Boulder, Colorado, 1979); Sam Dolgoff's *Fragments: A Memoir* (London, 1986) for the viewpoint of the libertarian left; Abe Peck's *Uncovering the Sixties: The Life & Times of the Underground Press* (New York, 1985); plus the valuable standard works: Todd Gitlin's *The Sixties: Years of Hope, Days of Rage* (New York, 1987); Maurice Isserman's *If I Had a Hammer . . . The Death of the Old Left and the Birth of the New Left* (New York, 1988); and Kirkpatrick Sales's *SDS* (New York, 1974).

For my knowledge of the '68 movement in Mexico (and other topics) I have drawn on César Gilabert, *El habito de la utopía: analisis del imaginario sociopolítico en el movimiento estudiantil de México, 1968* (Mexico City, 1993); Hermann Bellinghausen, editor, *Pensar el 68* (Mexico City, 1988), containing the recollections of a large number of participants; Elena Poniatowska, the author of *La noche de Tlatelolco*, for her evocative *Fuerte es el silencio* (Mexico City, 1980); Luis González de Alba, *Los dias y los años* (Mexico City, 1971); Gilberto Guevara Niebla, *Democracia en la calle* (Mexico City, 1988); and a curious volume of hippie memoirs by Armando Blanco, *20 años de aventuras HIP 70: El nuevo rock and roll en México desde 1968* (Mexico City, 1994).

My knowledge of gay history has benefited from Elizabeth Lapovsky Kennedy and Madeline D. Davis, *Boots of Leather, Slippers of Gold: The History of a Lesbian Community* (New York, 1993); Eric Marcus, *Making History: The Struggle for Gay and Lesbian Equal*

Rights 1945–1990, an Oral History (New York, 1992); George Chauncey, *Gay New York: Gender, Urban Culture, and the Making of the Gay Male World 1890–1940* (New York, 1994); and James D. Woods with Jay H. Lucas, *The Corporate Closet: The Professional Lives of Gay Men in America* (New York, 1993).

The essays of Václav Havel that I discuss—"The Power of the Powerless," "An Anatomy of Reticence," and others—can be found in various editions. I should mention a pamphlet that appears under the names of both Havel and André Glucksmann, *Quelques mots sur la parole, précédé de Sortir du communisme, c'est rentrer dans l'histoire*, with the first part by Glucksmann and the second by Havel (Paris, 1989). A discussion of Francis Fukuyama by Glucksmann appears in an interview conducted by Georg Kohler and Martin Meyer, which I read in the Madrid Socialist journal *Leviatán* (no. 55, spring 1994).

Cornelius Castoriadis's commentary on Fukuyama can be found in *De la fin de l'histoire*, edited by Bernard Lefort (Paris, 1992). The discussions between Alexandre Kojève and Leo Strauss appear in Strauss's *On Tyranny*, in the revised and expanded edition that was edited by Victor Gourevitch and Michael S. Roth (New York, 1991). I have also benefited from Michael S. Roth, *Knowing and History: Appropriations of Hegel in Twentieth Century France* (Ithaca, 1988), and from Vincent Descombes, *Modern French Philosophy* (Cambridge, 1980).

Index